The Divine Songs of Sage Poet Ramprasad

Ramprasad Sen was born in the second decade of the eighteenth century in Halishahar in (then) Bengal. He was a great saint in Shakta cult. But, he was too a natural poet and composer.

The songs are hymns to Goddess Mother Kali couched in rustic words and symbols of everyday life. Yet, most of this symbolism is a rare mosaic of the occult mystery of Tantrashastra and carry a double meaning. Thus, flying kites, the blind ox trudging routine endless circles of the village oil-machine (*ghaani*), the small town courtroom, the sailing craft of life—are all symbols of the highest mystic Shakta worship of Goddess Durga or Kali (Mahashakti).

The English rendering aims to echo the nuances of the original in its threefold uniqueness: (a) simplicity and rustic symbols, (b) their inner spiritual mystique, and (c) muse and rhymes. The volume will treat the English speaking world to a taste of this rare Indian spiritual songs and poetry.

Prof. Shyamal Banerjee is a student of English literature. Teachings of Swamiji and Sri Aurobindo. English (Hons.) and M.A. (Econ.) of Calcutta University. First in English in IAS. Former Sr. Professor, IIM (Joka), Kolkata. Author of many books and poems in English (and Bengali)—he took to translation spurred by a challenge to bring rare and unique Sanskrit and Bengali classics to the European reader without spoiling the savour and muse of the original. The result was his rendering into English of Michael Madhusudan Dutt's *Meghnad Badh Kavya* (original in Bengali); *Vidyasagar—The Ocean Man of Compassion* (*Karunasagar Vidyasagar* in Bengali); Kalidasa's *Meghadootam; Srimadbhagabad Geeta* (original in Sanskrit); and now *The Divine Songs of Sage Poet Ramprasad* (original in Bengali).

The Divine Songs of Sage Poet Ramprasad

Shyamal Banerjee

Munshiram Manoharlal
Publishers Pvt. Ltd.

ISBN 81-215-1085-6
First published 2004

© 2004, **Banerjee,** Shyamal

All rights reserved including those of translation into other languages. No part of this book may be reproduced, stored in a retrieval system, or transmitted in any form, or by any means, electronic, mechanical, photocopying, recording or otherwise, without the written permission of the publisher.

Typeset, printed and published by
Munshiram Manoharlal Publishers Pvt. Ltd.,
Post Box 5715, 54 Rani Jhansi Road, New Delhi 110 055.

Contents

Introduction   xv

Song
nos.

1	Who would nag you day and night	1
2	My days were lost in frolic and fun	1
3	Oh mind, do not crave for pleasure	2
4	I came to the world, I longed I would play at dice	2
5	Look, whose woman is it, dancing in dreaded stance	3
6	Tarry a moment oh Death, let me chant loud	4
7	Tell me, could you, my friend what happens when one is dead	5
8	I came just for coming, into this world I came	6
9	What profit, oh mind to Kasi sojourning	6
10	Oh Mother, don your robes	7
11	My luck; oh, Mother Tara	8
12	Oh, Lord of my life, the prince of mountains thou	9
13	Oh Mountain Lord, when my Uma is home this time	10
14	This thy balmy night has dawned	10
15	Who is it coming there, swinging	11
16	Oh Goddess Kali, how is it unrobed you roam	12
17	Oh Mother Kali, you became Lord Rashbehari	13
18	In a broken hut I dwell	13
19	My own Uma, She is no ordinary girl	14
20	Now I have hit upon the quintessence	15
21	Do I dread any in this world—me	15
22	Deliver thou, beseech, oh Tara	16
23	By whose wily words, oh mind	16
24	Oh mind, you have lost the warrant	17
25	Just think, oh mind, your own indeed is none	18
26	Is it just that Shiva's consort She	18
27	Mother Shyama you are flying kites	19
28	Jai Kali, Jai Kali—so you sing	19

29	His net cast the fisherman looks on	20
30	What use, oh Mother in trivial wealth	20
31	Do not touch me, oh Death, I've lost my caste	21
32	This time I will till my soil	21
33	Whose woman there, dancing in dour war	22
34	Who is that bewitching woman, on the brow	23
35	Who's that enchanting woman	24
36	Whose woman is that ravishing maid	24
37	Graceful as the nascent blue rainbearing cloud	25
38	Who is that woman, bewitching appearance	26
39	That enchanting woman, who is She	26
40	Is She just a woman, of many just one!	27
41	My poor mind, how is it amiss	28
42	Shame, my bumble-bee of mind, you let go the game!	28
43	Fie! oh mind, you are greedy of earthly riches	29
44	You turn, oh mind, your love to her	30
45	Will that day come, oh Mother Tara	31
46	Who, oh Mother, will fathom your sport	31
47	Mother Kshema, I am tenant of Her own domain	32
48	Being Mother is no idle word	33
49	Why should I, by the holy Ganges, dwell	33
50	Oh Mother Kali, all worries you wiped out	34
51	Beware, look out! The bark sinks	35
52	Nothing good is ever mine	36
53	Who knows how Mother Kali is	37
54	On the emerald rock of Kali's feet	37
55	Your saviour feet, you squandered all	38
56	This time, oh Hara, I will reckon	39
57	Tell me, Mother Tara, where do I tarry	39
58	Kasi, what use is it?	40
59	Mother, how long must you wheel me around?	42
60	Oh mind, you are so poor in the peasant's skill	43
61	Now I have mused on the quintessence	44
62	In the heart's lotus playground swings Shyama of fearful face	44
63	My cherished dream is unfulfilled	45
64	Oh Mother, it's over, my time of play	46
65	How long must I trudge on this fruitless toil	46
66	What marvel, oh mind, you came to do	47

67	Listen, Mother Tara, to my tale of woes	48
68	If the raft should sink, even then	49
69	Guess, what I'm dying to divine	49
70	Have pity on the poor, oh Shiva's queen	50
71	What treasure would you give me, oh	51
72	In my soul the queen of bliss	51
73	How often do I tell you, Mother, of all my endless woes	52
74	Why is it, mind, your illusion lasts	52
75	Chanting Kali's hymns day and night	53
76	The charming woman, radiant dark	54
77	Why are you, oh mind, so alarmed	55
78	Your saviour feet, all you gave away; none	55
79	Now the game is done	56
80	Am I afraid of misery	57
81	Where do I go at this unseemly hour	58
82	How you'd get rid of me	58
83	Away with you, you Yama's tout	59
84	I'll no more be swayed by sham deceit	59
85	What is it you vaunt, oh mother	60
86	What use this body, my friend	61
87	Oh mind, call Mother Shyama's name	62
88	That is why I love the darksome looks	62
89	I will call you Kali no more	63
90	I am so sore about that woe	64
91	Day and night bethink, oh mind	65
92	Tara, what more harm can happen	65
93	Locks unlaced, enrobed in space	66
94	Look there, who, that enchantress	67
95	On the body supine of Shiva supreme	68
96	That woman, what marvel, how she battles	68
97	Who is that woman doing war?	70
98	I pray, oh mind	71
99	For sure this day will end	71
100	The world is shoreless, there's no ferry across	72
101	How am I so much at fault!	73
102	Why commerce any more	73
103	Thou my tongue, sing, keep chanting Kali's name	75
104	Of the queen of charms it is fun supreme	76
105	Oh my mind, my forgetful uncle thou	76

viii Contents

106	Oh mind, do you fathom Her the Queen	77
107	My Mother, She abides in the inner niche of my mind	79
108	Mother Tara, thou oh queen Shankari	79
109	I dwell in the name of Mother Kali	80
110	So sweet is Mother Kali's name	81
111	Oh mind, at tipcat let's have a hand	82
112	That is why I grieve repine	83
113	Oh, thou my tongue, for once, call aloud	84
114	Tara's name is destroyer of all	84
115	Now, hence, oh Kali I'll take your count	85
116	Witness my chartered deed, oh come	86
117	Tara, deliverer of the woebegone	87
118	You, emissary of Death, better go back	88
119	Oh Death, what use your idle threat	89
120	Mother Tara, I'm not one of your timid child	90
121	Oh mind, what's your business that you came	91
122	I've reposed my soul on those fearless feet	91
123	That is why I bide under the tree	92
124	Oh mother, my destiny is to blame	93
125	Is it there, e'er, any fear, pestilence?	94
126	The mind bethinks it'll go on pilgrimage	95
127	Set me free, mother, with waving locks	96
128	Mother, now I'm vocal in my plaint	97
129	Mother, how so much you dance in war!	98
130	Loose vast hanging tresses	99
131	Home of charmer hopes, dread doom	100
132	Face as the moon without her stain	101
133	Who is there that ravishing woman	102
134	Shyama, the woman of legion charms	103
135	Lord Shankara beneath her feet	105
136	Shyama, that ravishing woman She	106
137	That graceful woman Shyama, who is she?	107
138	The gentle dame, she is naked stark	107
139	As the young lily the enchanting dame	108
140	Oh mind, is it that you do not know	109
141	What justice this, mother, fair play!	110
142	Why is it, for Kasi I should ask!	111
143	I abide immune out of bounds	112
144	The way in of Death is now shut out	113

145	Chant Kali, Tara's name oh, ceaselessly	114
146	It never left me, my evil fate	115
147	I'm none, no fugitive from law	116
148	That's why, oh mind, I tell you so	116
149	My mind, how you float on fancy, fun	118
150	When is it I would in Kasi dwell	118
151	Oh mother, I am so careworn distraught	119
152	In every nook and home there Mother dwells	120
153	I'll take refuge beneath mother's feet	120
154	Who is that woman, whose enchanting love	121
155	Oh my mind, I touch your feet, entreat	122
156	Oh my Queen, the metropolis is loud	122
157	I tell you this, oh mind, do worship, chant	124
158	Kasi, Annapurna's blessed land	124
159	Oh mind, call out Kali's name	125
160	Supreme deliverer of fallen soul	126
161	Oh my tongue, chant Kali Kali, chant again	127
162	All merciful! Who calls you all-benign!	128
163	Beyond all knowing, Unborn, Mother Thou!	128
164	The wretched soul has spread his empty plate	129
165	Thou hast broken up the fair, Mother Shyama	130
166	How longer must I toil round and round	131
167	How longer must Thou sleep oh Kulakundalini?	132
168	Look into yourself, oh mind	133
169	Will that day ever be mine	134
170	Do not wake her up my Jaya girl	135
171	Oh listen, that One He,—He is my groom	136
172	Should'st my mind be amiss, or err	136
173	Alone I came, I'll quit alone	137
174	No more, my child,—grieve, sulk resent	137
175	I do not shut my eyes for fear of that	138
176	Turn me insane, oh Mother (Brahmamoyee)	138
177	Put 'Her' in the niche of your bosom—caressing warm	139
178	I am not that dud moronic son of Thine	140
179	Come, Mother, let's have duel in the 'penance-ring'	141
180	How now, today oh Queen Kali	142
181	The daughter of the mountain King—her metropolis	143

182	My fond desire has gone in vain	144
183	The day's no longer far away	144
184	What shame is it, oh, how obscene!	145
185	Mother Kali, I've lost my caste	146
186	Mother Tara, Thou art the queen of thoughts	147
187	I've known, oh Kali, now Thy mental stance	147
188	When, alas but when	148
189	I'm most wretched, the meanest of the mean	149
190	Should I come by a rupee one crore purse	150
191	Today, Mother Kali, Thou hast assumed, as if, all-devouring form	151
192	Oh Tara, you Queen of thoughts	152
193	Deliverance is her 'Name'	152
194	Wake up, arise Thou gracious queen	153
195	Tell me oh Uma, my little child	154
196	Come mother, welcome Uma, little child	155
197	Is it that, oh Brahmamoyee	156
198	What is this game, oh Kali	156
199	This time I will sure go mad	157
200	Come, oh Mother, in my bosom dwell	158
201	It's now betimes, oh Tara, my prayer I submit	159
202	It's time, oh mind, you better call	159
203	Oh, it is not that wine I drink	160
204	Oh mind	161
205	Do thou get up, oh Uma, leave thy bed	162
206	Oh thou Mother Kali, ever ceaselessly	162
207	Oh Mother Kali with wreath of skulls	163
208	(Oh) you mist go—to tarry there's little time	164
209	Why not, oh Mother Tara, I so beseech	165
210	I wonder how oft you dwell in diverse moods	166
211	My Mother, She is the sea of joy supreme	168
212	Oh mind, what is this error on which you err	168
213	Tell me, oh *hibiscus flower*, how	169
214	Being mother thou, oh Mother Tara	170
215	I pray, oh mind, why not thou dost blossom	172
216	Durga Mother, be'est thou with Durga's page	173
217	When the child's in tears crying, 'mother'	173
218	Kali ever immersed in joy expansive vast	175
219	My Father, He is unvaried full of joy	176
220	My heart's in aching pain	176

221	Who bethinks of Tara's feet	177
222	Let's go, oh mind, we two together	178
223	Is it for nought that my soul so weeps!	179
224	If the world is full of grief and pain	180
225	Is it, oh Mother, thou wouldst send thy son	181
226	I call thee, Shyama, often and then again	182
227	You must save me, oh, thou saviour mine	183
228	That naked girl, her laurels care	183
229	Shyama, oh, who is that, below thy feet, supine!	184
230	The worlds dwell in Thee;— in thy marvel	185
231	I have got it, Mother, thy wily wish	186
232	This life, for ever it will not last	186
233	Oh Mother	187
234	Thou Mountain Lord,—Ganesh mine	188
235	Oh Mountain Lord, my Gouri, she did come	189
236	Aloft oh lift your limbs oh Mountain King	190
237	The dark dense cloud, in the inner firmament,— it loomed	190
238	Kali, how long like this time will lapse	191
239	What is the treasure I can offer Thee	192
240	That woman as the dark sombre night	193
241	What is thy 'name,' Mother by which thee I call!	193
242	How could you my little mother	194
243	Come, mother, thou Lord Bhola's spouse	195
244	She came just only yesterday	196
245	As tomorrow, Bhola comes	197
246	To this slave what grace, thou gracious Queen	198
247	Take me on to thy lap, oh, Mother Kali	198
248	Oh Kali, do this thou when Death doth come	199
249	There's no son so wretched as I	200
250	It is my fault I have cried and moaned	200
251	Let us set out, oh conscious mind	201
252	Whose dark swarthy maiden there	201
253	I have drawn the fence with Kali's name	202
254	What do I offer thee as worship	203
255	Where art thou, the world's deliverer	204
256	What dread have I of dreaded Death	205
257	Gaya, Ganga, Provas others Kasi, Kanchi who but yearns	205
258	I cling on to thy feet, Mother, even then	206

259	Oh thou, 'fish of life,' thy life is done	207
260	I have come to know, Shyama Mother's Court	208
261	Mother thou, deign the blooming lotus of thy feet	209
262	Jaya, oh, do not, I pray, so beseech	210
263	I have come to know, I ken so well	210
264	Should I breathe my last chanting 'Jai Kali'	211
265	Wake up thou, arise, oh mind	212
266	The fishing net cast well spread out	213
267	Into the Yamuna water I'll throw myself	214
268	Who is that your company, oh mind!	214
269	Get thee gone, oh Death,—what wouldst thou dare?	215
270	As the blooming lotus blue azure	216
271	Tara, pray now take me across the stream	217
272	Save thy son oh Saviour	217
273	Can I blame thee, Mother, oh?	218
274	To dwell in a place of pilgrimage, it's futile	219
275	How will it profit thee my errant mind,	221
276	When will it be that time will come, when	221
277	Tara! Thou art Supreme Mother divine!	222
278	Mother, you cast me, sure, out of mind	223
279	Tell me Tara, then, what use reposing trust in thee	224
280	Shiva's queen you mountain-maid	224
281	Who is that One who dwells upstairs	225
282	Take back your sack and gypsy gown	226
283	Do tell me, what kind is this stance	227
284	Lift thy head, thou Lord supreme	228
285	I'll let you know what's Mother's pain	229
286	By your ways and stance I now know for sure	230
287	The gnawing endless pain and tears	231
288	Howsoever I teach you, mind, alas, you ne'er learn	232
289	Do burn the passions	233
290	What fears oh mind, so why bemoan	234
291	Thou hast me bewitched becharmed	235
292	In the world's realm of thoughts	237
293	At long last now I have thought it right	238
294	What fears have I, oh Death, of thee	239
295	On the earth the joyous blissful soul is one	240

Contents xiii

296	Listen, oh my mind	241
297	Ignorant my absent mind, that's why	242
298	Oh mind, why but all these worries thine	243
299	This time, Kali, I'll thee devour	244
300	Oh mind, why not have a game of dice?	245
301	Oh mind, get wont to the saviour's feet	246
302	Mother, art thou everywhere!	247
303	Oh mind, even in error, absent mind	248
304	Oh my mind, must you take some potion, then	248
305	My mind oh, it so yearns to go, resort	249
306	I die of the load of thankless work in thrall	250
307	The elephant queen wild in must	251
308	Oh mind, do tell me, by what pain travail	252
309	Do not call out, seek, 'Mother' any more, oh mind	252
310	Listen, Mother Shyama, my yearnings hopes	253
311	Oh mind, let me but ask you this	254
312	Oh mind, hush, just keep quiet and calm	255
313	My Mother She is so concerned	256
314	My mind, is it, you have gone insane?	256
315	My mind, why, tell me, to Kasi would you roam?	258
316	As a porter I have spent all my days—oh Kali	259
317	Is it there still left aught of misery	260
318	You will no longer be born again	260
319	(Mother) pray, as life ends I do attain those feet	261
320	Have thy pleasure, oh Mother, I know thy way	262
321	What good turn you have done, oh Kali	263
322	The one who is daughter of mountain stone	264
323	The one who Tara's feet bethinks	264
324	You didn't care, oh mind, to obey my will	265
325	Crimson lotus in scarlet hands	266
326	Oh thou Death,—look, here I fearless stand	267
327	I shudder, my little mother, as I bethink	267
328	Pray, hearken thou, oh sombre Night	269
329	The withered Tree—it does not sprout	269
330	My heart, I've turned it desert—waste	270
331	Thou art, oh Mother so fond of desolate waste!	271
332	Shyama Mother, some device she has set up	272
333	If Shiva, Mother, is thy husband, Lord	273
334	Is it, my Shyama Mother	274

Introduction

MAN AND RELIGION

In any human system, in every clime and country, literature has given expression to the nuances of individual and social life. It is but natural, for, the emotional world of life as it is lived must find expression. This expression is both a joy and a compulsion. All emotions, yearnings are a charge, pent up fury that breaks barriers to come out in the open. The lava that erupts from out the crater of the volcano or the massive fluid that cascades as the mountain falls are victims of the same compulsion. And the joy is immanent. The colour and the sound and the smell of the millions of sensuous manifestations of Nature around us are all bubbling with the joy of creation. The longings of the inner being have an urge of reunion with its Creator, as He is revealed in the existential worlds.

Songs and poetry have ever served as the spontaneous vehicle of this conscious psychic life of man. In this inner bower of man's life religious devotion to a Power that is supreme—both immanent and transcendent—has always occupied a central position. Nothing else, it seems, lends any meaning to the life of the individual as we know it in this mortal world.

Devotional songs have enriched all literatures of the world. It is particularly so in Indian literatures in all of its many languages. The normal man has a passion for the supernormal. The reach must always elude the grasp, or, as the poet says 'what is Heaven for?' Nature is endowed with power, and so it is benign and beautiful. The ancient man perceived his God as the wielder of Supernatural power, the Fire, the Sun, the Rain, and the Winds who decide the destiny of man, against whom man was powerless, weak and insignificant. That is the beginning of all forms of worship.

As man's philosophic search for his Creator continued, God was bestowed with not only power but love, compassion, benign weal for all His creations. The Godhead was imbued with properties, virtues as He took immense and multitudinous forms. The Hindu pantheon of gods and deities came to be as wide as the relations of man with his Creator. The *rishis* (sages) of the Vedanta searched for the essence of this Godhead. The avenues were diverse, the paths of worship were many and God was perceived or realised in various ways. Advaitavada occupied a large stream of Hindu philosophy. There is only One God; all manifestations are merely His symbols as He is revealed. God is immanent in everything and everything is in God. Without God nothing exists. The whole of existence is but an image of the reality and Reality is God—infinite, uneroding, urborn, undying.

Along with this Vedantic approach to God, many streams of worship and philosophy went along and imbued man and society for ages. Taking off from Vedic legends the Hindu pantheon was overflowing with deities, endowed with various qualities, virtues and powers. Indra, Varuna, Surya, Vishnu, Shiva, Agni, Vasus, Usha and a hundred others. It is a curious phenomenon that the deities that filled the horizon of human perception,—they seem to be many and, at the same time, One. This vision is not one of polytheism; this is not indeed monotheism either, although the concept of the monistic Godhead seems to flow as a ubiquitous undercurrent. But the legion gods do not also submit themselves to henotheism. It is not the worship of One God of one's own psychic realm with realisation that there are many others. It is a worship of a deity, and then the deity seems to be one and the same as the Supreme Being, the One Almighty Godhead. And these gods are interchangeable, clearly conceived as different forms of the same Almighty Being. Thus Vishnu (Lord Krishna), the Goddess Durga or Kali, Lord Shiva and others in the pantheon are often realised as an image of the same Supreme Being.

In the poetry and songs of the period, in the last millennium these variations of worship and perception of Godhead are eloquently manifest.

LOVE AND WORSHIP

The image of the Godhead is bound to be coloured by the perception of humanity. The worshipper and the worshipped were bonded by common ties. The deities and the Godhead were humanised. They were superhuman Beings of course, and yet not free from the laws and virtues of humanity. The human soul marched toward Godhead for the ultimate reunion. Perception of the world as a playground of Godhead, with its littleness and essential futility, continued as an undercurrent of all sagely souls. Human relations with Godhead were overwhelmed with love and worshipful submission. The Being could easily interchange sex and gender. Indeed, the very concept of Godhead, had no element of distinction of gender. The Supreme is the only Male, *Purusha*. All creation was the will of God. God wanted to manifest Himself in Nature (*Prakriti*). *Prakriti* was conceived as the Female form, Mahamaya, the Goddess Kali or Durga—an image of God Himself, one and the same with God.

In Bengal right from the twelfth century, the Vaishnava cult of religion had a large sway. Countless devotees had filled the pages of literature with the sweet and loving relationship of Radha and Krishna in Vrindavana. With the advent of Sri Chaitanya in Nadia in Bengal worshipful songs and dances on the love and devotion of Radha for Sri Krishna had reached a culmination. The songs of the devout poets in Brajaboli—Vidyapati, Chandidas, Gobindadas, Sekhar and others and Jayadeva in Sanskrit had enriched Indian literature purely for their poetic qualities apart from their place in the devotional history of the land in which they are unquestionable landmarks.

Along with the Vaishnava cult of worship, seventeenth and eighteenth centuries religious life in Bengal saw the ascendance of the Shakti cult of worship. Goddess Kali, Tara or Durga was the most important Mother Goddess as the object of worship of philosophers, poets and sages in the last three centuries. One form of Goddess Durga was Uma, daughter of the Great Himalayas and mother Menaka. Uma is a daughter of the mountains, the sweet beautiful girl, who was married away to Lord Shiva. Uma is also Parvati in the great works of poet Kalidasa. She is ever the sweet charming daughter of every household in the sprawling land of India.

RAMPRASAD AND HIS POETRY

Foremost among the sage poets of the Shakti cult was Ramprasad. His songs and lyrics are of immense variety and are a phenomenal blend of the secrets of the sagely Tantric ways of worship with the sweetest relations of love and submission of the child and the mother. Ramprasad embodies the popular worshipful love and submission of the land to the Mother, as the Supreme Goddess in all her manifestations. The poet is aware that the only mission of life is love and worship of Mother Goddess and everything else is fruitless and futile:

> "I have lost my days in fruitless fun,
> My mission lost, charmed by bewitching time; . . ."

The poet is agonizingly conscious that all human relations are but transitory. The real and only life—selfless and eternal—can exist at the feet of the Mother Herself.

> "When oh, Mother Tara I earned riches
> At home and far away,
> Then friends, bothers, wife and sons
> Were mine, all obeying my words;
> Now my earnings gone, my age is over;
> Those selfsame friends, brothers, wife, sons
> Scold me all, alas, for lack of means. . . ."

Ramprasad uses the commonest of the common rustic lore and language, often, in his songs devoted to the Mother. He often uses symbols and metaphors taken from ordinary life. Thus he uses the symbol of the dice game in one of his songs:

> "I came into this world,
> I yearned I would play at game of dice;
> My hopes, alas, all shattered, a broken state—
> The first ever die the meanest 'five;'
> The die then read 'one and twelve,' then eighteen,
> Again sixteen, ages of matchless rounds;

> Then at last on 'twelve plus one'—alas,
> Mother—it got stuck at 'five' and 'six;'
> 'Six plus two for eight,' 'six and four for ten'
> Oh Mother, all outside my ken,
> My game gave me no fame, none—
> My stake, it's all over now;
> My last was my fourteenth lane—
> Stopped then at the blind alley;
> The fault was Ramprasad's—utter shame,
> The ripened die fell back alas
> To its raw state once again."

The song is a plea to the Great Goddess, symbolising the game of dice in which the poet seems to have lost in life.

Another symbol is the game of kite-flying. Song no. 27 (in this collection) throughout uses the various phases of kite-flying till the kite is cut off its strings and loses its moorings. The poet uses the simile as an image of life in its heart-breaking pursuit of the worship of the Mother.

Ramprasad's lyrics and songs are rich in imageries and eloquent sensuous description of the Mother. The curious blend of power and charm, the ravishing woman engaged in war—is exemplified in the songs, nos. 33 to 39.

The culmination of the Shakti cult was perhaps seen in the great sage of modern times Sri Ramakrishna. Sri Ramakrishna preached the oneness of all religions. He said again and again that God can be reached through every creed and religion. There are as many ways to reach Him as there are creeds. The seeds of this consciousness are also seen in Ramprasad's songs and poetry. Song no. 17 is an eloquent statement of the oneness of relations and the sameness of Godhead. Ramprasad declares—"Oh Mother Kali, you became Lord Rashbehari, as the amorous lover in Vrindavana."

There was inevitably some little rivalry between the votaries of Vaishnava cult and those of Shakti cult. Ramprasad shows the great awareness of the futility of religious fanaticism or conflicts among creeds and beliefs. He perhaps is the symbol and culmination of the immanent sublimity of the Hindu religion which embraces all religious forms of worship in its catholic unifying stream.

Ramprasad was a natural poet. His scholarship was well-known; his love of language made him proficient in many literatures including Persian, Urdu, Sanskrit and of course, Bengali. Most of his songs and lyrics were composed on the spot and have come to us through memorisation by his listeners and disciples. Many of the songs have great lyric beauties. They embody many secrets of Tantric *Sadhana* and sagely revelations of the progress of worship for realisation of Godhead. At the same time, the literary beauty and quality of the songs have made them immortal in the literature of Bengal. Among the common people of Bengal, throughout the rustic world Ramprasad's songs are on the lips of every devout soul. The songs reflect various emotional moods and relationships between the child and Mother, the devotee and his beloved Queen. The grace of the Mother, the sweetness of the Mother as a young girl as Uma, the daughter of the Indian household—the Supreme power of the Great Shakti, are all there in unforgettable lyric words and imageries through the songs of the great sage.

The attachment of the sage poet to the land of Bengal has captured the life and thoughts of countless people of the land, in a language that is their own and through symbols and metaphors which are bywords of village life and ex-perience.

LIFE AND WORSHIP OF THE POET SAGE RAMPRASAD

Ramprasad was born in the second decade of eighteenth century, in a distinguished family in village Halishahar in Bengal (now West Bengal), about 60 kilometres from Kolkata. His father was Ram Ram Sen and grandfather Rameshwar Sen.

The Sen family of Halishahar was known for its liberal traditions and devotion to the Tantric cult of Shakti (Goddess Kali) worship. Ramprasad was a talented child. He showed early signs of his spiritual nature and love of learning. His early studies included Persian and Urdu with a good deal of knowledge of Sanskrit and the Shastras.

At the age of 22, he was married to Sarbani. But that Ramprasad was not an ordinary person was evident from his early life. He showed little interest in the affairs of the world and concerns of the family. Even as a boy, he was often absent-minded, sad and melancholy for no apparent reason. Often he sought solitude and meditated. After his initiation by his spiritual teacher (*guru*), he increasingly delved into his spiritual life and the path of worship of Goddess Kali. At this time, the great Tantric sage Pandit Agam Bagish came to town. Ramprasad saw him in solitude and received lessons from him. From then on he was fast losing himself in his search for realisation of the Mother Goddess Kali.

The family had its fears and anxiety. Ram Ram Sen,— Ramprasad's father, was fast losing health and the affairs of the family got into serious financial difficulties. At this juncture Ram Ram Sen suddenly died leaving the burden of the impoverished family on the shoulders of Ramprasad.

The Struggle

The stark reality of life's struggle in the world now stared Ramprasad in the face. Unaccustomed to the burden of domestic life and not knowing any means of earning money, Ramprasad was miserable. He prayed to Goddess Mother for help but there was no relief.

Then one day in desperation he left for Calcutta to seek a means of livelihood. After some effort he got a job in the house of Durga Charan Mitra, a zamindar at Garanhata in Calcutta. His monthly salary was Rs. 30. Ramprasad was delighted and grateful to the Mother. But very soon the poet and seeker forgot himself and went about writing songs and hymns in the praise and worship of Goddess Kali across the pages of his accounts books.

Moved by the Great Mother's grace he wrote:

"Oh Mother, make me thy treasurer
I am not ungrateful Shankari, oh Mother."

From now on Ramprasad was lost immersed in chanting of Mother's name. Song after song filled the pages of the books of accounts of the zamindari of his master. Charged and overflowing with emotion and lest he should forget, the worshipful lyrics must be recorded as they came like fragrance from the churned petals of the jasmine flower.

It came to such a pass that Ramprasad's allotted work was neglected, errors started creeping in, routine tasks fell into arrears. His colleagues and seniors were unhappy and then angry. They reported to the master on Ramprasad's lapses. For a time the kind-hearted master took no notice. But one day, disgusted and worried he sent for Ramprasad. The officials took him to the master with all his books. The master picked up the book and was surprised—all over the book were written the name of Goddess Kali and Durga and devotional songs dedicated to them. The first song that the master read—

> "Oh Mother make me thy treasurer
> I'm not ungrateful, Shankari oh Mother,
> Usurps the treasure of thy feet everyone,
> I'm so aggrieved; the treasurer, thou hast named
> Lord Tripurari, so forgetful He;
> Lord Shiva, He so easily pleased—
> By nature bountiful—even so in His care
> You lodge your treasure immense rare;
> The estate is half and yet even then
> Shiva's wages are so high again;
> I'm thy valet with wages none
> The dust of thy feet, that's all that's mine;
> If thy father's footsteps thou shoulds't tread
> Then I'm lost, baffled indeed;
> If thou should'st tow my father's print
> Then thee I'd get, there is just a hint;
> Prasad says, I would be dead
> With the burden of such feet;
> If I attain such feet as those
> I would then escape my miseries."

The master was overwhelmed, his eyes filled in tears, he embraced Ramprasad and said, "Ramprasad, you are not meant for this humdrum work of the world. Go back home and do your worship and write your songs. You will get a monthly sum of Rs. 30 at your home."

Spiritual Development—Marvels in Ramprasad's Life

Relieved of his immediate financial straits Ramprasad went

about his spiritual pursuits with even more zeal. The sagely years of Ramprasad's life are a saga of spiritual growth of a human soul and is filled with marvels.

One anecdote goes—the fence around Ramprasad's cottage fell into disrepair. It was not mended for want of money. One day, Ramprasad started doing the fence himself. His young daughter Jagadeeswari was helping him with the binding chords sitting by his side. This went on for some time when suddenly Jagadeeswari left without telling her father. Ramprasad failed to notice it. However, the work went on and the binding chord was fed to Ramprasad as usual. After a while Jagadeeswari returned. Surprised, she asked father who it was that supplied the chords to him. Ramprasad equally lost said,—why you have been doing it all the time! When he was told that the daughter was away for quite a bit of time Ramprasad was overwhelmed knowing that Goddess Mother came as a young girl to help with his work.

There is another story of his life:

One day a young beautiful woman came to listen to Ramprasad's devotional songs. Ramprasad was then going for his bath. He asked the woman to wait for him. When he came back from his bath, he found that the woman had vanished. In wonder and fear he looked around for her. His eyes fell on the wall of the place of worship and read the writings: "I am Goddess Annapurna. I came to hear your songs. I cannot wait now. Do come to Kashi (Varanasi) and recite your songs to me."

Ramprasad felt miserable. He could not sleep. He decided at once to proceed to Kashi to sing his songs before Mother Goddess Annapurna.

On his way to Kashi at Triveni (in Hooghly district in West Bengal) he dreamt a dream: "You need not come to Kashi, you can sing your songs here itself." Filled with joy Ramprasad gave out his entire soul and sungha series of worshipful songs devoted to the Mother. The songs came out like a cascade of holy waters from heaven as if Goddess Saraswati herself sat on his tongue.

There is still another anecdote in his life: "The day after Kalipuja, at the immersion ceremony Ramprasad composed four songs standing neck-deep in the Ganges river. It is said that at the end of the fourth song when the words "the last rite is over (Dakshina hoyece)" were uttered the 'vital wind' from his being pierced the crown of his head and melted into eternity.

The life and work of sage poet Ramprasad as of his illustrious successor Sri Ramakrishna is a treasure-house of the metaphysical lore of the country. It sits on the crown of Bengali literature which is bound to shine with undiminished brilliance as ages wear on.

The Divine Songs of Sage Poet Ramprasad

❧ Song 1 ❧

Who would nag you day and night,
Oh mind,—knowing all yet so dense;
Whither your home—palace all,
When Death comes, oh tying you in toils;
Where then your father, your kinsmen all;
When you are dead, they will offer you
A broken pitcher, a tattered mat[1]
There, oh, then your 'name' is a dead account;
All your riches, wealth of men, but all in vain;
None, oh none, will keep you company;
Thus would urge Ramprasad,—renounce the cares
Of this ramshackle world,
Chanting Durga's[2] name upon your lips.

❧ Song 2 ❧

My days were lost in frolic and fun,
I've lost my mission by the spell of Time;
When, Mother Tara, I earned wealth at home and away,
Then friends, brothers, wife and sons—my word all obeyed;
Now, my earning's gone, my years are spent;
Those selfsame friends, brothers, wife, sons,
Scold me all, alas, for lack of means;
When Death's hand would sit beside my head,
Taking me by the hair on the brow,
Then on a cot of reeds with earthen pot, in coarse cloth[3]

[1] In Hindu custom the dead body of the common man is taken to the cremation ground, wrapped up in a mat along with a ritual earthen pitcher.

[2] Goddess Durga—also Kali—the divine Mother worshipped by sage Ramprasad.

[3] According to a Hindu ritual the dead body of an ordinary citizen is carried to the burning ghat in a bamboo-cot, on the shoulders of mourners, accompanied with a ritual pitcher of water.

They would send me off in a hermit's rag;
Then, with cries of 'Hari Hari,'[1] leaving me alone
At the burning ghat, they would return, each his home;
Ramprasad is dead,—all weepings over
They would eat their food with no pang or tears.

❦ Song 3 ❦

Oh mind, do not crave for pleasure
If thou should'st dwell at those fearless feet,
Even Dharma's son, losing at dice[2] left home for the wood;
The Lord of deities all—the wisest soul, even then,
Lord Shiva has beggarly ways;[3] She, Mother, merciful
To the poor devout; oh mind, seeking pleasure is bitter pill;
Oh mind, joy has seeds of sorrow; do not, I pray,
Resent these words; oh, there's pain in pleasure, joy in pain,
That's how the 'word' goes; the mind be thought
It would gain its ends by a sham pious stance;
Oh, it wouldn't work! She would count coins, split the pence,
No atom would escape! Oh mind, if indeed thou art Prasad's mind,
Then how so stupid thou, when it comes to act;
Oh mind, take pains, as thou must,
Thou would'st glean then the purest gem!

❦ Song 4 ❦

I came to the world, I longed I would play at dice;[4]

[1] In the Hindu custom, mourners carry the dead body to the burning ghat with repeated loud cries of the name of 'Lord Hari.'

[2] In the Hindu Epic *Mahabharata* Yudhisthira was locked in a game of dice with his rival brother Duryodhana. Yudhisthira was the god-son of god Yama, also known as Dharma. Having pawned liberty and kingdom as the stake in the game, Yudhisthira lost and had to take to exile into the woods.

[3] The great God Shiva is portrayed in Hindu mythology as clad scantily and attired in beggarly robes. The sage poet hints here that the Lord Shiva (consort of Goddess Durga) assumes this wretched attire as the great Goddess is fond of the poor and the fallen.

[4] The reference throughout is to the various vicissitudes in a game of dice which is likened to the struggles and setbacks in the spiritual path

My hopes belied, a shattered state; the first ever die,
The meanest 'five;' the die then read 'one and twelve,'
Then eighteen and then sixteen—a spell of matchless rounds;
Then, at last, on 'twelve plus one'—alas, Mother,—
It got stuck at five and six; 'six plus two for eight,'
'Six and four for ten;'—oh, Mother, all outside my ken;
My game gave no fame, none,—my stake, it's all over now;
My last was my fourteenth stake, stopped then at the blind alley;
The fault was Ramprasad's—utter shame,
The ripened die fell back to raw state again.

❦ Song 5 ❦

Look, whose woman is it, dancing in dreaded stance;
Who is it,—image as the young azure cloud;
What marvel, seated in Hara's lotus heart, clad in space;
Who but fashioned her in a niche, alone,
Feet surpassing purple lotus petals,—then,
How is it, the world so dark, so dismal—how;
I long, indeed, with love's own bonds,
Tie her fast, in deepest knots,
Seat her in my bosom's crystal lake,
Buoyant on its waves;
Who is it,—thighs becharming, shaming the round banana plant,
Blood, ceaseless, in cascading stream,
As if the lightning flash off the rain-laden cloud, in dazing wrath swooped down,
Singing, as the trident, the serpentcoil[1]

of the sage's life. The poet laments the ups and downs of the game till he seems to have lost his stake.

[1]According to Hindu Tantrashastra, the ultimate energy of the Godhead is enshrined in the human body in the spinal region. In the arteries in the body this unrevealed power is centered round six *chakras*.
  These are:
  (a) Muladhar: seated in the anus region
  (b) Swadhisthan: at the bottom of the genital organ
  (c) Manipur: at the root of the navel
  (d) Anahata: in the heart

At the root of the navel-lotus; who is she—
The swollen budding bosom;
On the blooming lotus face the buzzing bumble bee
Racing roams around,
As if on the snowy lotus bloom in the lush woody bower;
What lips sublime, what rapier rolling tongue,
The yearning of Lord Hara,
As if nascent youthful charm swims in trance of war;
Who is it, the facial orb veiled in toils of flowing locks, long,
   kissing the earth;
Thereon the arch of eye-brows with the arrow aimed on it;
The half-moon on the brow, quivering forehead locks
As playful birds, what marvel—giant pearls
Smiling in the youthful rays of the sun;
What phantom sprites—male and women—
Dancing Bhairabis—Yoginis[1] bursting in lurid laughter—
Bowlfuls of divine wine going round and round;
Divines Ramprasad—it is wayward waging a war
With this woman indeed—beneath whose feet Lord Shiva
Himself supine, as if a lifeless corpse.[2]

♀ Song 6[3] ♀

Tarry a moment oh Death, let me chant loud,
Mother mouthful, let me see if, in my dire days
Brahmamayee—Mother—She has come;

   (e) Vishuddha: within the throat
   (f) Ajnachakra: between the eye-brows
   A little above the Ajnachakra is the lotus seat of the All Soul (Brahman) known as Sahasrara lotus. The supreme energy is coiled as a serpent in Muladhar.
   [1]In the Hindu Shakta concept the great Goddess Kali (Shakti) is fond of dwelling in *smashana* (deserted burning place of dead bodies) in loud company of denizens of the spirit world.
   [2]Lord Shiva, the great God and consort of Goddess Kali (Shakti) is depicted lying prostrate on His back, as a corpse, under the feet of the Goddess Kali—a philosophical symbol of the Brahman carrying in his bosom the manifest Energy of the created worlds.
   [3]The song is a symbol of the sage poet's faith in Goddess Kali. The poet challenges Death. Since he is armed with the name of Tara (Goddess Kali) he has no fear of Death.

You would take me along with you—of that why
Do I worry at all; then were it useless
I wear round my neck the charmed necklace of Tara's name;
The great Goddess is my sovereign King, I'm tenant
Of her own domain; sometime I owe, I'm owed
Sometime—I'm never stuck in paying my debts;
Prasad divines—can others know Mother's playfulness;
How, ever I fathom Her,—one who is mystery
To Lord Trilochana Himself!

☙ Song 7[1] ☙

Tell me, could you, my friend what happens when one is dead—
This is what's argued—endless—by one and all;
Some say you'll be phantoms, fiends in the spirit world;
Others, you'll go to heaven; still others say
You will live with God; and yet others, you'll unite with Him;
The Vedas hint, of Infinity you are the vase,
Death is the name when this vessel melts;
Oh, virtue, vice is an empty count,—of it they are awed
In wishful void; the elements, five of them,
In the same house they dwell—in some accord,
Then, when it's time, each one will flee
On his own unto his appointed place;
Prasad divines, you will be when Death overtakes
The same you have always been; as the image in water
Rearing off the water, melting as water
Back into water itself.

    In the Hindu mythology Lord Shiva is the consort of Goddess Kali. Kali is imaged as standing on the supine body of Lord Shiva, feigning as if he were a corpse.
    Mythologically Kali is the Eternal Space and Shiva (Mahakala) is Eternal Time. Space and Time uphold the existential system.
    [1]The song is sage poet's message on the human state after death.
    Each man embodies a soul; this soul is a particle of the All Soul—the Absolute God. The human body and mind are built up of five elements— Earth, Water, Fire, Wind, and Space. These elements evolve within the Absolute and when the body *dies* they get back to devolve in the Absolute. Ramprasad has no doubt of the infinity of the human soul and its merger with the All Soul, as it leaves its body in flesh and blood.

☙ Song 8[1] ❧

I came just for coming, into this world I came;
This sojourn, alas, futile;
Just as the bumble bee, charmed,
On the painted lotus, stuck;
Oh Mother, by wily words, you made me swallow bitter *neem*
In sugar's garb, oh Mother, allured by sweet
All my day was spent in bitter taste;
Mother, you duped me—sent me down on earth,
So you would play; and yet the game you played
Left me in utter despair; divines Ramprasad,
In the sport on earth, whatever destined has happened;
Now that the dusk draws near, Mother,—
Do take home your nursing child.

☙ Song 9 ❧

What profit, oh mind to Kasi sojourning,
Mother Kali's feet—sole, absolute alone;
Legion holy shrines—thirty crore and half again
All dwell at those two Mother's feet;
If vespers you have learnt,
The shastras—their mantle you have donned—
Then what use, to Kasi[2] you repair;
Meditate, seated still in your lotus heart

[1]The sage poet laments here of the futility of the earthly life.

According to the Hindu Shastra all our thoughts and actions are guided by divinity. Man is a mere instrument. The Doer is the Absolute.

The poet has wasted his life in frivolous worldly pursuits. And the Mother Goddess is to blame.

She has tempted him to the illusory charms of life.

She has hidden the Truth from him of the useless futility of all pleasures and riches.

The poet draws the image of the bumble bee which takes the painted lotus as the real flower and gets lost.

Finally, the poet pleads that, at the end of life, She should take him (poet) back in her lap as he is the hapless child of the Goddess Kali.

[2]Kasi, also Varanasi, in Uttar Pradesh, is famed in Hindu religion as the holiest place of pilgrimage and the last resort of the devout Hindu when it is time to leave this world.

The four-armed Mother[1]—with flowing locks;
Ramprasad will attain in unbroken strain
Holy Kasi, seated still in his own domain.

❦ Song 10 ❦

Oh Mother, don your robes—
Don your robes, Mother,
Beseech you don your robes;
Hibiscus flower anoint with sandalpaste,
Oh, I would offer at your feet;
In Holy Kalighat[2] you are Kali;[3]—
In Kailasa,[4] oh Mother, Goddess Bhavani;[5]
In Vrindavana[6] you are Radha,[7] beloved
The milk-maid oh in Gokula land;[8]
In the netherworld, Mother, as Bhadrakali[9] you dwelt—
Legion deities worshipped you, oh, with human sacrifice;
To whose abode you had been, oh Mother,
Who has worshipped you; that's how,
Red sandalpaste I ken upon your brow;
At your feet, oh Mother, crimson hibiscus;
In your right hand, Mother, you vouchsafe refuge;
In your left the open scimitar;

---

[1]The image of the great Goddess Mother Kali is depicted with four arms.

[2]Holy Kalighat: A shrine in Calcutta of Goddess Kali, a place of Hindu pilgrimage.

[3]Kali: Goddess Kali.

[4]Kailasa: The legendary place in the Himalayas, the abode of Lord Shiva and Goddess Bhavani.

[5]Bhavani: Another name (image) of Goddess Kali.

[6]Vrindavana: A noted place in Uttar Pradesh of Hindu pilgrimage, where Lord Krishna and his beloved Radha spent their childhood and youth.

[7]Radha: The beloved of Lord Krishna, another image of the great Goddess Kali or Shakti or Bhavani.

[8]Milkmaid of Gokula: Radha who was the foster-daughter of Nanda of the milkmen community.

[9]Bhadrakali: Another image of Goddess Kali whose abode was the netherland (under the earth).

Oh Mother, you 'have severed Asuras' heads,[1]
Countless heaps of them;
Blood streaming off your sword, Mother;
String of severed heads around your neck;[2]
Bowing, look oh, Lord Bhola at your feet;[3]
The golden crown on your head, Mother,
Touches the blue inane;
How is it, thou art unrobed, Mother[4] beside thine own child;
Crazy thou, thy Lord insane,[5] oh Mother, there are others still as mad—
Mother, mad too, Ramprasad yearning for thy feet.

☙ Song 11[6] ☙

My luck; oh, Mother Tara,
It is not good, it is not good, Mother,
It has not been ever good;
When a child my father died,
Oh Mother, my kingdom then you stole;
Of small wisdom me, you let me lost at sea;
Like the moss afloat on speeding waters,
Mother, I am drifting on the sea;
People say, oh save him—none dares into the deep;

[1]Goddess Kali: In her war against the Asuras (the demon clan, the legendary enemies of the Suras, i.e., the gods in heaven), she had slain countless Asuras by severing their heads with her famous scimitar.

[2]Goddess Mother Kali: This image is depicted with a long string of severed heads of Asuras, worn as necklace round her neck.

[3]Lord Bhola: Lord Shiva, the consort of Goddess Kali, who according to Hindu religious belief lay like a corpse, supine under the feet of the great Goddess Kali, as a symbolic posture.

[4]Goddess Kali: is worshipped—her idol stripped and naked, the symbol of the unbounded space.

[5]Lord Shiva: The great God's way of life and traits, as epitomed in Hindu shastras and legends do not obey the ordinary conventions of sanity.

[6]This song is both a lament and worship to the Goddess Mother.

The poet alleges that his early life was lost, orphaned, through the neglect of the Mother. He has drifted in life as the floating moss. No one came to his rescue. Now he pleads that he would worship Her with red hibiscus, *bael* (wood-apple) leaves and wild flowers—all so loved by the Mother Goddess.

Bael leaves with wild flowers in worship I'd give,
Oh Mother and, besides, my head;
Red sandal, crimson hibiscus, I'd offer at Mother's feet;
To Ramprasad's these prayerful words,
Do listen Mother Narayani,
As the day ends of this mortal frame,
Oh, pull me on to the holy Ganga waters.

❦ Song 12 ❦

Oh, Lord of my life, the prince of mountains thou,[1]
My limbs tremble in fear,
What is this dreaded news I hear—
Darkness indeed in warm daylight;[2]
Spreading out his tiger-skin, Mahakala sits within
At the portals well installed
Calling loud often—"emerge oh Ganesha's mother;"[3]
Of pitiless rock thy person,[4]
Within the flesh my life of stone—
That's how it is there so long, it hasn't split;
Mine own daughter—to other she belongs,
One knows, yet the mind does not own,
Alas Almighty, what's this thy conundrum;
Prasad's these woeful words
Oh royal Queen of the snowy mountains
Are like the female bird pining for the moon
Sad, despairing at break of dawn.

    The poet pleads that She will rescue him at the end of his mortal life by taking him on to the holy Ganges waters.
    [1]According to legend, Menaka, mother of Goddess Durga, is the consort Queen of the Himalayas, the mountain lord.
    [2]Mahakala (the eternal time) is another name of Lord Shiva. According to Hindu mythology, Lord Shiva, the prince of sages, is clad in and seated on tiger skin.
    [3]Lord Ganesha is the son of Goddess Durga, the consort of Lord Shiva.
    [4]Reference is to the Himalayas, built of rock.

☙ Song 13[1] ☙

Oh Mountain Lord, when my Uma is home this time
I won't send her back again;
Let people decry, if they will,—
I would, sure, listen to none;
Should Lord Mrityunjaya come in quest of Uma's return
Mother and daughter this time would contend,
Heedless he is son-in-law;[2]
Ramprasad, twice-born, wonders how
One should endure this agony
Lord Shiva,[3] alas, erring in eerie lands,
In cremation grounds—of home careless, unconcerned.

☙ Song 14[4] ☙

This thy balmy night has dawned,
Thy charming daughter is home, oh receive her—
With welcome open arms;
Come, behold the face, sweet as the moon,
Thy sea of sorrows will flee—melt, swoon,
The mellow smile of the Diana face, dripping nectar dews;—
Hearkening to these halcyon words, hastens the royal Queen,
Locks unbraided, flowing robes in disarray;
With emotions worn, tears cascading down—

---

[1]The song is a loud cry of Menaka, the spouse of the great Himalayas and Mother of Uma, another name for Goddess Durga. The daughter Uma, who has returned to her mother's place is now being taken back to her husband's home for which her husband, Lord Mrityunjaya (Shiva) has come personally to collect her.

[2]In the Hindu home the son-in-law is treated with the greatest attention and affection. Here Menaka, the mother-in-law pleads that she will not oblige and allow Lord Mrityunjaya to take back Uma, his wife, even though he is the son-in-law.

[3]Lord Shiva, the consort of Uma, Goddess Durga.

[4]This is a different kind of song, of which there are a few in the bunch of songs sung and written by the sage poet which have survived. Goddess Kali is also known as the girl Uma. Uma is the daughter of the Great Himalayas and mother Menaka. Uma is married off to Lord Shiva whose ways are beggarly and irregular. The Himalayas are the King of Mountains and, that way, Uma is a princess daughter.

The Mountain Lord behind her—she weeps,
Weaving her arms round her scion's neck;
Then seating her on her lap
Looking deep into her charming face,
Kisses her ruby lips; then proceeds—
"The Mountain is thy father,
Thy Lord, born beggar,
Thee I gave away alas, my charming lass,
To one robed in empty space!"
All companions, friends—in joy overwhelmed
Throng, clasp her hands in joyous laughs;
They beseech, 'for full one year unremembering
Where, we wonder, all this love you put away;
Oh lift your face do speak, we are dying indeed;'
Poet, Das Ramprasad, inwardly so amused,
Exulting in the sea of joy;
With Mother's advent, rejoice all worlds
Oblivious of shifts of day and night—lost in the ocean of bliss.

☙ Song 15 ☙

Who is it coming there, swinging,
Tresses long and flowing, drunk,—languorous;
The woman rushing headlong in war
Smashing demon hordes
Swallowing them in elephantine gorge;[1]
Who is she, the dark person bedazzling in blood,

According to Hindu legend, Uma returns to her father's place four days in the year when the greatest Puja in Bengal is celebrated. In the present song mother Menaka is emotionally obsessed at the return of her daughter after long separation. Her beloved daughter Uma had been married to the beggarly, ill-clad Shiva. As the loving mother she overwhelms Uma with love and kisses on her brief sojourn to her mother's place.

The song is a symbol of Bengal's girls who are married off to the distant spouse, returning home once in a while. The loving mother often misses her and often regrets that the husband is beneath her expectation.

[1] Goddess Kali is depicted as the dour Mother Goddess in war with the 'demons' (the forces of evil) slaying them by the hundreds and devouring them with her wide open mouth.

As on the dark river Kalindi, buoyant the crimson *kinshuka*;
Who is that woman, as the azure lotus, the gracious face divine,
The sickle moon on the forehead shines;
Who is that, as the blue sapphire absolute,
The teeming finger nails the darkness devour;
Who is that, in blinding grace unleashes lightning flashes,
Booming rolls of thunder mount the heaven;
The sons of Diti,[1] all, their hearts timorous,
Rock, tremble, terrror-struck;
Oh Mother, thy rage abjure, vouchsafe—
To thine own abode repair;
Thus implores Sri Ramprasad thy lowly humble page.

☙ Song 16 ☙

Oh Goddess Kali, how is it unrobed you roam,
Such disgrace, you have no sense of shame;
Mother, you are sans clothes—or ornament,[2]
And you boast you are princess of royal descent;
Mother, oh, does it behove, is it right for your lineage;
On the person of your Lord you mount your feet,
Naked yourself, no less your husband so,—
You amble in moors and cremation lands,
Oh Mother, we all blush, die in shame—
Don now my girl, we pray, your clothes;
Forsaking wreaths of gems, oh Mother, you 'dorn'
With corpses, heads your gracious neck;
Prasad avers, oh Mother, awed Lord Digambara[3]
Of that your fearsome countenance.

---

[1] The 'demons' are the sons of the Mother 'Diti' just as the 'gods' are the sons of Mother 'Aditi.'

[2] The image of Goddess Kali is unclad and naked, overwhelmed by long tresses of hair, and the large apron of necklace of severed demons' heads; the infinite open space is indeed the shroud and symbol of Mahakali.

[3] Lord Shiva, the consort of Goddess Kali, is equally naked, clad scantily in tiger's skin around the loin. Another name of Lord Shiva is Digambara, meaning in Sanskrit 'clad in open space.'

❦ Song 17 ❦

Oh Mother Kali, you became Lord Rashbehari,
As the amorous lover in Vrindavana;
Diverse your manifest Divinity, varied your playful pranks,
Who but knows this abstruse Word!
Radha, angelic damsel parcel of your very own;
Yourself the Being, the cosmic Woman yourself;
Bare round the waist it was,
Now the loins yellow-clad,
Tresses flowing, the princely crown,
The flute between the hands adorns;
It was, with arrow looks off eyes askance
Lord Tripurari[1] you becharmed;
Now, you Being Supreme,—with graceful limbs
With arched glance, the love-lorn lass you beguile;
It was, dark lurid laughter, frightening all three worlds,
Now, it is mellow smile, the Braja maid[2] entranced;
It was then, oh Shyama, in the sea of blood you danced,
Now, the Yamuna-waters, azure, your love;
Prasad now amused, buoyant on the sea of bliss—
Has got it all, oh Mother, by a little thought;
Lord Krishna, Being Supreme,—Shyama, Mother,
Dark of hue—
All One and the Same;
That's what alas, one fails to know.

❦ Song 18 ❦

In a broken hut I dwell,[3]

---

[1] This lyric is a perception of the sage poet that God is one in many forms in different climes and ages.

[2] Sage Ramprasad is a devotee of Goddess Kali; but he perceives and proclaims that the same Goddess Kali also assumed the image of Lord Krishna (also known as Lord Rashbehari) in the land of Vrindavana. The poet then sings of the becharming transformations and the playful traits of the One God in different images—of Goddess Kali and Lord Rashbehari or Lord Krishna.

[3] This frail mortal body in which 'I' dwell, is compared to a broken hut open and vulnerable to marauding forces.

That's why, Mother, frightened, thee I call;
It sways with the slightest swing,
Stands propped, alone with Kali's name;
As night falls those felons six[1] the mud-walls scale;
Quelling them—far from it, oh Mother,
I'm scared, flee them all;
Prasad dreads—by some false step perchance
Lest him they should trap in toils.

Song 19[2]

My own Uma, She is no ordinary girl;
Oh Mountain, our daughter she—
That's not all, not all at all;
What I dreamt in my dream, passing strange,
I fear to tell; someone four-faced He,
Another with five-some heads—
Uma sitting on their crown;
Discoursing, smiling face,
As the Queen of the prince of Kings;
The Lord on Garuda's mount, dark-hued,
Her, worships with folded hands;
Prasad avers—the sages whom can't reach, fathom
In Yoga, meditation—oh Mountain,
A maiden as this your daughter own,—
You are blessed indeed, great virtue yours—

---

[1] The six vices are foes within a man's self: desire and lust (*kama*), anger (*krodha*), greed (*lobha*), confusion—non-discernment of good from evil (*moha*), arrogance (*mada*), and jealousy and hatred (*matsaryya*). These are evils, waylaying in the path of spiritual progress of man.

[2] This lyric is the sage poet's vision of the great Goddesshood of Uma—same as Goddess Durga or Parvati in Hindu mythology. The words in the lyric are from the mouth of Menaka, mother of Uma, who to the mother is but the beloved child. The mother beholds the true image and greatness of her little daughter who is no less than the great Goddess, worshipped of the great Gods in the Hindu pantheon.

☙ Song 20[1] ☙

Now I have hit upon the quintessence;
My soul I have yielded to Kali's fearless feet;
I have got the scent from the Being Supreme,
With which I have charmed the fount of essence all;
That's how renouncing anger, hate, greed
I have turned my thoughts to pure serene;
Tara's name the elixir
Tied it fast in my tuft of hair;
I have made crystal of Durga's name
By uttering Durga, Durga, Durga—ceaselessly,
I've come to know for sure, I must depart
That's what Prasad deems,
I've done my parting chores—I now abide—
With Kali's name, of the voyage as wherewithal.

☙ Song 21[2] ☙

Do I dread any in this world—me
Whose Lord is the great Goddess Mother,
I dwell in joy, in the hallowed Mother's own domain;
There is no surveying the land, no earnest seized;
The estate not sliced in lots, oh Mother;
The mystery I cannot fathom—Lord Shiva, a hireling He!
I have no worries—none oh Mother,
No levy, none to pay;

[1]The sage poet sings here the joys of his devotional worship. The sage has now realised, to his immense joy, the right path to salvation. He has abjured the petty foibles of life and immersed his soul in the final Truth. The Truth is the name of Mother Goddess. The poet is no longer afraid. He now knows that the name of Goddess Kali is the invaluable support and salvation of his sojourn in this world.

[2]The song professes the sage poet Ramprasad's faith in Mother Brahmamoyee as the saviour. The words of the song observe the symbolism of the tenant living in the realm of the landlord. This whole world is the Zamindari of the Queen Goddess Maheshwari. Prasad has earned his right as freehold tenant with no fees, rents and taxes, and the *subah* of the Great Goddess, is ever flowing with wealth and treasures. But then the poet also knows that by sheer devotion he could buy up the Queen's Zamindari, such is the power of devotion.

My savings—fast secure in Durga's triumphant name—
Whence my revenue I draw,
I have no longing, oh Mother, in my mind—
(So divines Ramprasad—twice born)
I could buy out with my ardent love
The Estate of the immanent Queen—of the created worlds.

❦ Song 22[1] ❦

Deliver thou, beseech, oh Tara,
Mother of the Worlds;
The worlds thou hast emancipated,
Yet me thou hast ruined;
Am I, oh Tara, then none of the world;
As the day ended, the night was dark—I swam
With the name of Sree Durga upon my tongue,
My vessel worn, oh Mother, thou at the helm,
Yet my craft brimful dipped sank submerged;
Ramprasad, twice-born, baffled, at his wit's end,—
Being Mother, how didst thou banish me to the Aunt's!
Where is it you had been that you learnt this way,
Being Mother, yet oh Tara you so forsook your son.

❦ Song 23 ❦

By whose wily words, oh mind,
You are so becharmed;
Oh my dear beloved bird,[2]
Dwelling in my own inner niche,

---

[1]This song is the sage poet's awareness that the world is a sea in turmoil. The final aim of the human being is to reach salvation at Mother's feet. The poet is afraid and lost and uses the metaphor of a sinking craft. The poet feels insecure, radarless, in an old, dilapidated vessel—amid the dark turbulent sea.
But the poet now seeks the blessings of the Goddess for safety and restoration.

[2]The mind is the beloved bird of the human being—yet as fickle and wayward as the winged creature. The poet here is remonstrating with his 'mind' seeking to turn it, and its wayward ways, to the chanting of the name and to the path of Goddess Kali.

Yet me you thus beguile!
I have cast you, cosy content inside the cage
That you may chant, oh Kali's name meditate;
Oh mind, you cheated me—
Rejoicing at the foeman's joy;
My mind—Shiva Durga Kali's name
Utter ceaseless, silently;
Your afflicted limbs will cool, allay—
Just once you sing Mother Shyama's name.

❦ Song 24 ❦

Oh mind, you have lost the warrant
Of your occupation,[1]
Day and night you sit brooding
On ways of amassing wealth;
The round coin is but sham illusion,
Shyama, mother thine is the vessel
Full of Gold,
You have bartered gold away
For the price of broken glass;
Alas, oh mind, shame to thee,—
Indeed accursed thou,
Whate'er is destined by the chain of deeds[2]
Whoever can ever reach beyond;
Futile you roam at home and alien worlds,
What's written by Destiny
Is all across your brow;
All-eroding Time in Your bosom ensconced—
It burgeons apace as the sal-tree bud;
Oh, destroy that rapacious Time, take refuge
In the Mantra's healing balm.

[1] The sage poet remonstrates here with his own 'mind.' He complains that the mind has forgotten its mission; it has set about the useless pursuit of amassing wealth and earthly possessions forgetting the path of God.

[2] According to Hindu philosophy a man's soul is bound by the 'chain of deeds' through his never-ending circles of births and deaths till he is freed by the grace of the Supreme Being.

Prasad says, do you divine, oh mind,
Of the five horsemen[1] you are the mount;
Those five are rogues, an assorted lot,
They would rack you up and down, torment.

❦ Song 25 ❦

Just think, oh mind, your own indeed is none,
It is meaningless, this world you roam;
Do not forget Dakshina Kali, Goddess Supreme;
Trapped in the toils of illusion, sham—
For a couple of days or three, on this mundane world
They call you master; and then this master
They'll discard when the Master arrives of Eternal Time;
For whom you pine, worry yourself to death,
Would she, indeed keep you company;
That same dearest love will splash a charm[2]
Lest it should be boding ill;
When Death (says Sri Ramprasad) will seize you by the hair
Then chant, Kali Kali—loud,
What then Eternal Time, Death can do?

❦ Song 26 ❦

Is it just that Shiva's consort She,
Whom the ordainer of Eternal Time adores;
Across the six-some knots, seated She
On the lotus seat;[3] of Her companions all
She is the crown—She dwells on the thousand-petalled
    bloom;[4]

[1] The five physical senses, which are the roots of all sorrows.

[2] According to Hindu belief a death in the family often leaves behind the lurking spirit of the departed which may cast an evil spell.

[3] According to Hindu Tantrashastra, the seat of the Supreme Energy (Mahashakti) the Goddess Kali is spread along the spinal cord in 'six circular knots' These are: (i) Muladhar—(in the region of the anus), (ii) Swadhishthan (at the bottom of the male organ), (iii) Manipur (at the root of the navel), (iv) Anahata (in the heart), (v) Vishuddha (in the gutteral region), and (vi) Ajnachakra (at the centre of the brow).

[4] On top of the six circular knots, rests the ultimate seat of Brahman, the Sahasrara—the thousand-petalled lotus seat in the crown of the head.

Naked herself, rooting out foes, She abides
In the bosom of Mahakala;
Oh, could you tell, my mind, how is but She,
On the chest of Her Lord She stamps Her feet;
Prasad says, 'Mother's pranks, playfulness,
I know all are her arch banditry;'
Oh my mind, wary watchful—persevere,
Hallowed beatitude you will secure.

☩ Song 27 ☩

Mother Shyama you are flying kites[1]
(Amid the world's market fair),
Look there, the mind as kite in the breeze of hopes—
To that tied the attachment-string;
Framed in flesh and bones—in which
Lie the ribs and legion arteries;
The kite built from out of self-born traits,
The skill, workmanship par excellence;
The abrasive paste of possessiveness,
With which you've toughened the flying string;
Kites snap—in a million one or two,
You clap, oh Mother, your hands in joy;
Prasad says, in the sweet south breeze,
The kite will flee—free-
Beyond the ocean of worldly life,
It will tumble rolling presently!

☩ Song 28[2] ☩

Jai Kali, Jai Kali—so you sing,—

---

[1]This lyric is a symbol of man's existence and his sojourn through life. The simile and the symbol is that of a flying kite. The mind is the kite, the worldly attachment is the string, the wind is the breeze of hopes, the abrasiveness of the string is supplied by the mind's possessive trait. Only one in a million, the 'kite' is severed and freed from the string—and then it flees and tumbles pleasantly at the Mother's feet.

[2]The poet has given up all worldly interests.
    He is mad, beside himself, in the name of Goddess Kali. The ordinary man finds him unusual, unworldly, almost insane. The poet assures

Let people say, if they will, you've gone insane;
Let them make fun, if they will—
What then, it is none you lose;
There are two words 'good' and 'bad;'
It is good to do what indeed is good;
Sever all ties, infatuation,
By summoning up the scimitar of Kali's name;
Torn on the rack of sham illusions
Ramprasad in misfortune doomed.

☙ Song 29 ❧

His net cast the fisherman looks on,[1]
What in this world, Mother to me will befall;
In unfathomed waters down the fishes dwell,
The fisherman has cast his net across the world;
Oh, whome'er when he chooses he tucks him
By the hair; there is no way from out the snare;
How do you escape, oh mind, you are whelmed
By all-consuming Time; Ramprasad says,—
Invoke Mother, she will arrive,—
And then will rout the God of Death.

☙ Song 30 ❧

What use, oh Mother in trivial wealth;
Who weeps, oh, without the treasure, thou;
Should'st thou, Mother Tara, grant riches trite,
It will lie lost in the cottage nook;
But should'st thou grant thy feet, the sole refuge—
I'd install them in my bosom's lotus seat.
My great guru deigned, oh Mother, graciously—

---

himself that his way is the right one; let others say what they will; let them ridicule! Ramprasad will sever all illusory ties, and reach the ultimate aim.

[1]The fishes are the creatures of the world. The all-devouring Time will ensnare all;—no one can escape his all-embracing net. Mother's name alone can save man from the lowering hands of Death.

The wealth that he poured into my ears;[1]
Even that, my Guru's treasured 'word'—let waste
For want of ardent pains; Prasad says,
If thou dost deign, still shower grace—
It shall be, oh Mother, thine own compassion;
When my days end, Jai Durga, I'd proclaim—
Grant me then, I pray, a niche at those feet.

☙ Song 31 ☙

Do not touch me, oh Death, I've lost my caste[2]
The day the gracious Mother granted me Her Grace;
Listen, oh Death, I'd tell you how my caste I lost,
I was a householder—that dark ruinous woman[3]
Has made me sannyasi; my mind[4]
My tongue as well—this twin in Her name combined;
Hearing this the foemen six[5] have left the sailing boat;[6]
The strength on which I am deemed outcaste
Is e'er undimmed; Prasad says, let not
Yama dare near him who leaves this world so outcaste.

☙ Song 32 ☙

This time I will till my soil.[7]
Oh, in my sojourn in this mundane world;
Just drop a dew of your grace benign,
Then sit behind, watch, oh royal queen;
Rank is the growth in this fleshly soil,

---

[1] In Hindu philosophy and the path of worship of God the *mantra* (the sanctified 'word' for repeated chanting, and meditation) is passed on by the 'spiritual guru' to his disciple. This *mantra* is the highest treasure that a man can possess in his spiritual life.

[2] The poet claims that by clinging to the great Mother's feet he is no longer a subject of the domain of Death.

[3] This is an affectionate worshipful reference to the Goddess Kali whose image is dark and who ruins the householder's worldly attachment.

[4] An ascetic who has renounced the world.

[5] The six enemies within oneself.

[6] The symbol of the body sailing on the sea of the worldly life.

[7] Throughout the lyric the symbol is of this life on earth as field for

Beyond me, Mother, to till it all,
If a tiny bit, oh Mother, is sown
I swim indeed in the sea of joy;
Luxuriant weeds as crop of sins
Within the bosom abide;
What legion barbs of sorrow bruise the feet,
Deliver, oh Mother with flowing locks;
Oxen six—'passion,' 'rage' and others too
Toil ceaseless, day and night—;
I would sow seeds deigned by guru's grace,
Would glean harvest lush, profuse;
Prasad says,—the mind set on farming—
Fruitless; deep down
I yearn to merge with Mother Tara's
Those divine vermilion feet.

☙ Song 33[1] ☙

Whose woman there, dancing in dour war,
Naked She, beaming,
On the person of the robeless Lord;
The gracious limbs the nascent streams uphold,
The pool of cascading blood,
Is it, the ruby *kinshuka*, buoyant
On the dark Kalindi waters;
Face as the taintless moon,
Smiles dripping nectar dew;
With dark grace,
Extinguishing dark dismal gloom—
Heaving mass of them; poet Ramprasad,

sowing and harvest. The 'seed' is the worshipful *mantra* and chanting of Mother's name. The 'harvest' is of spiritual fulfilment ending up with the merging with Mother Tara's vermilion feet.

[1] This lyric is of a different kind. It is the poet's realisation of the image of Goddess Kali. In Hindu metaphysics Goddess Kali is the symbol of Energy, the moving power behind the existential system. She is robeless, dark in space. Her person is smeared with blood of demons that She has killed. She wears a necklace of skulls.

And even then, She is the repository of all bewitching charm and beauty, the refuge of all sages.

To the lotus-feet of Goddess Kali, submits,—
The Yogi's heart swimming buoyed
For final deliverance.

۴ Song 34 ۴

Who is that bewitching woman, on the brow
The blooming moon—graceful, enchanting;
The woman roaming in war, locks in molten roll,
Person, spark of the dark cosmic night;—
The maiden unclad,—slender slight;
The right palm vouchsafing safety,
On the left skull and scimitar;
What splendour, look, the Prince of the demon race;
The divine woman, or is it the demon maid,
Or still is She the serpent queen
Or just the human dame;
The Mighty Lord on whom I lean
That my battle I may win—
He, that Lord, feigning as dead
Lying at Her feet, Mahakala,
So bewitched with the sombre Grace;
She in many wily illusive stance
Enchants by the flicker of a glance askance,
In a trice assumes a gigantic frame,
On the lips wears a lurid grin;
Now on the earth, hurtling in a flash,
In a moment in the heavens soars;
Swallows, legions, chariots charioteers-
Steeds, warring elephants;
Ramprasad avers—for that's the truth,
You never know Mother's grace divine—
She is the image of the awakened soul,
Immanent, the Queen of the Lord of Creation;
Lord Shyama (Krishna) the self-same He[1]
Is the Goddess Shyama—the woman queen

[1] Lord Krishna, also known as Shyama, and the woman form, Goddess Shyama, of the Supreme Being are One and the Same.

A mere shift in verbal form,—
The suffix changed, once again,
The scimitar resumes the form of flute.

♀ Song 35[1] ♀

Who's that enchanting woman,
In loud uproar in war;
Who's that bewitching woman, graceful
Charmer of the demon lust—
The Moon usurping the solar glow;
The entrancing grace with the trinal eye—
Person as lotus petals creamy dark;
This youthful woman, naked,
Tresses billowing down to earth—
In battle excels—of virtues ocean,—
The essence Prasad avers, of whom afore the deliverer,
Routing Death with beat of drums.

♀ Song 36 ♀

Whose woman is that ravishing maid,
Complexion liquid as the rainbearing cloud;
Look, oh royal prince, the Lord Supreme
Himself prostrate as dead,—
Oh His chest adorns Her charming feet,
The shining nails as the crystal moon
Shed lustre ceaselessly,
Is it Lord Hari, four-some face[2]
Murmuring sweet—oh Shankari
Quit your warring stance—;

---

[1]This song is a spontaneous overflow of joy and wonder of the Sage Poet in the image of Goddess Kali.

The metaphors are taken from charming symbols of the world. The Goddess embodies violence, power, destruction and charm—all at once.

The poet is puzzled by the union of these conflicting qualities in the Mother Queen.

[2]Lord Hari, another name of Lord Krishna, prayerfully implores Goddess Kali (Shankari, spouse of Lord Shiva—Shankar), to quit Her warring stance and resume Her gracious appearance.

Drunk with the wine of war
Mover of the worlds you torment
The mountain at your feet;
The king of serpents quakes, e'er in fear,
Is this the 'cause' of the final doom;-
Prasad, Her humble page implores—
Your own vassal, deliver;
The 'mind,' alas, an 'elephant' in must
E'er drunk with the wine of earthly means—
Unwise wandering erringly,
Wilful, ne'er contained.

❦ Song 37[1] ❦

Graceful as the nascent blue rainbearing cloud
Wno is that bewitching woman, oh!
The moon in the darkest night,
The youthful sun at break of dawn—
As twins gambol at those charming feet;
The mellow light of million moons play upon
The enchanting face, voice reproaching
Sweet ambrosia—ears as ornaments,
Long tresses billowing down surpassing glorious youth,
Handsome necklace pendant around the neck,
Radiant hued reposing on the thighs
Immanent; in the left palm of the woman sublime,
The scimitar, the parted human head—
On the right, boundless bounty grace; the beaming moon
Upon the brow—
Buoyant on Eternal Time,
Rolling often in dark booming laughter;
Sings Sri Kavi Ramranjana, in my mind I've yearned—
On me thy gracious eyes turn benign,

---

[1]This song is the poet's 'hymn' to the beauty and power of the Goddess Kali.

The image is charming, enchanting. All the glory and beauty of the world is incarnated in the person of the Queen.

The sage poet prays that the Mother remove all evils and darkness and take him to the realm of bliss.

Vouchsafe, uproot all sins, evil stains;
Whoever chants Thy name beloved he,
In the world it's so renowned.

Song 38[1]

Who is that woman, bewitching appearance—
Reproaching the blue lotus—liquid stance
In battle form—unrobed!
The ravishing woman roams in rolls of laughter,
Churning the bosom—the charming lass—
Of the God of amorous love;
The rolling clouds in thunder roar
As in the hour of final doom,—
Lour, frown in sinister scowl
Constant, in measured howl;
Charmer of the universal mind, the sister own
Of the God of Death—of pride the arch tamer—
Ushered into the shastras' world
Overwhelming lessons in youthful years;
On whomever She turns Her frowning eye
He is doomed to the realm of Death—
"Oh Goddess Mother, Jagadamba"—Prasad chants,
"In battle annihilate the swarm of foes,
Wind up your warring stance, resume your grace,
Have mercy—shield the sagely souls."

Song 39[2]

That enchanting woman, who is She

---

[1] The song is a symbolic revelation of the Mother Goddess.

Goddess Kali is the annihilator of all evils, the slayer of demons and the saviour of the devout. She wears Her charm and beauty and dour look in immanent glory.

The poet craves that the Mother abjure her frightening countenance and take a kindly look at her hapless child.

[2] This is also a song of wonder and joy at the sage poet's perception of the Mother's image.

The Goddess is a warrior Queen. All that is dark, evil and illusion—vanish with the name of the Mother. She, as if, is at war with the force of darkness and deviance.

With billowing locks unrolled;
Companions in wanton fun—
The *bhairabis*, the *yoginis*—
Wageth war in passion wild,
What joyous smile, unabashed style
On Lord Mahesha's bosom dancing;
In dire war locked, all robes hath shed
Swallowing elixir in rapturous trance;
In gay abandon moving in swinging gait;
'Hold me, oh'—so says in welling laugh,
Whose woman is that I cannot guess;
She has me entranced in her robeless stance,—
Who is it, you worship else,
At those two feet you lose yourself;
All ten corners with Her grace illumed,
What use in battle fray—in my mind
I so divine; Prasad avers
To Kailasa let us all repair.

☙ Song 40 ☙

Is She just a woman, of many just one!
Swallowing hemlock, by whose name
Mahesha still alive;[1] 'creation,' 'upholding,'
'Annihilation'—by the wink of an eye
She brings about; the limitless created worlds
In Her womb entombed; at whose feet
The gods take refuge in peril;
Under whose feet recumbent Mahadeva,[2]
God supreme of all the godly race;
Prasad says, as warrior Dame

   At the same time, she wears a vouchsafing smile offering refuge to all devout souls.
   [1] According to Hindu mythology, when the great ocean was churned in ancient times by the gods and demons a vase of hemlock came up. It had to be consumed and since none else could or dared, it was lord Shiva (Lord Mahesha) who swallowed it! The great lord could still survive as He had taken the name of the great Goddess Kali.
   [2] Goddess Kali is depicted as standing on the recumbent person of Her Lord, Shiva.

She joins the fray decimating
Shumbha, Nishumbha in thundering roar.

☙ Song 41[1] ☙

My poor mind, how is it amiss!
Thou art, oh Shyama, the sorcerer's lass—
Thou call'st the tune and it dances;
Thou art the purpose—virtue, sin—
That's the truth one knows for sure,
Thou art the earth, Mother, waters thou,
On fruit-trees thou growest fruits;
Thou art Power supreme, devotion thou,
Thou art deliverance—that Lord Shiva avers;
Oh Mother, thou art 'sorrow,' thou art 'joy,'
That is as the Chandi says;
The 'chain of deeds'—Prasad says—
In this the spindle spins the yarn;
Embroiled in this 'illusion's chain,'
The 'being' plays its game insane.

☙ Song 42[2] ☙

Shame, my bumble-bee of mind, you let go the game!
You chose the bane of worldly riches
Giving up the honey of Kali's lotus feet;
Among the crowd you are supreme,

[1] The poet is charging Mother Goddess Shyama in this poem.
    The Hindu shastra believes that the human mind is a slave to Nature's Qualities. Nature is the total existential system, a mere reflection which mirrors the absoluteness of the Almighty. The 'Still Brahma' turns kinetic through His other 'face,' which is Mahamaya, Goddess Kali and of whom Poet Ramprasad is the devotee.
    Man goes astray; the human mind is besieged with the million turns and twists of the earthly world. The poet claims, and pleads to the Mother, that for all these errors the 'mind' is not to blame. The mind is the plaything in the hands of Mahamaya, Goddess Kali. It is Mother that is behind everything that happens and all the 'thoughts' that are thought, and errors and aberrations. The worldly being is dancing merely to the sorcerer's tune of which the Mother alone is the cause.

[2] This song is a series of images and metaphors used by the Poet to introspect his own mind.

They say you are the royal king;
You consort ever with the vile,
You are king no doubt,
Your ways are mean;
You roam drunk with haughty airs,
As if you are the Judge's steed;
A time will come when you'll learn,
You'll hit the wall and have full fun;
Youth, infirmity, doting age,—
They come in turn with passing days;
Then one, who loses his mind in the den of thieves,
He dotes on the drunken bull;
Prasad says with bated breath,
As old age creeps the priest will come;
When, mace in hand, Death will drag you,
What then you'll do, my dear friend.

❦ Song 43[1] ❦

Fie! oh mind, you are greedy of earthly riches;
You know nothing, you obey none, to none you listen;

> The human being is an atom of the universal soul. He possesses sense organs which respond to Nature's Playfulness. Mind is the controlling organ which causes all desires and attachments to worldly things.
> The poet compares the 'mind' to the bumble-bee. The bee collects honey from flowers. The mind forgets that the Mother's feet are the honeyed lotus flower and then roams the world, futile, in search of honey and happiness.
> The poet is puzzled how the mind behaves like this. After all the mind belongs to the sage and should know that finally, its obsession with worldly pleasures is bound to end up in drunken misery. The poet realises that it so happens because the mind keeps company of wicked allies, which are enemies of the human soul. Ego, self, desires, meaner thoughts, all cause confusion and lead the mind astray.
> The sage poet reminds the 'mind' that devouring Death will come at the end of it all and that it should mend its ways while there is still time.
>
> [1] It is the poet's spiritual soliloquy. Perhaps, it is not quite so. Because, the Hindu philosophy, in fact philosophies all over the world, recognise that Mind is a different entity from the Self.
> The sage poet is part of the immanent Being. The world is a source of confusion (*bhrama*). The illusion is created by the Great Goddess Mahamaya (Goddess Kali). Nature's Qualities (*gunas*) play on the human

With the holy-unholy twin you dwell so well
In your blissful home;
If the twosome wives will live in love
Mother Shyama will be thine;
Virtue, vice—the twin ewes,
You tie them up to the meanest peg;
Then, as the two you sacrifice
With the falchion of spiritual light,
You will reach reunion with the Absolute;
The enlightened lore that bringeth weal,
Of her scion counsel seek;
Oh, the Illusion's yarn is the yarn that splits,
Chase it off, you banish it;
The two as your soul's offering, give them
Up to Mother She;
Then at last, says Ramprasad Das,
You merge into Brahman's bliss.

༓ Song 44[1] ༓

You turn, oh mind, your love to her,
Who sails you safe across the earthly main;
Your commerce, what's the use of it,—all arid, vain;
Your craving for wealth, kith and kin, fruitless—
You've forgotten bygone times,—

Mind. The Mind then goes astray, coveting worldly treasures and entangled by desires. The inner 'self' of the poet, in this song, is quarrelling with his own mind. The Mind is like an errant boy running away from the 'real home' which is the feet of Goddess Kali.

The present song is the poet's lessons to the Mind as to how it should behave itself, and keep clear of all the forces of errors and wickedness.

[1]This song too, is a dialogue between the poet's 'self' and his 'mind.' The poet reminds the Mind as to what the Being in the 'person' of the poet really is. The worldly pleasures are all useless and futile. The Mind is caught in the lap of a sorcerer and sinks in the great illusion that is this world.

Anger, attachment, desires, the ego-self and all that dally with the Mind day and night—are mere wanderings away from the real home of the 'being'—getting lost in the labyrinth of transient trifles.

The poet advises the Mind to meditate the name of the Great Goddess, the Supreme source of Bliss and Salvation.

Whither you had been, where you are,
Where, from here, you'll go;
The world is all a house of glass,
You dance to the sorcerer's tune,
You are in the Witch's lap, in dungeon lost;
Vainness, malice, ire,—doting on wayward ways,
What you've lost you can't revive,
The day about is past and wan,
In your treasure-isle Shiva's consort contemplate
Ceaseless in your citadel of bliss;
Durga's name, Prasad says, sweet abode of deliverance,
Chant it constantly, sweeten your tongue with heavenly bliss.

❦ Song 45[1] ❦

Will that day come, oh Mother Tara,
When chanting Tara, Tara, Tara tears will flow in streams;
The lotus-heart will bloom, the mind's darkness flee.
Then on the earth my limbs will roll
Overwhelmed chanting Tara's name;
All discord I will renounce, will vanish all lament,
Oh listen,—shashtras, Vedas endless Truths,
Mother Tara is formless One;
Shri Ramprasad proclaims, Mother's there everywhere,
Thou, oh blind of eyes, behold Mother,
In darkness of the darkest hue.

❦ Song 46[2] ❦

Who, oh Mother, will fathom your sport,—

---

[1] The song is a typical worshipful 'hymn' of the poet to the Mother Goddess Kali.

The poet regrets that this precious human life that he has been vouchsafed is wasted in frivolous pursuits of the world. The poet craves that the Mother takes him into her lap and give him devotion. The poet avers that all knowledge, all shastras, and all formal worships are useless. The Supreme Consciousness that Mother is immanent, everywhere, that all is Mother and nothing else exists, but all is suffused by Mother—is the ultimate bliss.

[2] This song embodies the mood of the poet when he perceives the

What you take away and what restore;
It's you who give,—withdraw, that's you,
Whether it's day or dusk;
Your endless work all ordained,
Each his measure as destined;
Entrapped at your guileful feet, Lord Bholanath,
E'en He forgets;
Just as you show so I see, even on waters you float a rock;
To me your wiles will never work, Mother,
He knows the tricks of all those charms,
For, Ramprasad is your own son.

❦ Song 47[1] ❦

Mother Kshema, I am tenant of Her own domain,
Kshemankari, there She is my sovereign King;
You do not know me, oh Death,—
If you did you'd be chastened then;
I dwell in Mother Shyama's Court,
Bear the burden of Her fearless feet;
I abide in Kshema's demesne,
From drought or flood the estate immune,

playfulness and the all-existence of Mother everywhere in this manifest world.

Nothing happens in the world,—no grass grows, no flower blooms, no fruit ripens without the will of the Mother. It is She, the absolute Goddess, that runs this worldly show with Her magic wand.

It is the universal message of Hindu philosophy, the Cream of the *Gita*; it tells the human soul that there is the Power and the Truth and the Being, that shows itself everywhere and makes everything happen. The human being is the mere instrument through which the Supreme plays His tune, moves and evolves the world, in His eternal Cycle of Creation.

[1] Here the poet Ramprasad comes into his own. He dares Death to do him harm. He is well assured in his rights,—rights that he has gained through his absolute devotion to the Mother Goddess Kali.

This whole world, as if, is the Zamindari—the domain—of the Goddess. Ramprasad is the tenant who has owned his right of tenancy perpetually through his worship of the Goddess. Since Mother is munificent, all-powerful Ramprasad has no fears of the predatory hands of the God of Death and Destruction (Yama). The poet enjoys the birthright of his soul as the free-hold tenant of Goddess's own domain.

Look, the sandy stream beneath the sand,
Even then the Estate is lush and green
Prasad says, oh Death, you carry burden for no gain,
By whose gracious feet you own your seat,
You are innocent of their joy and fun.

❦ Song 48[1] ❦

Being Mother is no idle word,
(None is mother by just delivering the child)
If she does not share the child's agony;
Mother has suffered ten months and ten days then,
Now that he starves, you do not ask where is the son,
Where he has gone;
The child has sinned, so say the parents, and that's the end;
Look, there, mace in hand, the devouring Time,
You are pitiless even then;
Ramprasad, twice-born asks, whence this trait you learnt;
Were it, it is your ancestral ways, then pray,
Do not don the name, "Mother of the World."

❦ Song 49[2] ❦

Why should I, by the holy Ganges, dwell,
I would sit at home and sing Mother's hymns;
Leaving my own domain why should I live in other's realm;
At the feet of Mother Kali,
Legion holy Gayas, Ganges I will ken.

---

[1] The sage poet reminds the Mother, in this song, of Her responsibilities to Her own Child.

Mother, in Hindu tradition and philosophy, is a sacred word. Mother is all blessing, all protection, all caring of the errant child. She is the saviour. It is not enough that the mother conceive, carry the embryo in the womb till the child is born. Her duty to the child goes on throughout till the son returns to her lap at the end of his sojourn. The child can always err, go astray, but the Mother has no right ever to forsake him.

[2] These five lines of the song are an expression of faith of the sage poet in the Mother's Saving Grace.

According to the poet all pilgrimages, paying homage to holy places,— are all useless, waste of time and life. The Mother alone is the end of all worship and devotion. And Mother abides everywhere. The poet is a

Song 50[1]

Oh Mother Kali, all worries you wiped out;
Vedas, Tantras—Shiva's Words, this, would you own or not;
You cherish waste, desolation,—jewelled mansion you so spurn,
Oh Mother, as you are so is your lord,
You've never been rid of stirring *bhang*;
Whoever worships you, he wears a different look,
His waist's without a loin-cloth,
Clad in bark, with matted locks;
You brought me on to earth, Mother, beat me, black and blue,
Even then I call, loud, 'Kali',—hail my pluck, so true;
It has spread, it's now 'talk' of town,

tenant of the Mother's own Kingdom and his devotion lies at Her feet. All shrines and holy places are all there at the Mother's feet. The poet has no reason to proceed on pilgrimage so long as he has installed his faith and submission to the Mother.

[1] Ramprasad's songs are unique among all metaphysical 'hymns' in Hindu shastras. Hindu metaphysics is rich and hoary. The Vedas, the Upanishads, Brahmanas, Aranyakas, the *Gita*, the various shastras and then the two great Epics—the *Ramayana* and the *Mahabharata*—are monuments of spiritual analysis and flights of the richest perception of the Abstract in human life and the universe.

The Tantrashastra is called a Science. It is Science by its nature and logical progress. It bridges the latent power of the body with the infinite Energy of the spirit. The infinite Energy of the spirit is housed in the body—because for the living being the body is the house and the temple. If the spirit has infinite Energy how is that the limited, flimsy body can house such a power? This is the eternal conundrum. This is the mystery.

The Tantrashastra explains it and that by a series of logical steps. Because it is logical, Tantra is a Science. It explains the dormancy of this infinite energy. But it also tells, step by step, how this dormant Energy can be realised.

The limitation of the Tantra Science is that it has, perhaps, no laboratory where the experiments, the realisations—can be demonstrated. It is well established and demonstrated in Tantra literature, but it cannot be displayed on the screen or to spectators or witnesses around the ring. It has to be practised and realised—and the experience is unique to the one who does it. It cannot be transferred to the viewers or listeners. That is how the mystery continues, a large misunderstanding persists.

Ramprasad's songs are unique by the close proximity, the deepest contact with which his words are charged when it comes into union

Sri Ramprasad is Kali's son;
This is just a matter of Mother and son,
This who's there to understand.

❦ Song 51[1] ❦

Beware, look out! The bark sinks,
My mind, you are inane, the day has waned,
You never worshipped Hara's Queen
You bought and sold deceitful wares, loaded full the craft;
On the ghat you tarried all day long, took the ferry at dusk;

with the Abstract and the esoteric Energy. Sage Ramprasad had reached to the end of the Tantra Science. He practised it, realised it. And that is why his words are revelations, realisations and charged with power and reality on the one hand and wonder and assurance on the other.

Rishi Sri Aurobindo in his several monumental works has explored the path of progress of the human soul. His ardent followers had asked him whether *Savitri* could not be written more simply, with greater transparency, with less abstractions. For, the epic *Savitri* is difficult reading for the uninitiated.

Sri Aurobindo's answer was that he was as simple as the human language (he chose English) would permit. The human words are humdrum. Words enshrine infinite Energy. But, by their repeated usage on trifles of the human existence, they lose their power for the human perception. The rishi added, he was speaking from vision—from what he experienced—and he was converting this profound vision into a language and words which have their wings clipped. They can no longer soar. Perforce, he had to use symbols and silhouettes which are not circumscribed by what they say but reach out to the infinite space and time and spirit of which they are symbols. The difficulty of *Savitri* (written by Sri Aurobindo) is that the readers fail to reach the vantage point from where the vision can be shared with him. He confessed his helplessness.

Ramprasad is unique because the uses simple rustic words—metaphors and symbols—which are clothed with the power of the highest communion, the final union with the spirit in the image of Mother Goddess Kali.

The present song is one such example. The ultimate 'says' in our shastras, are all embodied in Mother. She is the manifest Absolute and She is playing with this infinite Energy, making man a tiny toy of her playfulness. At the same time, She has put the spark of the immanent power into her toys, who struggle through the maze and illusions of the world, to reach back to the ultimate source, the Mother.

[1]The sage poet uses the metaphor of a sailing raft to return after the day's bargains.

Your sailing craft is old and worn, and then it's laden with sin;
Should you sail, oh mind, the worldly sea, install Mother at the helm;
The six oarsmen, all, have fled, of the wild tumult of waves in dread;
Now, oh mind, turn to Guru Brahma, Prasad vows Mother's behest.

⚜ Song 52[1] ⚜

Nothing good is ever mine;
If weal were mine, why then my mind should roam in sin!
Oh Mother *Dashabhuja*, on this earth my body a burden now,
To You with hibiscus, bael and Ganga waters, I haven't homage done;
Nor, in this world of my sojourn, to Gaya, Kasi I have gone
When Death'll come, lay his hold, then,—Kali Kali, I would call.
Dwija Ramprasad says, as reed on water rudderless I drift,
I cry out, oh hold me up,—me, who on the shore would lift!

    The world is a fair where million give-and-takes of trifles go on. The day is the life. At the end of the day when life is ebbing out, the sojourner must return home. And then he finds that there is the violent sea which he has to cross and that his sailing raft is rotten and dilapidated.
    The human soul is rudderless without the helmsman. The sage poet knows that Mother Goddess Kali alone can steer the human soul across through this turbulence. He invokes Her and is assured, the all-merciful Mother will save him and take him back. No matter if the six oarsmen (the six senses—the five physical senses and then the Mind) have fled in fear. Saviour Mother is unfailing.

[1] In this devotional song the sage poet is confessing his regrets to Mother Goddess.

    This human body is the highest form of Being. The *prana*, lodged in the body is the gateway to the Supreme. Even gods in the heaven can reach the Supreme Being through human powers of *yoga* and meditation.
    The poet is penitent that he had wasted these precious years of human existence without worship or devotion.
    But the poet is assured that since he has taken the 'name' of Goddess Kali, death and decay will not be able to claim him.

☫ Song 53[1] ☫

Who knows how Mother Kali is,
No one can fathom Her with six-fold wisdom's ways.
In the lotus grove, as Queen Swan
Kali sports with the Swan King
Sages muse, ever, Her in Muladhar, in Sahasrara in bloom,
Kali is the Soul of Being, the mystic *Om* the cause
    Supreme;
Mother Tara abides in all,
As the Ordainer's all-pervading will;
The Mother's womb, where repose the cosmic worlds,
Is vast, know this well;
Mahakala knows Kali's quintessence, who else does it so well!
Prasad divines, people laugh,—
It's swimming across the main!
My being knows, yet the mind revolts,—
Dwarf, he would yet seize the Moon!

☫ Song 54[2] ☫

On the emerald rock of Kali's feet
Tie secure the tusker mind,
Tear up the bonds of work
With the sharp sword of Kali's name;
On your head you carry worthless wares,
Steeped in worldly games;
The load on you of the five elements,
And then you drudge with work all vain;

---

[1] This 'hymn' is the poet's realisation of the nature of Goddess Kali. She is the ultimate of spiritual pursuits of the highest Yogin. The realisation of Brahman—the joy and bliss of the final reunion—is concealed in the image of the Mother. The sage who reaches this realisation alone can find the real Truth,—the immanent repository of all in Mother's image.

[2] This song is Prasad's typical regret at the wasteful use of this precious life.

    The human life is a supreme gift endowed by Almighty to the human soul. But a very short life-span is given to man in his single life in the cycle of endless births and deaths. It behoves the 'man' to use his life well and wisely. Instead man wastes his life absorbed in worldly trifles.

The vale of the heart is split,
Ever singed by the trinal bane.
By harassing new-born clouds,
The life eroding wanes;
Sojourning to legion shrines,—
Sweating walk is all you win;
At home at ease you'll gain four fruits,
Lapping misery, oh, don't you ken!
Ramprasad says, nothing pays,
Rummaging shastras, all in vain;
Let now, chanting Brahmamoyee's name,
The vent of the crown burst in flame.

❦ Song 55[1] ❦

Your saviour feet, you squandered all;
For your own son, left none at all,
Of a generous father born, lavish yourself,
You learnt, Mother, in father's home;
The way your parents bounteous,
Are you so to me your son!
The Lord who's master of the Store,
He, at your feet, supine;
Ever drunk with *bhang*, Lord Bhola,
Pleased with leaves of *bael* alone;
Even as Mother, on me what pain
You gave Mother, through legion rounds.
Prasad divines, as I die this time
I'll proclaim you the Cause of Ruin.

---

[1] In this song, the poet is in a different mood.
The poet claims Goddess Kali as his own Mother. And now the poet pleads with the Mother that She has betrayed him (Her child). For, She has already sold Herself to Her consort Shiva. All Divinity is pledged and stored in the custody of Great God Shiva. What is left then for Her poor child, the sage poet himself?
The poet pleads that the Mother has only given him grief and sorrow in his mortal existence. In his sense of thwarted injury the poet tells the Mother that in his next birth he would not call her Mother but he will invoke Her as the 'Queen of Doom.'

Song 56[1]

This time, oh Hara, I will reckon
I'll seize Mother's feet, hold them fast
I' ve caught Bholanath in the wrong,
This I would tell all, everyone;
If Bhola cares for His good,
To me let Him deliver up my Mother's feet,
Father-and-son coveting the same and one!
This I'll tell Him the moment we meet;
Being Father, how does He, Mother's feet,
Hold them down on to His heart!
To Mother's wealth the son is heir,
By what means He that wealth purloins!
Usurping Mother's feet, Bhola, whom does He cheat with sham decease!
Should I say it's Shiva's fault,
It hurts me, as if it were my own;
Ramprasad avers, he has no fears
With the warrant of Mother's guarding feet.

Song 57[2]

Tell me, Mother Tara, where do I tarry,
I've none, whosoever here, oh Shankari;

---

[1] This song is in a similar vein as the previous one (Song 55); but the poet here takes a different stance.
  The poet finds that Lord Shiva (Lord Bholanath) is his competitor. The poet claims the Mother as his own. But Shiva, lying supine at Her feet, has already claimed Her lotus feet. And this is an error of Lord Shiva that the devout poet has spotted. Shiva is the consort, Lord God of Mother Kali. How does the husband lie prostrate at the feet of his queen consort? Poet Ramprasad argues that the wealth of the Mother (Her precious feet) belongs to Her son; that is the age old custom of inheritance. Shiva has no claim to Goddess Kali's treasures. He is a usurper.
  But then, well, the poet finds fault with the conduct of Shiva! Shiva is his father too. It hurts the poet to blame the great father. But then, finally, the poet assures himself that he has the refuge of the Mother's guardian feet as the reward of his absolute devotion.

[2] One unique quality of the sage poet Ramprasad's songs is his dialogue with the Mother as an intimate person. The poet is suffused in his love

With mother's fond love goes father's care,
That's quoted often everywhere;
The father who holds step-mother on his crown,
Counting on such father is in vain.
If you do not deign your grace,
To step-mother then shall I turn;
If step-mother would take me in her lap,
Then would cease my agony.
Prasad says, the Vedas, Shastras—all—
These words recall—
Whoever chants your name, Mother,
He is destined to rags and begging bowl.

☙ Song 58[1] ☙

Kasi, what use is it?
'Gaya, Ganga, Varanasi'—all abide at Mother's feet;
In the lotus-heart as I muse, I swim in the sea of bliss,
Look, the 'ruby lotus at Kali's feet,' legion holy shrines;
With Kali's name, what sin is there,
There's no headache if the head's nowhere,

for the Mother as Her own child. He talks to Her, as the fond child does in the human world to his loving mother.

In this song Ramprasad pleads a dilemma with the Mother. He knows that the love of the father for the child largely depends on the Mother's love for him. The poet is assured of the love of Mother Goddess Kali. He is, thus, quite confident of Lord Shiva's attachment to him. But then, a doubt torments the poet.

Lord Shiva carries the Great Goddess Ganges (the sacred river 'Ganga' of the Hindus) on his braided locks; that is the Hindu legend. In a way, Goddess Ganga is the step-mother of the poet. Proverbially, a step-mother, in Hindu society, is seldom fond of the son of the other wife of her lord. By this token Prasad is not sure of the love of the step-mother, Mother Ganges.

But the poet tells Mother Kali that if She does not take care of her child then he might as well seek the refuge of the step-mother.

But then again, the poet knows that all shastras enshrine the wisdom that any one who seeks refuge at the feet of Goddess Kali,—he must suffer from all worldly agonies. This knowledge assures the poet in his steadfast devotion to Mother Kali.

[1]This song embodies the quintessence of Hindu Vedanta philosophy.

Just, oh, as the flames consume cotton piles.
At Gaya, offering food to fathers dead,
One repays the ancestral debt.
To one who meditates Kali's name,
To him oh, Gaya is a trivial fun;
Who dies in Kasi does salvation reach,
This, in truth, is Shiva's words.
Devotion, that's the seed of all,
Salvation, oh mind, is her slave;
What use *nirvana*,—what profit is it!
In water oh doth water mix,
Look, it's no good being sugar,
I would love to taste it so!
Prasad says, as if in jest,
By the sea of love, by Her grace
All 'four goals of life' are in his easy reach
Who but contemplates 'Mother with flowing hairs.'

    The Vedantists know that the whole of the universe is 'One and the Same.' The material universe is what the philosopher calls, *akasha*. Every atom and the largest stellar body—every bit of matter,—animate or inanimate—is born of this *akasha* and, after the *kalpa*, will melt into the *akasha* and thus go on the existential cycles.
    Now comes the Energy. This Energy is the *prana*, the kinetic essence of existence. This *prana* suffuses every Being, living or non-living, all universes—air, water, fire, earth or space.
    This is the concept of 'Brahman,' the Absolute Godhead as perceived by the Vedanta.
    Poet Ramprasad gives a lyrical expression, with his usual rustic metaphors and in the common man's language, to this absolute unity of life and matter.
    He knows that once he has put his soul, whole being into the meditation of Goddess Kali, there is nothing else, no other worship, no penance, no pilgrimage—that is necessary.
    But the poet is also aware that sharing Mother's playfulness is an eternal joy and bliss. For the sage poet it is easy to merge into the Absolute. Water can always mix with water in the eternal ocean. But then, the poet divines, that he would prefer enjoying the duality and share the bliss and the supreme joy as the devotee of Mother Goddess. He would much rather taste the sweetness of sugar than dissolve in the sweet immanence.

☙ Song 59[1] ☙

Mother, how long must you wheel me round?
As the blind 'ox at the oil-man's wheel;'
You have tied me up to the worldly tree
And, Mother, ceaseless mill me round;
For what sin of me, oh, you made me slave
'Of the vile team of the oil-men six;'
For eight million births I've travelled on
As all kinds of birds and beasts;
And yet I haven't escaped the mother's womb—
I'm dead with pain and agony.
The word 'mother' is full of love,
The weeping child, she takes him in her lap;
This I ken in all the worlds,
Is it, Mother, I'm out of it?
Chanting—Durga, Durga, Durga,—
Legion sinners have escaped;
Take the veil off my eyes,—just once, Mother
Let me look at your fearless feet;
Many a son is wayward, Mother,—
But never so a 'Mother' evil
(Prasad, I know, your worthless son,
Beseech, you keep him at your feet)
Ramprasad, Mother, has this cherished aim,
He lie lowly at your feet when comes the end.

[1]This is a typical song of the sage poet.
    The metaphors are all humdrum, from worldly life. But each metaphor is glowing with symbolism. The cycle of fruitless days and nights of man in this worldly sojourn is like the blinded ox that moves round and round in the village oil-mill, churning the oil-seeds into the liquid oil.
    This repeated mutation of births and deaths is an eternal cycle. Life in this world of the common man is full of pain, sorrow, worries and agony. The poet asks the Mother why it is that the loving Mother should so punish the hapless child continuously in Her playfulness. The poet prays that this blindness of the soul, who goes on in this world forgetting himself and his final salvation, be once removed. The veil may be lifted from the inner eyes so the poet can realise the Truth and partake of the bliss of the Mother's saviour feet. Finally, the poet pleads that he as the hapless son may be errant and wicked, but it never behoves the Mother to avenge on the son. The poet leaves his prayer to the Mother's feet that

☙ Song 60[1] ☙

Oh mind, you are so poor in the peasant's skill,
This precious soil of human life you left sterile;
It would yield gold if you were to till it well.
Fence it round with Kali's name
This harvest then were out of harm;
Of her with rolling tresses, the fence stubborn
Even Yama dares not near it draw.
Today or in a million years
It may be seized, you never know;
Now that your mind to your harp is tuned
Why not reap the harvest to your heart's content
Sow the seeds deigned by Guru's grace,

at the end of this life She should receive the child and give him refuge at Her feet.

[1] This is another immortal song of the sage poet. The *yogi* has to combat the worldly barriers and realise the Truth.

The poet compares this life with a fallow land. The human life is the stepping stone to Divinity. According to Hindu philosophy a man can reach Godhead in one life—in six months or even in six weeks. That is what Swami Vivekananda declares in his *Rajayoga* while talking to his American students in his Vedanta classes.

The poet pursues his simile of the good farmer. The fallow land of this human life must be fenced properly and this has to be done with the *name* of Goddess Kali. This will protect the crops against burglary or pilferage.

The land is also freehold, because it is in the domain of the Mother Queen. The tenancy is sound and there is no chance of bankruptcy or forfeiture.

Then seeds must be sown. And what are the seeds? The seed is the *mantra*—the powerful 'word,' which by mere repetition and meditation, will yield the richest harvest. But then irrigation is needed, and where is this precious life-giving water to come from? The poet has no worries, because his devotion is the holy water which will quench the soil to enrich the crop.

The Poet is aware that cultivating this life, a fallow land full of barbs and weeds, is a gigantic task. That is why the poet tells his mind that if it (the mind) cannot do the farming job alone, let it take Ramprasad as his ally and companion.

Let us note that, in the Hindu philosophy, the Being in Man is a different identity—which possesses all the sense organs, including the Mind as the sixth and most powerful controlling organ of life.

Then water it with devotion's rains;
If you fail, oh mind, by yourself, alone
Why not take Ramprasad as company.

♱ Song 61[1] ♱

Now I have mused on the quintessence,
Have learnt the truth of an enlightened one;
I have come by one from over the land
Where dark night, Mother, there is none;
By day or evening fall,—to me all one,
The eventide sterile I have turned;
Slumber has left, do I sleep again
I'm wide awake in worship, meditation;
Now giving up sleep to whom it keeps,
I've put dark sleep itself asleep;
Mixing borax, sulphur,—I've set gold aflame.
I'll scrub clean, pure the temple of gems,
In my mind I cherish this dream;
Prasad says,—devotion, salvation, twin
I've placed them on my crown;
Knowing that Shyama's name is Brahma supreme
I've abandoned rites and rituals all of them.

♱ Song 62[2] ♱

In the heart's lotus playground swings Shyama of fearful face,
The mind's wind, oh, day and night, it sways;
The arteries two,—Ida, Pingala by name—

---

[1]This song blends poetry and philosophy in a rich baroque of beauty and charm.
  The poet is dreaming of the land of bliss. In such a land there is no darkness, no night, no gloom or sorrow. This, the poet has learnt from someone who knows. There is no slumber in that domain. With the charm that the poet has gained, he has put slumber into sleep. He has learnt the alchemy of turning the dross into gold by a divine chemistry. The poet has united devotion with salvation; he has resigned this world of action and steeped himself in the Name of the Mother as the essence of Brahman.
[2]This song enshrines the cream of experience of the yogin.

The charming Susumna in between;
Within them laced, Shyama, the termless Absolute,
Smeared in crimson blood, how sublime her person looks;
Passion, other illusions all, at the sight flee post haste;
One who has witnessed Mother's sway,
He has Mother's lap his way;
This word of Ramprasad,
Rolls loud by beat of drums.

♥ Song 63[1] ♥

My cherished dream is unfulfilled,
My grief is mute within myself;
My days are past, a string of woes,
There's little left now, of hope of bliss,
What do I tell, oh Queen of all mercies,

According to the *yogin* eternal Energy is ensconced in the spinal chord of the human body. Along the centre of the spine is a capillary channel which is Susumna. To the left of Susumna as one moves upward from the bottom of the spine toward the centre of the brain, is Ida, the artery carrying the Energy of Wisdom. Along the right of Susumna proceeds the other channel, Pingala, which carries the Energy of work (*karma*).

Just as an energy, like electricity, needs wire for transmission, these 'Ida' and Pingala carry energy from the centre at the bottom of the spine upward through the heart region, to the centre of the brain. But the *yogin* can, finally, get rid of this need for channels and proceed through the empty passage of Susumna, which moves along the centre of the spine.

Goddess Shyama (Kali), the principle of Brahman stretches Herself along the Susumna and is ensconced at the lotus seat at the crown of the head.

'The poet is perpetually craving for the bliss that is the Goddess Kali's feet. Constantly, he regrets that the desires, attachments and worries of the world are taking him astray from the path of Truth and tranquil Bliss.

The qualities of Nature disturb the human mind continuously. These Enemies have been defined in Hindu philosophy as: *kama* (desire and attachment); *krodha* (anger and rage); *lobha* (cravings, greed and avarice); *moha* (the loss of discrimination—*vichara*; the power of judging right from wrong); *mada* (vanity, ego and the nagging *aham*—'I'); and *matsaryya* (jealousy, loathing, hate and ill will for others, *anista chinta*).

The poet says in the song that these six *ripus*,—the wicked enemies,— they spoil and destroy continuously the soul's craving for salvation—its

With me are six of them who spoil my deeds;
Shri Ramprasad says, oh Mother,
I'm lost with cares in wilderness;
Giving myself up to your fearless feet,
I am discomposed, all upset.

♀ Song 64[1] ♀

Oh Mother, it's over, my time of play,
It is the end of sports, oh *Anandamayee*;
I came into the world for a round of play,
I did my game of play with dust and clay;
Now, oh mountain maiden, in his chosen hour,
All-consuming Time draws near;
The childhood years spent full of fun,
Days were waste to purpose none;
And then with wife in nuptial pranks,
The vital breath was spent;
Now, old infirm with age,—Prasad says,
Pray, tell me what now I am to do;
Oh Mother, with devotion's potence
Pull me into the sea of deliverance.

♀ Song 65[2] ♀

How long must I trudge on this fruitless toil,

---

joy and peace. Finally, the poet trusts the saviour feet of Mother, for he is utterly discomposed and all his world has turned topsyturvy.

[1] This song is a typical stance of Sadhak Ramprasad. He pines for the Mother's feet, the beauty and bliss of the final Truth. And yet he knows that his days in this world have all been spent in useless pursuits. The sage poet was born into this world and got into the playful swirls of worldly life. Most of his life the poet has spent by playing with dust and useless playthings.

Now his life is drawing to an end and eternal Time is closing, in the shape of death. The childhood was spent in meaningless play; the youth went by in pleasures with the loving wife; the old age has now set in and the fragile body is weak and wasted.

The poet craves that the Mother should take him now, at the end of day, back and drag him to the ocean of bliss and salvation.

[2] The song is the poet's regret that his spiritual cravings have been

Oh Tara, tell me, how much would you make me drudge;
I cherish one, what happens is else,
Mother, there is never bliss;
I'm driven away in five-some ways,
By the five elements within these limbs;
Oh Mother, those six foes have then aligned,
As slaves to the Elements they have signed;
Coming into this world's sojourn,
Got here full share of miseries;
Oh Mother, whose bliss should have been mine,
That Mind is not alas after my mind;
In the name of sugar you served me bitter *neem*,
That bitter taste in the mouth lingers on;
Why, Prasad, physician thou, so sad of mind,
Having taken refuge in Kali's gracious name!

❦ Song 66[1] ❦

What marvel, oh mind, you came to do,
Setting sail the human raft in primeval flood!
You came for commerce, oh mind,
On the rivers of the earthly realm;
Some made two for one,
Some lost both capital and gain;
Earth, water, fire, wind, space,
Of these the hold of the craft is full;

thwarted by worldly desires. And the foes are all within. There are the five elements,—earth, water, fire, wind and the inane—of which the earthly body is composed. They are all frail and prone to mortal disarray. Then, there are the other six enemies within—lust (*kama*), rage (*krodha*), greed (*lobha*), ignorance (*moha*), vanity (*mada*), and jealousy (*matsaryya*),—who constantly bedevil the mind. The poet complains that the Mother is at fault; for, who but She has caused, all these misfortunes for him!

[1]This is typical of poet Ramprasad who often talks of his highest spiritual experience in terms of metaphors.

The poet compares this world to a place of merchandise. The world is like a wide turbulent stream. Merchants negotiate it on their crafts. They lose although a few may gain as well.

The wares are all trivial—made up of frail five elements,—earth, water,

Oh, the six oarsmen pulled six ways,
Kicked and sank the craft ere it sailed;
Trading errant in five-some wares,
When five will melt dissolve in five,
What'll happen, that's what Prasad divines.

♀ Song 67[1] ♀

Listen, Mother Tara, to my tale of woes,
My home is not benign,—oh, thou supreme;
Those with whom I run my house,
Their ways, alas, are wayward, extreme;
The *five*, Mother, pursue their five-some ends,
They share alone the spoils, the cheers;
Having done a round of eight million homes,
It's my turn to amble in a human haunt;
In this motley world cloaked as a clown,
My raft is laden with chagrin;
Heed, oh Mother, Ramprasad's appeal,
In such a home, oh, to dwell;
The lord of the House has a wavering mind,
The *six* of *them*, upon it, wreaking ruin.

fire, air, and the sky. And the oarsmen are all errant—pulling the craft criss-cross; the craft sinks before it has a chance to sail. The six oarsmen of the 'song' stand for the six qualities of the mind that buffet it astray. They are: lust (*kama*), rage (*krodha*), greed (*lobha*), ignorance (*moha*), vanity (*mada*), and jealousy (*matsaryya*).

The Poet avers that this worldly trade in trivial wares will end up in naught and melt into the five elements.

[1]The poet addresses the Mother Goddess and tells her all his miseries. The world is a household. The poet abides here for ages. But all his people are errant and wicked. His five companions—the five elements—earth, water, fire, air, and the sky—have all their distinct cravings. They are not with him nor wish him well. The poet, as the lord of the house, spends his days as a clown tossed about in miseries. And then the poet tells the Mother of his final woe; his own mind, who is lord of the house, is himself so unstable! He (the *mind*), is buffeted by the six hostile forces,—*kama* (lust), *krodha* (anger), *lobha* (greed), *moha* (confusion), *mada* (vanity), and *matsaryya* (hate and malice).

♣ Song 68¹ ♣

If the raft should sink, even then,
Row on, oh mind, my sailor wench;
Pray, oh mind, do not let go the helm,
Take heart, you can still steer on;
Mind, look, the oarsman's depraved, most vile,
By its winks it works its woe as it beguiles;
Shyama, she has cast her snare truly well,
The daughter, she, of the sorcerer;
Set aloft, oh mind, devotion's sail,
On the winds of reverence;
Ramprasad says, —never forbear.
Chant the chain of Kali's name.

♣ Song 69² ♣

Guess, what I'm dying to divine:
By whose name darkness pines
At whose feet Eternal Time supine,
How is it she so sombre, dark!
There are legion dark, swarthy hues,
But this one darkness is passing strange;
Who, when installed in the bosom,
The blooming lotus in the heart illumes;
In complexion dark, the name is 'darkness'

---

¹The poet Ramprasad is constantly fond of metaphors. His highest spiritual songs are often couched in common experience of the world. The image of a sailor sailing, in the turbulent stream of life is one of his favourite symbols.
    The poet assures himself that faith in the Mother will finally save his craft. He knows that the eye of the oarsman often eludes. For the whole show is set up as a snare by Mother Shyama, Herself the daughter of a magician.
    But the poet does not feel disheartened. He knows that constant chanting of Mother Kali's name will lift him out of all perils.
²The image of Mother Kali in Hindu pantheon is dark and sombre. The poet wonders, what kind of darkness is this that, when the Mother's dark image is installed in the heart, it is illumined in lambent light!
In this song the sage poet has used the Hindu symbols that go with the conception of Goddess Kali and Mahakala (Lord Shiva).

Darker than the darkest hue;
Whoever has seen that grace has lost himself,
For other charms he never cares;
Prasad says,—lost, amazed,
Whither had this woman been!
Without a glimpse, by her mere name,
The mind unites with her as one.

꣸ Song 70[1] ꣸

Have pity on the poor, oh Shiva's queen;
You are so carefree; Your fallen son
In this world, he drowns;
There is no ferry in this *ghat*,
How do I ride this earthly waste!
Mother, do deliver me, or else,
Your name, 'Durga,' will be disgraced;
I call you again, and then again,
You listen and yet never hearken,
On earth you follow your father's trait;
What profit then,—'Jai Durga'—my morning call
By which I take your refuge all!
Shri Ramprasad says,—oh Mother,
No shame or harm will come to me;
Mother,—Kasi, your holy place of deliverance,

The cosmic creation is divided into two eternities—Space and Time. Lord Shiva, Mahakala, is the symbol of Termless Time; the epitome Kali is Space in its infinite vastness.

In the Hindu shastras the Infinity is one, but when it manifests itself in the visible creation, it assumes the dual form,—vastness of Time and Space, embodied in the presence of Lord Shiva and Goddess Kali. The Two are One and the One is revealed in Two.

[1] The sage poet is in a mood of reflection in this song. Goddess Kali is the poet's mother. The poet is so close to his mother that he accuses her that She is not delivering her son from the troubles and miseries of this world.

He tells Mother that if Her own son should suffer like this, then who would take Her name and submit to Her refuge in the world! The poet warns the Mother that if She is so indifferent to Her son then the harm will come only to her; no one will call Her any more the deliverer of the world.

Annapurna—your gracious name,—
People of the world will then disown.

☙ Song 71[1] ☙

What treasure would you give me, oh,
What precious wealth have you left?
Your gracious look, your lotus feet,
To Lord Shiva, they are forfeit;
Is there any more a way, Mother,
Of redeeming those lotus feet?
Now, pray, oh, do your best, deliver
Lest should sink this house of reeds;
Should you say those feet are priceless,
I can't reckon what is the price;
Yielding up life, disguised as corpse,
Those feet Shiva has possessed;
Whoever has ever lost his right,
His claim to father's property!
Ramprasad divines—I'm a wayward son,
That's how I have been dispossessed.

☙ Song 72[2] ☙

In my soul the queen of bliss,
Is ever doing her sports, pastime;
In whichever way or how I am,

---

[1] The Poet here is in a different mood. He is so close to Mother Goddess Kali that he charges Mother that She has little love for Her son.
  In the Hindu mythology Lord Shiva lies supine under Mother's feet. The lotus feet of the Mother are thus pledged, tied to Her Lord Shiva. Her gracious looks are fettered by Her attention to Her lord. However, Shiva is also the father of the sage poet. And the poet claims that he has full claim to his Father's weatlh, and the wealth is the lotus feet of the Mother. Is it that the poet Ramprasad has been deprived of his share of the treasures because he is a bad son!

[2] This song is an expression of joy of the sage poet. He is rolling in delight as he feels within himself the bliss of the presence of Goddess Kali. Mother Kali is playful, sporting with Her creation. The poet's heart is the playground of the joyful sports of the Mother.

I never forget that Name sublime;
And then as I close my eyes I see,
The goddess, inward, with necklace of skulls;
Worldly wits, I've lost them all,
Me insane all people call;
Let them call me what they will,
At the end, I would, I'm with my silly girl;
Shri Ramprasad says, Mother dwells
In the lotus in hundred petals blown;
I take refuge under the feet,
Pray, do not turn me out when comes the end.

☙ Song 73[1] ☙

How often do I tell you, Mother, of all my endless woes,
I'm adrift in the flood of sorrows like weeds in a racing stream;
Alas, oh, Mother, I have no moorings, none,
I'm stuck somewhere, yet elsewhere I am bound;
From all six ends pull the six-some foes,
In between I'm caught in deathly throes;
Sage Ramprasad says.—Mother, are you so unkind!
Pray, appear for once in the lotus-heart,
Vouchsafe one last look ere I quit this life.

☙ Song 74[2] ☙

Why is it, mind, your illusion lasts,

The poet has lost all sense of earthly pleasures and possessions. That is why the ordinary people call him insane. But the poet is not worried. He is careless of what the others say of him or how they look at him. His only prayer is that at the end of this life's sojourn he should not be deprived of the lotus feet of the Mother.

[1]The world is like a turbulent stream on which the poet is drifting like the moorless moss. He is buffeted by the pulls and violence of the six enemies. These six enemies are the wicked traits with which the human mind is ever distressed. They are: *kama* (desire); *krodha* (rage and anger); *lobha* (greed); *moha* (illusion); *mada* (ego and vanity); *matsaryya* (hatred and jealousy).

However much the poet tries, these six-some foes tear at him from all sides in his fragile craft of life.

[2]This is a rare song of the poet. Ramprasad was a devoted worshipper

You had no real look at what Kali is;
All three worlds are 'mother's' face,
You know it, oh mind, and yet you miss;
What shame is it, her earthen form
You make and cherish, worship then;
The 'mother' who adorns the world
With gold, gems and jewels all,
Oh what shame, you would her 'dorn'
With *sola* and tinsel ornaments;
The mother who feeds all three worlds
With legion food and delicacies,
What fun that you would offer her
Sun-dried rice and soaked grams;
All worlds with care are nursed by 'mother',—
Is it e'en this that you do not know;
Then how is it you'd sacrifice
Young kids and sheep and buffaloes?

❦ Song 75[1] ❦

Chanting Kali's hymns day and night,
Rapping armpits in wild joy delight,
Sail this carnal craft calm quick and fast;
What of worldly cares! Make you, mind the sailor

of Goddess Mother Kali in her image. At the same time, the poet is conscious of the highest Hindu philosophy of the Absolute Oneness of God. He is both transcendent and immanent. He is above everything, indwelling in the smallest and the largest of the cosmic creation. In this song the poet asks the question,—since Mother is everywhere, anything that happens in the worlds is Her wishes, why it is necessary to build idols and images of the Mother and then worship her! Why it is necessary that one should sacrifice animals at the altar of Mother! And then, when all three worlds are fed and nursed by her, how is it that one should offer humdrum food to her in worship!

[1]In this song, the poet is in a joyous mood. He is buoyant on his assurance that the world will go merry, the life's boat will sail mellow on the worldly stream. The name of Goddess Kali, chanting Her praise is like the friendly breeze that will take the raft of life across the stormy seas. The shastras like Aagama and Nigama—which are words of Lord Shiva himself, declare the same assurance; the poet avers that Lord Shiva's words cannot be wrong. And then before the puissant name of Mother Kali all contending forces of evil will flee in mortal fear.

The southerly egging wind from behind will hail,
Termless Time will stand mute and stale;
It's no lie, hark, what Shiva says,
The subtle powers all are his slaves;
Prasad says, the contender, Evil,
He will flee, hie, post haste.

❦ Song 76[1] ❦

The charming woman, radiant dark,
Lord Tripurari's heart she roams;
As lotus in the morning sun, the feet fair and sheen
With nails as spots of shining snow adorned;
The woman laughs roaring loud,
Swallows darkness in rolling clouds,
Elixir swims in endless rains;
The busy bumble bees—nimble,
Prey upon the maiden's lips
Blundering for bunch of crimson lotus;
Nature's, lythe lissom youthful form,
Enchanting robeless unadorned,
Sans compassion, heart of stone;
The quick glance askance the heart usurps,
As sharp missiles it rains—oh legion;
Poet Ramprasad divines,—dark Mother's form
Musing it, ceaseless tears cascading rain;
To laze on the petals of the lotus feet
That's what my mind unceasing yearns.

---

[1]This song is of an altogether different kind. The poet is charmed by Her womanly image. The description of Mother Kali as an enchanting Maiden shows basic poetic genius of the sage poet.

The rhythm and the rhyme are in the best tradition of Bengali worshipful songs of love and praise—which as pioneering work remains in the Vaisnava literature; exponents being Vidyapati, Chandidas, Govindadas, Sekhar and then, Jayadeva.

But then the song shows the rare power of the poet to blend romantic poetry with highest worshipful stance without lightening the sublime ambience of devotional song.

☙ Song 77[1] ☙

Why are you, oh mind, so alarmed
Like, as it were, the orphan child;
Having come to this world you worry alone,
Afraid of the Lord of the final doom;
Oh listen, Shiva, Lord of eternal Time,
Who ordains the final end of Time,
That eternal Time lies low at Mother's feet;
Yourself the hooded cobra, you fear the frog,
It is indeed so passing strange;
Is it that you dread eroding Time,
Being the child of Brahmamoyee supreme!
How, oh, you're utterly lost as one insane;
Who has his Mother, Brahmamoyee herself,
Of whose threat is he afraid;
Why for naught you fret in grief,
Chant ceaseless Durga's name;
On mind, in Durga's name all fears flee,
Of all worrries the mind is free;
Dwija Ramprasad says, in erring thoughts
You worry, oh, yourself to death;
Now hold on to the seed by Guru taught,
What will the son of the sun-god do?

☙ Song 78[2] ☙

Your saviour feet, all you gave away; none
You left, Mother, remembering your son;
Daughter of a generous father, lavish yourself,

---

[1] The sage poet is talking here to his own Mind.
   The mind is worried about decay and death. The sage poet is surprised. Lord Shiva, in Hindu metaphysics, is known as Mahakala—the ordainer of Time. And that Lord Shiva lies supine at Mother's feet. And the poet is the son of that great Mother.
   With this, how is it that the poet's mind should be afraid of Kala, the great annihilator!
   The poet tells the Mind to forsake all worries. Let it take the name of Goddess Durga ceaselessly, and then there is no fear at all!

[2] The sage poet in this song, is in a different mood.

You learnt, Mother, in your father's home;
The way your parents were bounteous,
In my own case so have you been?
The Lord who holds charge of the treasury;
He prostrates himself at your feet;
Ever inebriate, swallowing *bhang*,
Lord Bhola, pleased with just leaves of *bael*;
As mother, oh Mother, what agony
In legion births you showered on me,
Prasad says,—as I die this time
I'll call you the 'queen of ruin!'

༈ Song 79[1] ༈

Now the game is done,
What sport is this, tell me, oh mind;
The chess-board my chief playground,
The five players they let me down;
Now lodging faith on the move of the pawn
The bishop trapped got killed betimes;
The elephants two, the horses twin,
At home sat idle listless, losing time;
They are mobile, can move to every room,
And yet how, stay put, they got deadlocked;

The poet is the son of the great Mother. But then, the poet complains that the Mother has given away all her wealth in the coustody of Her consort, Lord Shiva. She has kept nothing,—no treasures, for Her son. And then Lord Shiva, who is Mother's treasurer, He is himself mad; He is pleased by a simple worship of *bael* leaves and then he forgets all else.

The poet is bitter that being Mother, She still causes Her son such miseries; the poet promises that in his next birth he will call Her, not Mother, but the Ruinous Queen.

[1]The sage poet talks here in the symbol of the Game of Chess to describe his worldly state.

The poet is a constant loser in the battle of the game. The five elements—the five physical senses—are all his enemies; they have destroyed the *Minister* out of turn; and the two *Horses* and the two *Elephants*, they too have let the poet down. In fact, they could move freely but chose to stay put as imbeciles. Then the poet had two crafts. They too did not set sail with his merchandise, even though the breeze was so cool and friendly.

The twin boats with laden salt
Never flew with sails aloft;
Oh, hail, e'en with such friendly breeze
The barge on the quay ne'er harbour left;
Sri Ramprasad laments, alas at last
Was it this, then, in my lot destined;
Oh, then at the end, in the corner room
The game was lost, checked by the tiny pawn.

♀ Song 80[1] ♀

Am I afraid of misery;
On earth you give me pain, mother, as you please;
If, mother, I go somewhere,
Back and forward grief keeps company;
Then, with load of pain on my crown,
I settle claims with agony;
I'm poison's worm, in plague I dwell,
Poison ever my staple diet;
I'm, mother, such poison's pouch
I wander with load of pestilence;
Prasad pleads, oh Brahmamoyee,
Unburden my bag of woes;
Let me, I would, have some repose;
Look, people vaunt their happiness,

The poet regrets that this is his lot; with all his wherewithals he lost the game of chess by one stroke of the pawn.

The *pawns* are the wayward forces of the mind that take *bishop* or *minister* (the wise intelligence) astray. The two elephants (*gaja*) of the chessboard is steadfastness, which is the tower of strength. Then the two horses (*ashvas*) are the versatile puissance of the Mind who is the King or the soul of the human being. The two boats or crafts are the body and the senses on which sails the ship of life.

[1]The poet here is in a mood of introspection.
He tells Mother, that he is not afraid of misery. In fact, he abides in misery, misery is his merchandise and his total stock.

The poet is like a worm which constantly dwells in poisonous mire. He lives in hemlock, feeds on it, and carries its burden.

The poet urges Mother Brahmamoyee that She unburden him for a time; others proclaim their happiness, the poet is content to be proud of his agonies.

I proclaim, proud, my miseries.

❦ Song 81[1] ❦

Where do I go at this unseemly hour,
I've wandered daylong here and there;
The day, now, declining, wanes,
As I ken, I shiver at the void inane;
Thou, as refuge of the homeless One
Deign me a niche, oh Mother of the worlds;
I have heard it said, the Lord's own words,
Thou art the giver of the foursome[2] ends;
Ramprasad says, beneath thy feet,
Pray let me abide, that's all to it!

❦ Song 82[3] ❦

How you'd get rid of me,
Wretched though, this time I'll see;
It is no candy in the hands of the child
That you snatch, devour it, by your wiles;
I'll so conceal myself, mother,
You'll hunt for me and never find;
Just as the cow behind her calf,
So after me you will run up;

---

[1] The poet here is worried and melancholic.
The day is near its end and the dusk is about to set in. The poet is afraid; he has no refuge, nowhere to abide.
The poet tells Mother that he knows about Her consort Lord Shiva—who ordains life's mission, himself supine at Her feet. The poet pleads that Mother give him refuge at Her Feet; that is all his cravings!

[2] The foursome ends in Hindu philosophy are *dharma* (piety), *artha* (prosperity), *karma* (all that is cherished), and *moksha* (the final emancipation).

[3] This is a typical song of the sage poet. He is the son of Goddess Mother Kali. He challenges here Her Mother—let Her get rid of her child! The poet warns Mother that it would not be so easy that She should escape his claims.
The poet threatens that he would go into hiding; and then the Mother would be in torment for Her lost child; just as the mother-cow runs after her calf.

Prasad says, mother, you could cheat,
Were it, perchance, I was an idiot;
If you won't, mother, deliver me,
Shiva, Father, for sure, He'll intervene!

❦ Song 83[1] ❦

Away with you, you Yama's tout,
I'm Brahmamoyee's son, never doubt;
Tell Yama, your royal King of doom
How many like me has he taken out?
I could be as well your Yama's doom,
Brahmamoyee's radiance should I count;
Prasad warns, you herald of Time
Watch your words before you shout;
With might of Kali's name should I tie you fast
And chasten you, who would thee protect?

❦ Song 84[2] ❦

I'll no more be swayed by sham deceit,
I've pitched my tent on the fearless feet;
For no fear or threat I'll waver or tilt;
I will not wallow in the well of woe,
Stuck with, wedded to worldly wealth;
Pain and pleasure are all the same,
Knowing that I won't set the mind aflame;
With passion roused for fortune, wealth,
From door to door I will not plead;
Obsessed by the craving winds,

Finally, the poet tells Mother that She should never try to play tricks with him; and if she were to do that, Lord Shiva would turn on Her.
[1]This song is another mood of the poet.
Yama is the God of Death and Destruction. The poet is threatening Yama here and scaring Him away. He tells Yama that he (the poet) is no less than the son of Mother Brahmamoyee. And that's why Yama, should better be careful. If the poet so wished, by the power of Mother Kali's name, he could tie him (Yama) hand and foot, and punish him; and then no one could save him (Yama)!
[2]In this song the poet has reached his mission and purpose.

I won't reveal my cherished dreams;
Tied fast with illusion's trap,
I will not hang from passion's tree;
Ramprasad says, I have tasted milk,
I won't swallow stale turbid whey.

❦ Song 85[1] ❦

What is it you vaunt, oh mother,
I know your causal roots,—
What is there you boast about?
You are mad yourself, your lord insane
You dwell in crazy company;
Your primal stock, that all I know
You were lavish when, in which descent?
Torn with strife, man and wife,
You're ne'er at peace in own abode;
Why is it, mother, with a begging bowl
Your man roams from land to land;
Prasad says, I call you names

    He is no longer swayed by the illusions of the world. He has secured the refuge of Mother's Feet. He won't waver in fear; no longer any attachment for him of the poison of worldly possessions; to him joys and sorrows are all the same and the mind is still, tranquil,—unsinged, untouched by passion. He would no longer long for wealth and move around from door to door.
    He would bid hopes adieu, would not allow attachment to tie him up, and would not hang himself from the tree of worldly love.
    Finally, the poet avers that he has tasted milk; he would no longer be cheated by watery curd.
    [1]This song is typical of the sage poet. The intimate relation of son and mother pervades the song. The son is here quarrelling with the Mother. He tells Her that She has nothing much to boast about. Ramprasad knows Her very origin and family history. His Mother herself is mad and wanton; Her husband (Lord Shiva), is half-naked and insane. Between the Mother and Her consort there is constant quarrel.
    In the Hindu mythology Lord Shiva is depicted as beggarly, scantily clad in tiger's skin, with a snake coiled round his arms and addicted to *bhang* (chutes of hemp burnt and smoked for intoxication).
    But then the sage poet's quarrel and complaint to the Mother is about Her stony heart which is due to Her father who is the Mountains. The poet's father, Lord Shiva, He is sagely dwelling in Holy Kailasa, the sublimest shrine of the Hindu pilgrim.

Just for your sire's deeds;
Oh mother, should one take my father's name
One adorns the Kailasa realm.

♣ Song 86[1] ♣

What use this body, my friend,
If in Dakshina's love it does not end;
Oh fie on this tongue, a thousand shame,
If it does not chant Kali's name;
Kali's face which do not ken,
I call those eyes vile, in sin;
Oh, that mind is wayward, ill,
In Kali's feet which does not dwell;
Let thunder strike those blighted ears,
What use, why, they are there,
Which hearkening to that gracious name
Do not fill eyes with flowing tears?
The hands that the stomach fill
Who cares for them,—baleful, ill,
Unless they hold in folded palms
Hibiscus, sandal, leaves of *bael*?
What use these feet that day and night
Work fruitless without respite
That do not hasten eagerly
Where Kali's image is installed?

[1] In this song the poet is questioning the errant ways of the senses.
    The tongue is useless if it does not take the name of Goddess Kali.
    The eye has no use if it does not witness the grace of the Mother.
Let the ears be destroyed by lightning, which, with the Mother's name, do not fill the eyes with tears.
    The hands are depraved if they only help fill the stomach and do not offer worship of flowers sandal and leaves of *bael* (favoured by Lord Shiva) to Mother and Her great Lord.
    The legs and feet have no use if they toil endlessly but do not travel to where Mother abides.
    The mind too is errant if it does not sink into the lotus feet of the Mother.
    The poet regrets that his own senses are deviant and stubborn; how then would he propitiate Mother Goddess! When the tree is wrong can it bear the right fruit?

One whose own sense-organs go astray,
Him, will ever the gods obey?
Ramprasad says, does it yield
Ever mango on the wild basil?

❦ Song 87[1] ❦

Oh mind, call Mother Shyama's name,
See devotion, deliverance on your palm;
Give up passion for worldly wealth,
Worship those red lotus feet;
Disappoint, spurn mortal time,
Listen,—oh, heed this lesson;
Ocean of compassion, Kali's name,
Your yearnings all will be attained;
Bide then in blissful joy,
For half the full round of day;
Das Ramprasad this soulful swears,
Vanquish the six-some foes
Sound Mother's drum, shun all fears,
With the loud cry,—"it's all useless sham."

❦ Song 88[2] ❦

That is why I love the darksome looks,
Shyama, the world's charmer with flowing locks;

---

[1] Here the poet is talking to his own mind.

The mind is proverbially uncontrollable. It is like an unbridled horse. The Being of the man, his will and aspirations are not fulfilled by his mind.

In this song the poet remonstrates with his errant mind so that it should behave. He assures the mind that if it should turn to worship of Goddess Mother there is no doubt that it will attain bliss. He tells the mind that it must vanquish the six enemies that lie inside the Being—*kama* (desire); *krodha* (rage and anger); *lobha* (greed); *moha* (illusion); *mada* (ego and vanity); *matsaryya* (hatred and jealousy).

[2] In Hindu philosophy, the image of Goddess Kali is dark. Her complexion is dark blue like the dense rainbearing cloud.

The poet says that the sweetness and charm of the dark complexion is unparalleled. Lord Krishna, another incarnate God in Hindu philosophy, who had his sports in Brindavana (north India)—was dark complexioned

Shuka, Sambhu, Devarishi,
The spell of darkness, they know so well;
Among all gods, the one Supreme,
In this bosom the dark idol dwells;
The dark hue is Braja's life,
The Braja maiden lost bemused.
Leaving flute, with sword in hand,
Banamali wore dark Kali's form;
Mother's companions, all equal age,
Among them all my Mother dark,
Shines as the moon in the full-moon night;
Prasad divines, knowing all is one,
Darkness rolls with darkest forms;
Oh, one is five, the five-some one,
Bear no ill, oh mind, quarrel with none.

☙ Song 89[1] ☙

I will call you Kali no more,
You are a maiden, yet you took the sword,
Stark naked, fought the raging war!
One 'calling' me you deigned,
You gave it,—that too you stole away;
There was that poor innocent lad,
Being mother, him, you depraved;
Oh mother Kali, Ramprasad divines,

too. And then the poet avers that Lord Krishna with the proverbial flute in hand and Goddess Kali with her scimitar—they are one and the same. A remarkable trait of Ramprasad's sagely worship of Goddess Kali is its catholicity. He is conscious that the great Almighty is One, indivisible and absolute. It is He who appears in different forms. This awareness puts at naught the fruitless quarrels among religions and sects within the same religion.

The philosophy and religious vision of Ramprasad is of immense relevance today when factionalism, sectarianism and fundamentalism,— are so rampant in the world and are the cause of widespread bloodshed and misery.

[1]This is another typical song where the poet is charging Mother Kali that She has not looked after him well. Anything that the poet does is the Will of Mother. That Mother, dire and unrobed, is engaged in war but She neglects Her son and does not give him salvation!

What is it you have done this time!
Lading full this withering broken craft,
You have sunk both capital and gain.

❦ Song 90[1] ❦

I am so sore about that woe,
That you, my mother, being there,
There's theft at home when I'm awake;
I so desire, I chant your name,
Then forget as time wears on;
I now own, I've got a home,
I have known your wily game;
You gave nothing, none you won,
You asked none nor a morsel munched
—Was that all my sin!
Had you given, had you won
Had you taken or swallowed some,
I would have fed or given
All that is your own!
Fame or shame, virtues, vice,—
All qualities are yours;
Oh Queen of playful fun,
While you swim in merriment,
Why break the world of charm;
Prasad says, you've bestowed the mind
With looking at it askance,
Mother, your charm is scorched by evil eye,

    She has given him a broken raft (the physical existence) and then filled the raft with useless things, so it sinks with all its merchandise.
    [1]The poet here is talking to Mother in his inimitable style.
    He asks the Mother how, when She is present, everything is stolen from his house. The house is the poet's mortal existence and the treasures stolen are his devotion to Mother.
    It is only due to Mother's negligence that thieves enter the house of the poet and burgle his treasures. He tells Mother that the final loss is Hers'; if Mother had given him devotion and the real thing of life he could have served Her better,—he would have offered all his devotion and treasures to Mother. But what happens, the Mother has cheated Her son with spurious entertainment and the poet is lost in this jungle.

I roam it round as the sweetest pie.

༆ Song 91[1] ༆

Day and night bethink, oh mind,
That dreaded countenance;
Mother's look is dark nimbus cloud,
Tresses flowing, her robes the empty shroud;
She roams between the Muladhar wheel
And Sahasrara in lotus bloom;
Don't you know, oh mind, as Swan Queen
E'er in the lotus-pool, blissful She swims!
Install her, the Queen of joy,
In your bosom in utter bliss,
Why not light up your enlightened flame,
Then witness Brahmamoyee's countenance;
Prasad says, I so entreat,
Fulfill the longing of the soul devout;
I would rather unite with thy incarnate form,
What fun dissolving in the Supreme sublime!

༆ Song 92[2] ༆

Tara, what more harm can happen,
Oh Mother, Shiva's Queen;
What will you rob, wrest from me,

---

[1]This song is the essence of metaphysical *sadhana* in the Hindu Tantrashastra.

The poet has the eternal dormant energy inside. Along the spine there are eight knots or centres,—which, when awakened, evolve the immanent energy of the Goddess (Mahashakti) and takes the *sadhaka* (the worshipper) to realisation of the Absolute. On the crown of the head is the Sahasrara (the thousand-petalled lotus), which is the seat of Brahman. Brahman is epitomized as the Swan, who roams this region of ultimate realisation and the union of the human soul with the All-Soul.

But the poet does not seek annihilation of his human soul and its merger with the All-soul; He would much rather seek the bliss of his reunion, with Her incarnate form; he would enjoy the supreme tranquillity and peace of witnessing Her glory and grace.

[2]This song is another singular mood of the poet. He is challenging

The most, my life you will take away;
If I live or if I die,
It matters none either way;
If my mind should rest on those fearless feet,
Why do I then suffer torment?
By mounting show of surging waves
What more do you show, oh, Shiva's queen;
Is it an amateur boatman that you ken,
That he should fear the raging storm!
If I should sink myself my raft
In the world's tempestuous sea;
E'en then at your fearless feet I'd sink,
Drink off the pool of elixir;
I'm lost, is there any else to lose,
What more is there from out this world;
I'm here a mere wooden frame
A dummy just for counting name.

꠆ Song 93[1] ꠆

Locks unlaced, enrobed in space,
Kali, grant my heart's desire;
The craving that I cherish deep,
Of that, mother, I see no trace,
Would or would you not on me have grace,
Do tell me right upon my face;

Mother on what harm She can do to him. At most She can take away his life. But the poet does not mind. He is not enamoured of worldly pleasures. The turbulence of the worldly scene does not frighten him. The poet claims he is an expert sailor. He is not afraid of storms and rough sea. Unless he sinks his own raft, no harm can come to him.

Even if he drowns, he would still hang on to the fearless feet of Mother and drink all the honey of the lotus feet of Mother.

The poet is not worried about his physical being. He knows far better and would never be taken away from Mother's bliss.

[1]This is a prayer. The sage poet is the devotee of Mother. He enjoins on Mother that She fulfil his soul's desire.

He gives a final warning to the Mother; let Her tell him whether he will reach his coveted salvation. Mother only knows the cravings of his soul; and let her tell him if his longings would be fulfilled.

The longing that I harbour in me,
That I have told you openly
And barring you, in all three worlds
This agony no one knows.

♀ Song 94[1] ♀

Look there, who, that enchantress;
Rolls of lightning, liquid waves,
Image radiant in emeralds, gems;
Arch charmer, demon-slayer,
Shamer of the lily bloom;
The seas seven, the worlds seven,
The seven-and-twenty temptress eyes;
The crescent moon the crown adorns,
Mahesha in his bosom borne,
Hara's queen, she is alone;
On the foil of the forehead the firebolt flames
On the nasal ring the diamond gleams;
What marvel! What grace I ken;
Just look, oh royal King supreme,
The visage, a well of elixir;
Where the dead are burnt she dwells,
She laughs roaring loud and wild;
Her hairs as foaming swollen clouds,
The winsome wench warm in war,
The fright of fiends and Lucifer;
She's there so near I shiver with fear;

[1]This song is another vision of the poet of the grace and dour countenance of the Mother Goddess.
  The language and words of the song are both metaphysically symbolic and poetically rich. The Mother's person is luminous like lightning, more beautiful than the lotus, beaming with gems and sapphires.
  And yet, She is the exterminator of the demons. She abides in the bosom of Lord Shiva—as His enchantress. She alone adorns the person of Lord Shiva; She is the fire on His brow and the halo on His person.
  She abides where the corpses are burnt (crematorium), with frightful attire. The evil spirits and the demonic forces are frightened of her, but Ramprasad is not afraid. He knows Her grace and Her infinite kindness; he has called her Mother and no harm could befall him.

Prasad counsels abjure despair,
Danger looms, far and near;
Your self, you are ne'er your own,
She's all grace, that's all well known
Chant her name, of Mother Supreme.

❦ Song 95[1] ❦

On the body supine of Shiva supreme
Stands the woman of grace serene;
The streak of sanguine stream of blood
Shines as lightning in looming cloud;
What is it I ken, surpassing strange!
Shiva's corpse She has made her stage;
The dream of thoughts in woman's frame,
The world's charmer bewitching maid.
The Sun, the Moon, the Fire in her eyes,
The moon on the brow of the moon-like face,
The nails on the toes are the rays of the moon,
Portly gait as the elephant queen's
Srikaviranjana, he divines
The image of the dark rain-laden cloud,
Muse, bethink ye, all, devout
Ceaseless, ever, day and night.

❦ Song 96[2] ❦

That woman, what marvel, how she battles;

---

[1]This is another description of Mother Kali as the sage poet perceives.

The poet is puzzled that the beautiful woman is mounted on the body of Lord Shiva himself (in Hindu mythology Goddess Kali is imaged as standing naked on the supine body of Her Lord Shiva).

Her whole body is strewn with cascading blood; it looks like lightning on the dark clouds (Mother's person is dark like the clouds). The poet is puzzled with these contradictions. The sun and the moon in her two eyes, and the mellow moon is lambent on her brow. Her gait is like the elephant queen and on the nails of Her toes there is gleaming lambence like the cool rays of the moon.

The poet yearns to witness this image of the luminous cloud day and night!

[2]This is another song of rare lyrical beauty.

The dour charmer in raging wars,
'Neath her feet the earth in full tremor;
The chariot, warrior, charioteer,—
The horses too she gorges, wild
Her person vast Eternal Time;
In Termless Time her forehead shines,
Her hair benights the diurnal sun.
In terror hie the elephants
As the fleeing insects in the sun;
Meseems the moon is going to fall
Shivering in fright and in thrall;
Unequalled in radiant charm,
Wrapping Brahman in her arms,
Swarms of mighty demons hordes
She swallows, gulps, in giant lumps;
Bhairabis, they strum their jowls,
Yoginis, in tune they howl;
What music, marvel, swelling waves,
Songs fill out the open space;
The wise damsels, they surround,
They shower honey, all around;
Swings the mellow moon-like face
With faint smiles of charming grace;
Cherished desires of everyone
She has wiped them off with nonchalance;
She has usurped cravings all as sham
Lest back to them they should turn and swim.
As the last essence, Ramprasad divines
Chanting Shyama mother's name,

    The Hindu sage Ramprasad often wonders at the grace and beauty of Mother, as a woman of bewitching charm and enchantment.
    The woman is in war with the demons; The earth trembles under her prowess. She devours warriors with chariots and horses. Her person is cloaked in eternal Time. Her dark flowing locks mellow the sun.
    The rebels in war flee in fear like worms in a storm.
    The power of Brahman suffuses Her person. The woman is in company of the lowering spirits and demi-gods who sing and play lurid tunes around her. The mellow grace and sublime kindness in Her eyes and face never turn Her devotees away. She is the last refuge of all who would submit their soul in devotion to Her.

In blessed joy with beat of drum
To Kailasa let's all march on!

☙ Song 97[1] ☙

Who is that woman doing war?
The maiden girl, supreme charmer
Of all three worlds; the eye on the brow
Primordial Fire aglow,
The leftern aural orb the crescent moon
The right a sailing boat,
The facial ring emerald green
As blemishless pure mirror sheen,
Hue as nascent rain-laden cloud;
As Mandakini coursing down
In Shiva's heart in frosty shroud;
The earth radiant in heaving waves,
On that the twin feet installed
As lotus red, the nails arrayed,
In comely rays; the night bedewed
In balmy elixir divine;
Warbles, chants poet Ranjana—
Gracious mother shower thy grace,
Thou Hara's charmer queen in space,
Thou maiden of the Himalayas,
Refuge of the all three worlds
Bower of my life, oh Mother grace.

---

[1]Here is another song in the manner of the sagely vision of poet Ramprasad.

The blending of the lour and fright in her visage with the grace and assurance of Her eyes and face—is a rare combination of the Mother's form. The woman is in war. The God of Fire himself is on her brow and in Her eyes and again Her face is as cool and reassuring as the first rainbearing cloud. She flows as the warbling Mandakini river in the bosom of Lord Shiva lying supine under Her feet. Her feet are like full blown lotus with the nails of Her toes sharing mellow light of the moon.

She is an enigma—gracious and luminous. Who ever takes refuge in Her attains his fulfilment.

☙ Song 98[1] ☙

I pray, oh mind,
Let's together sit alone.
Let's plan it out, heart and soul,—
We would make a haunt at guru's feet,
Just so, and then by stealth beneath those feet
Will drink off the elixir;
Couldn't care less for Yama's father;
After all, what is he?
You say, oh mind, what this swealth,—
Its import you don't quite see!
Oh, the wealth that guru has given,
The saviour feet sublime—
How is it I make its use?
What Sri Ramprasad bethinks—
He would cut the thorns and make it clean;
Then go to the land of elixir,
Drink off the manna-dew, holding
Fast in heart to guru's name.

☙ Song 99[2] ☙

For sure this day will end,
This day destined to end,
Else the world will loud proclaim
Shame, on Tara's name;
Legion stains will remain;
Into the world's crowded fair I came,
I sit upon the *ghat* my bargains's done,
Mother, now sets the radiant waning sun,
Do take me, pray, on your craft!

---

[1]The poet here is in a reflective mood.
He is asking his own mind to have a quiet exhange of thoughts with him. The poet advises the mind to drink deep off the grace and nectar, staying fast at guru's feet; this will be his forte for protection. And as the mind so drinks ambrosia there is no fear of the God of Death. The *mantra* (seed) that he has received from guru will help the mind cut through the barbs of life and drink deep off the honey of the message of Guru.

[2]Here the poet is in a mood of melancholy. He harbours a grievance against Goddess Mother.

The craft full with the wares of sundry men,
It leaves the wretched one behind,—
Mother, from him they ask the fare,
He will get it, oh, tell me, from where!
Prasad says, oh *maiden of stone*,
Pray turn your eyes, a seat you deign
Chanting your name, oh, I now set sail.

❦ Song 100[1] ❦

The world is shoreless, there's no ferry across,
The hope, the gracious feet, the abiding treasure,
Thou saviour in peril, pray, do deliver;
I witness tumult of waves, the fathomless sea,
Lest I should drown, in fear my limbs do shiver;
Tara, I'm your slave, you deign your grace,
By your feet as sailing craft save me this once;
The storms rage, there's no respite,
My person shakes, quivers day and night.
Grant thou my dream, I'll chant Tara's name;
Tara, thy name is the seed of the worlds.
Time has slipped, Kali, worship undone,
Prasad says, fruitless, life has gone;
These worldly chains, pray, do unshackle;
Unless, Mother, deliverer thee—
On whom shall I this burden leave?

The days go on and then life is wasted. Mother is not helping Her son to attain his heart's desire. What will happen; only shame will attach to the name of the Mother. The poet has traversed the market place of the world; at the end of the day he sits alone on the bank of the river watching for the last ferry. The sun is about to set; the ferry comes and goes with the wares of others, leaving alone the wretched person of the poet. The boatman asks for the fare, but where is the means of the poet with which he will pay the passage.

The poet prays to Mother—who has but a stony heart (in the Hindu legend Goddess Kali or Durga or Parvati—is the daughter of the Himalayas, the Mountain of stones and snows). The poet finally submits that he would chant the name of Mother and the Mother must ferry him across the ocean of the world.

[1] It is a typical song of the poet.

He was born a man of the world. He has witnessed the storm and turbulence, the sorrows and miseries of existence in the world. But the poet has moored his sail on the anchor of Mother's feet. He prays that

♀ Song 101[1] ♀

How am I so much at fault!
For, each day the day wears on
So heavy and woebegone,
I keep on weeping oh, Mother,
Alone throughout the day,
Often I wish, I desert home,
I'll abide no more in this wretched land,
But then the potter's wheel was set wheeling
By the orderly, 'worries' by name
So often I decide, I'll give up home,
Sit quiet contemplating Mother's name
But Mother Kali has so set up her trap
I'm tied hand and foot in attachment's web
The wretched Ramprasad
In dire agony, he floats
As flotsam on Kali's feet.
That Mother Kali, she's mine,
But the soot and dust of my mind,
By that I'm tainted black
By attachment to earthly things.

♀ Song 102[2] ♀

Why commerce any more;

the Mother should come and rescue him from the storms and high waves that torment the sea. Lest the poet should drown, Mother should provide him with the craft that will help him sail across the sea.

The poet is shivering with fear and constantly taking the name of the Mother. And then days go by and the longings of the poet's soul remain unfulfilled. His prayer to Mother is that She should rescue him and make him free from the fetters and turmoil of this worldly life.

[1]The song is a regret that the sage poet submits to the Mother. The sage wants to quit this world and its useless worries. His whole being seeks solitude with his dear Goddess Mother; he wants to forget himself in chanting her name and worshipping her feet. But then Mother Kali has laid a trap in this world. The sage poet would much rather break away from the toils of the world's joys and sorrows. Finally the sage poet craves the indulgence of the Mother that She remove all the dark sins and desires from the mind of her devotee and give him the safety and bliss of her golden feet.

[2]This song is a unique blend of symbols and experience of the working world.

Oh my mind, do tell me so.
My debtor She, Queen Brahmamoyee herself,
To that 'bliss,' even alas, you said, 'no;'
The breeze ensconced as it is fanned,
As it moves, it's all revealed;
Oh my mind, Brahmamoyee dwells in thee
In slumber, do awaken Her aglow.
Should water enter the aural adit,
One takes it out at once who knows the trick,
Alas, oh mind, mixing water
In that self-same water,—
How then all worries of the mortal world!
The supreme treasure is in your home,
What illusion, so, you care for glass;
Oh mind, listen, embrace the Truth
Bestowed on you by Lord Supreme,
Why not with that open the door
Of the profound weird device.
The grandchild was born nonpareil,
Old grandfather, by him grandma slain.
Hark, oh mind, thou art profane
Impure, ever since you were born.
Worship, Vespers, all in vain;
Prasad avers again, and then again,
You've ne'er known yourself, alas, oh mind,
Marked vermilion on the widow's brow,
What shame, indeed, how insane!

The poet tells his own mind as he often does that it should not get immersed in worldly commerce. The great Mother Brahmamoyee (Mother Kali) herself owes to it the poet. Why is She so indebted to him? Ramprasad is a great devotee of the Mother. And his devotion has earned the poet a claim on the divine Goddess for Her grace.

The great goddess ever dwells within the poet's inner soul. Only that She is dormant. And She is dormant and slumberous because the mind is not clear and pure in its meditation of the divine feet. The mobile wind is everywhere but it is revealed only when it is fanned. And how does one wake up the dormant divinity within oneself? It is only with the help of the divine Grace itself. One knows that when a film of water enters the ears one can take it out only by putting a little more water in the ears and then shaking it out.

☙ Song 103 ☙

Thou my tongue, sing, keep chanting Kali's name,
In Death's own form Destiny has opened up her Womb.
When dwells Kali in one's heart,
What use to him is then debate;
It's all sham playthings meaningless words.
Get your tongue to play the game,
The divine deathless elixir of Shyama's name,
You sing, you chant, you drink
Off that everlasting bowl of elixir,
Kali's Name is immanent bliss,
It is the realm supreme of calm and peace,
How is it with your hands in knot
Beads of Kali's name you do not count,
What shame outrage blasphemy!
Set your ears to hearken on to the tune
Of the two-lettered word you contemplate
In your mind constantly;
Prasad avows upon his faith, bide your time,
Oh, listen, with Kali's name on your lips.

The poet regrets that his poor mind forgets the gems and treasures that abide within himself and is chasing all the time useless broken pieces of glass by pursuing worldly pleasure. The poet pleads with his 'mind' that it should abandon all formal rituals and worships and then concentrate on the name and image of Mother Kali. His own 'mind' is foolish as it chases absurd aims as if to put a vermilion mark on the brow of a Hindu widow (a practice which is taboo in Hindu custom).

Lord Shiva and His essence is the sole purpose of life and the seed is always within the human being.

The sage poet remonstrates with his own mind and his physical senses. The tongue is urged to constantly utter the name of mother Kali. He reminds the tongue that 'Kali' herself dwells within him. And when that is so what is the use that the tongue should waste its efforts in debates and dissertations!

The name of mother Kali is the final bliss of the being. Why then the mind should stray and wander on worthless thoughts and desires.

Prasad pleads with his mind that it should dwell on pure thoughts of the two-letter word (Kali) of Mother and bide his time in joy and bliss. And that is how it will attain its final salvation.

Song 104[1]

Of the queen of charms it is fun supreme;
One who is caught in attachment's web.—
Alas he is fugitive,—the one who is free
Usurps merrily all the bliss;
This is me and this is mine,
The one who like this divines.
Is so naive; oh, my mind
You feign courage take stoutly heart,
Taking it, all amiss, for sole essence.
Who is me and who is mine
Who is there, else, alone save me!
Oh mind, Oh listen, who cares
For whom, it's for nought you pine,
For pleasures, suffer pain.
Lighting up the lamp in the chamber dark
If one attains the sole essence,
Oh my mind it is only then
You gain salvation absolute;
And then remember nothing remains.
In the royal home of enlightenment;
Oh do abide,—your own self yourself you ken;
Ramprasad avers,—Oh lift the veil
Remove the curtain and then behold
Thee thy own countenance.

Song 105[2]

Oh my mind, my forgetful uncle thou,

---

[1] This is a song of resignation and supreme enlightenment. In the Hindu philosophy, all worldly attachments are a chimera; they are all transient. There is no reality but the all-soul, the absolute Godhead. Mother Kali is the symbol of the Absolute. It is an error that we believe and call our near ones our own. Indeed,—no one and nothing in this world is our own.

This 'science' is the true enlightenment. This knowledge is veiled from us by *maya* just as if we hide ourselves behind the mosquito net. Ramprasad reminds himself that the light of enlightenment must be lit up; then only one will be face to face with oneself.

[2] In his songs, the sage poet Ramprasad quite often uses symbols to

What goes out and what comes in
Even that you do not know!
The day you were born, deposited on the earth
E'en then you were lost, written off as expense;
Oh, set out right—expense, income,
And then subtract and put three noughts,
If what remains is subtrahend
It's minus sum the cash is short,
When the treasury is poorly stocked
Bankrupt, it is cruel deceit,
Then the accounts go on you have no end!
Prasad avers, ponder, bethink yourself
What are all these expense accounts,
In whose account the incomes come?
Rather, thou oh mind, reflect for once
Cast your thoughts within yourself
On Kali, Tara, Uma, Shyama
There, effulgent, all they dwell.

Song 106[1]

Oh mind, do you fathom Her the Queen,

couch his spiritual and worshipful thoughts on his beloved goddess mother Kali. The Hindu Tantrashastra is the most profound exploration of the cult of Shakti (Energy) immanent but dormant within our body. Once this coiled Energy is roused and the *sadhaka* (sage) proceeds unfolding the seats of the successive levels of spiritual power, he approaches the Absolute ensconced on the brow of the human body.

The sage poet often talks to himself—his own mind,—of his pains and travails, his visions and urges—on his way to salvation. And he uses symbols and metaphors from common life. The game of dice and chess— the fun and frolic of kite-flying, commerce and voyage, buying and bargaining in the village fair,—they all serve the poet as subtle sources of symbols and similes.

For sometime Ramprasad had worked as a clerk in a zamindar's office, keeping the accounts books of his master. In the present song he uses the books and methods of accounts as his language of lyric. The debits and credits—and the art of drawing balances serve as models of keeping accounts of our earthly life. But the poet-accountant sets puzzling—whose assets and what incomes and expenses is he talking about? The world is all a chimera; all our earthly gains and losses and our endless calculations are all illusions, unreal. The only lasting asset is mother Shyama installed in the human being.

[1]Ramprasad often reveals the urges and impatience of his soul for

In the dark wild chamber insane!
She is the essence of thought,
Without it, were it, She ever fathomed
Sans profound contemplation;
Do tame, oh mind,—thus within
The wild lunar realm with thine
Coiled cream of dormant flame;
Oh remember within the chamber
There is the recess deep concealed,
There she will hide beyond your ken
E'en as the dark night should dawn
Beyond beholding of the six-some lores
Of agama, nigama of the Tantra's cream;
She loves to bide in devotion's roll
Oh, She dwells there in her inner attic
Rolling e'er in eternal bliss.
She is *yogin* supreme ever longing
For love forlorn; in *yoga* immersed
In meditation from aeon to aeon;—
As love, devotion well up in foam
She embraces, pulls it on
As loadstone does the iron ore.
Prasad avows, the One whom
I quest as child the mother, contemplate,
Do I spill it out in open lawn?
That, you guess, oh mind through tips and hints.

Mother Kali, to his own mind. Again and again he takes his own mind to task. It is the mind that takes the 'being' astray—into the blind alleys and dark byeways of this worldly life. There are the six foes—*kama* (desire), *krodha* (anger and rage), *lobha* (greed), *moha* (confusion), *mada* (pride and vanity), *matsaryya* (spite and jealousy). These foes are the product of *gunas*, "the qualities of nature." These plays of the *gunas* work through the six-some foes,—their victim is the mind of the 'being,' The being in the poet is in constant search of the divine 'Mother.' but is swayed and betrayed by the errant mind.

In the present song the sage poet catechises, remonstrates with the mind; he explains to his mind the secret of enternal bliss and salvation. The Mother is the symbol of the Absolute. She is ever with us, in-dwelling, abiding in us. It is love, devotion and craving of the 'being' for the Mother—that is the only way to attain her Grace. Ramprasad is Her own child, tied with deep bonds of affection and total surrender. But is it that the poet has to reveal all his deepest attachment for Mother,—in open and in public? He holds his treasures close to his chest and let the mind guess it by hints and nuances.

☙ Song 107[1] ☙

My Mother, She abides in the inner niche of my mind.
(Who says, Oh Shyama, in-dwelling thou)!
Thy heart is stone, thou art mountain-maid
Deadly charmer sorceress thou.
How you thrash and rinse this lowly page!
You assume five-some virtual forms
As one worships you by diverse creeds;
But from one who knows all five
And yet kens they are Same and One,
From him, Oh Mother, how but you escape!
One that doesn't discern and seek refuge
His burden you would feign and shun;
But one who knows the worth of Gold
Would you enchant him, how, with trivial glass?
Prasad avows—my inner soul
Is lambent pure in lotus mould
Do, mother assume that mould
And dance your rhythm as the charmer maid.

☙ Song 108[2] ☙

Mother Tara, thou oh queen Shankari;
For what sin, what justice this
You passed decree on me of endless miseries !
One accused, pursued by bailiffs six
Oh, tell me, Mother, how I contend them all,
How I so yearn all six I kill

---

[1]The poet declares in the song that his beloved Mother Kali, She is within himself.

But, as he says so, he remembers the confounding charms of the supreme Mahamaya. Mother Kali assumes five-some forms to the Hindu worshippers. But the poet is wise. He knows, whichever way and form She appears, She is the One and the Same, the Absolute Godhead.

Mother Kali cannot escape Ramprasad, Her devotee, who knows this essential truth. The poet knows the value of gold and therefore he cannot be cheated with broken glass. He declares that his own bosom is a clean and crystal mould. Mother Shyama, universal charmer, can do her dancing in that same mould.

[2]In this song, the poet uses throughout the language of the criminal court.

By ministering mortal poisoned pill;
Krishnachandra, the Bailiffs' Lord
In his name the auction called,
There, that Krishnapanti who lives by betel-selling
That fellow, to him you gave away your wide estate.
Do I appeal to His Lordship, but how,
Where is the money that I can vow?
Making me a pauper by deceitful means
Thou art seated, careless, princess Queen;
The one who is my counsel before the assize
He makes compromise, pleads such wise
Very like, his case lost dismissed,
As for sure, I should very like lose.
I have nowhere to flee, oh Mother else
Tell me, oh how, what is it I do;
My only refuge was those fearless feet,
That too has been usurped by Lord Tripurari.

☙ Song 109[1] ☙

I dwell in the name of Mother Kali
What worries then are mine!
Oh, the dark confounding night is gone
The morning begins to shine,
As the nascent sun arises.
The web of darkness melts away.
Listen, oh,—the lotus in the lotus-seat,

Mother Shankari or Kali, —She is the ordainer of all decrees and judgment in the living world. Ramprasad complains to Mother,—why She had to pass the judgment of misery on Ramprasad.

He is the only accused but there are six bailiffs the six-some vile propensities of the mind; and the poet is helpless. The decree of auction has been passed; all assets of the poet have been passed on to other hands. The poet is penniless; He has no money even to pay the court fees or to make a petition. The Queen Mother is watching his miseries and his plaint is dismissed.

The poet laments that he has nowhere to go or take refuge. He had only one place of safety, which was Mother's fearless feet; but that too has been usurped by Lord Tripurari. The allusion is to Lord Shiva who lies supine at the feet of the Mother.

[1]This song is a great piece of poetry and metaphysics lambent through the veil of sublime symbols.

That's your end, it's so proclaimed
By herself Lord Shiva's Queen;
Those blind agents of the six-some lore
Have thrown dust in your eyes, so sore,—
Oh, hearken, if you do not ken
Your inner seats of Jyeshtha, Mula
Who would end your aimless sports;
Where there's rolling mart of joy and bliss
There's no guru no disciples
No lessons, no learning, none,
Oh, the players are His who mounts the Show
By debate who the truth will know!
The deep devout soul that has tasted bliss,
He alone, to that realm, has access
Ramprasad divines, the illusion's gone
Who will hold the flame in rein!

❦ Song 110[1] ❦

So sweet is Mother Kali's name
You chant it drink it all the time,
Shame to thee, oh tongue, e'en then
Thou seekest dainty porridge bun,
Formless or incarnate, the primal Being
She is home, refuge of everyone,
Oh hearken,—pleasure emancipation
Their destined home is the Name,
What is there beyond, you tell me then !
In whose bosom Mother Kali dwells
There, in him the holy Ganges bides;
When time comes, he quits the world.
He is one again with Lord Mahakala,

    Philosophy and metaphysics have caught the genius of sagely scholars of all ages. Hair splitting analysis and discrimination on the nature and identity of Divinity is meaningless to the Poet. He has contempt for all such scholarly dissertations: He declares that the Absolute is within the person. It is only that we are unconscious of the Godhead within us. The devoted worshipper who has realised the in-dwelling presence of the Absolute does not need any scholarship or debate. He himself has tasted the bliss and joy within himself.

    [1]Here the poet Ramprasad is questioning his own tongue and then his

As he claps his hands to consuming Time.
Light up the flame of enlightenment
In Thee, forswear virtue. vice and all;
Turn your mind as holy *bael* leaf
Distil your ceaseless worshipful care.
Prasad declares,—all doubts and conflicts then
Will melt away in blissful harmony
In your inner bosom's realm;
This my earthly body is forsworn
To Dakshina Kali, to her name
Bequeathed and sealed as divine realm.

☙ Song 111[1] ☙

Oh mind, at tipcat let's have a hand
Save with you I ne'er play the game;
I will put it here, I will lift it there
I'll hit it round and round,
Dusts will fly and pollens cry
As the game in pitch does mount;
In the name of Kali I'll hit out the stick
The skull of Yama I'll crack;
You took counsel from those six
That's how you forgot yourself,
Oh Ramprasad you spoilt the game.
The tattered rag the beggar's bag

own mind. He scolds his own tongue that it is fond of sweets, cakes and pastries forgetting to chant the name of Kali which is much sweeter and satisfying. He reminds his tongue and his mind that within himself the great Goddess Kali ever abides. She is the deliverer of the being from death and annihilation of termless Time. He advises his mind that it should light up the flame of consciousness and worship Mother Kali installed in the mind. He is at peace because his own body has been dedicated to the worship of Mother Goddess Kali.

[1]This song is typical of sage poet Ramprasad. He often takes a worldly game, fun or frolic as the symbolic structure of his sagely realization.
In this song he tells his mind to play a game of tip cat. And the poet warns the mind that he will only play the game with it (i.e., his own mind) and with no one else. The poet is himself an expert in the game and he will trip and lift the tapered piece and hit it so hard, by taking the name of Mother Kali, that it will break the skull of Yama, the God of Death. The poet reprimands the mind that it has taken counsel from the wicked 'six' and therefore has lost its right vision. The poet refers here

You made them wreaths round his neck.

❦ Song 112[1] ❦

That is why I grieve repine
You have made me, mother, a worldly man;
Without wealth, money this earthly life
Is vain futile for every man;
Even thou, mother, thou didst quarrel
For Shiva is a mendicant;
It's true pursuit of knowledge enlightenment
Is the highest form of bliss
Yet higher still is giving alms
Sacrifice and charity;
Oh mother, that Queen of Brajaland
Had not been across to Mathura
But that she had done penance of giving away;
Artless poor thy camouflage
Oh mother, transparent thy veil,
Wearing ashen ornaments
On thine effulgent limbs;
Oh mother, how, where dost thou put away,
Conceal thy treasures of the lord of wealth.
How is it, oh mother, thou art
So chary, grudging miserly
In bestowing thy grace to poor Prasad,

to the six traditional foes in our being viz., *kama* (lust and desire), *krodha* (rage and anger), *lobha* (greed and avarice), *moha* (confusion and loss of vision), *mada* (ego and vanity), and *matsaryya* (hatred and jealousy). The mind has betrayed the poet and spoiled his game of tip-cat, making him don the beggar's robes.

[1]The poet here is in a different mood. He complains to his Mother Goddess that she had made him a worldly man; but then he is poor, without money. Without money this worldly life is a waste. And the poet proves his point by telling Mother that, Mother Kali too had quarrelled because Lord Shiva was a beggar. The poet supports his point; he says that the virtue of wisdom is high indeed, but charity is supreme. Even the queen of Brajaland (Sri Radhika) had to pay her alms when she had gone to Mathura. Mother too wears a false robe of ashen trash. In fact she has concealed Her immense treasures. Prasad knows it and then he complains to his Mother that why then she should be so chary and not give him a little bit of her grace. Prasad submits to Mother that she should keep him at her feet, then he could bide his time in peace, away from all peril.

Should'st thou grant refuge in thy feet
I would hold on well and fast to it
Wary ever, safe, from all peril.

☙ Song 113[1] ☙

Oh, thou my tongue, for once, call aloud
Full-voiced, Kali Tara's name,
What fear hast thou of Death, oh, tell me then?
What use then, oh, of pilgrimage
To Ganga, Kasi, in whose bosom dwells
The image awake of Elokeshi!
What need has he of penance worship sacrifice
Who knows the essence of Her, the queen supreme.
Has faith in hymns, in chanting name,
Hopes absolute of release profound;
Of Ramprasad, this is the plight
Wavering torn between two minds.

☙ Song 114[2] ☙

Tara's name is destroyer of all,
What remains alone is the beggar's bag,
The blighted rag and that even
Is frail fragile, impermanent;
The way the goldsmith purloins the gold,
The gold removes the base alloy
Thy name, oh mother, has the self-same way,
One can't tell the other from the one.
The soul that in the household loud
Calls, mother, Durga's name.
Lost afraid in mortal fear;

---

[1] This is a typical song of the sage poet.
He enjoins on his tongue to chant the name of Kali full and loud. Then, the poet assures, there is no fear of death. Then there is no need for pilgrimage to Kashi on the bank of the holy Ganga. When Mother Kali with her flowing locks dwells within oneself, that person does not need any worship or rituals.

Ramprasad is in such a stage when he has given up all puja (worship) and is immersed in the image of the in-dwelling Mother.

[2] In this song the poet tells mother that taking her name makes one a

Mother, in-dwelling Thou, wide awake
Thou shoulds't know when it is time;
One whose parents, alas, wear ashen robes
Dwell, abide under the tree;
How, oh mother, their son should last
In his earthly home, that's cipher
Coy, indeed a conundrum;
Prasad is now overwhelmed by Tara's name
Grace eludes him far away.
Oh, my brothers, friends,—pray, hearken,—
On Prasad cease to reckon, count.

❖ Song 115[1] ❖

Now, hence, oh Kali I'll take your count;
I will work out the account, fathom
Kali's dark profoundest lore.
She is dancing Kali ever so fickle
Shifting stance so constantly.
I wonder ever how I her confine;
I'll mount the tune in my mind's instrument,
Set her dancing in the lotus of my heart.
I'll teach you the way, oh my mind,
The stance, the tune of Kali's feet
And those other six, the wily wicked team
I'll cut them down to pieces everyone
Kali alone I will contemplate
Till I am dark withering bare bones,
I will chant Kali's name and bide my time;
I'll paint black his face,—put to shame

beggar. Only the beggar's bag and the tattered rag remain,—and that too is so transitory.

The goldsmith steals gold and mixes alloy. Likewise, taking Mother's name removes all worldly treasures and makes her disciple a total wretch.

The poet tells Mother that she dwells within. But then, The Poet's own parents adorn their person with ash and live under the tree. For the son of such a Mother dwelling in a house must be strange indeed.

Ramprasad warns his own friends and kith and kin that they should give up all hopes of him because Mother Tara (Kali) has overwhelmed his whole being.

[1]In this song the sage poet vows to deliver the accounts with Mother Goddess Kali.

Death, emissary of Eternal Time
And quit this world at the end of my sojourn.
Prasad craves, why mother
What more, oh tell me, do I reveal,
I am hurt though I conceal my wound
Yet, I won't cease chanting Kali's name.

꣹ Song 116[1] ꣹

Witness my chartered deed, oh come,
I am Mother Kali's son.
You, Yama's bailiff, go and tell,—
I dare you, your Yama, royal King;
The *firman* signed by Lord Ganapati,
Approved and sealed by queen Parvati
Lord Sadananda, omnipresent, my bail,
Nandi Himself witness without fail;
The *firman* dwells in my bosom's niche
Its throne is just as the *firman*, rich
On that has signed in His own hand
Himself Digambara, Lord Supreme,
I got the *firman* from Mother own
Could there be a mischief e'er therein!
Prasad dares Death—if thou should'st frown

    The song uses the Bengali word *kali* in different meanings and nuances with a pun on its different senses. Kali is the name of the Mother; again kali in Bengal refers to measurement and a third meaning of *kali* is blackness—all with a little difference in spelling.
    The poet puzzles how he will retain the mobile and dancing mother in the lotus of his own heart, But then the poet knows the propensity and the desire of the Mother. That is why he promises to cut down the six wicked forces inside viz., *kama, krodha, lobha, moha, mada, matsaryya*. He would then go on taking the good name of kali till he himself is black with fatigue. Then when time comes and death appears the poet will paint the face of death black and quit this world happy with Mother's name.
    The poet concludes that he cannot say any more of his plan of things.
    [1]This song is the poet's challenge to the God of Death.
    Death is inevitable and he overtakes every mortal man. But then Prasad warns Death that he has a *deed* signed and sealed within him. And Lord Shiva Himself is the security of the deed, which has Goddess Parbati's approval and delivered by Lord Ganapati (Lord Ganesha) Himself. Further, the witness to the deed is the great Nandi (Lord Shiva's right-hand valet).

I would proceed, report to Mother's throne.

❦ Song 117[1] ❦

Tara, deliverer of the woebegone,
Thy name, mother, is the essence of all,—alone
Biding moorless in the open inane
I now know, mother, the way of thy reign;
Sage Vashistha had learnt your charms
He blew a baneful curse with broken bones,
The Queen Serpent, as if, ever since
Rages without the gem on the crown.
Thou had'st met your match in the noble sage.
Thy ways are free from the chain of cause;
'Un,' 'Sa,' 'Ta,' 'Ra,'—coiled in charm
Your alphabet is conundrum,
It's true, the path of ten is straight and even,
But the walking sticks of ten is a load on one
The load of ten is burdensome,
It's just playing pranks with the mind.
Duped by the word of the one insane
Wasted time in worship so long;
The bond of slavery I've signed,
There's nothing now which can be done.
My nose I rub, I beg your pardon,
Deliver, oh mother, thy sermon;
Thy witnesses all, they're liars and knaves
With them the corridor's full and dark.
Thou dwell'st on the lotus of sixteen leaves unfurled
Will so reveal thyself in all three worlds;

With this kind of 'deed' in his own possession, signed personally by Lord Shiva,—there cannot be any error or omission. Therefore the poet tells Death that he has no claim on him (poet); if he (Death) should misbehave then the poet would appeal to the Court of Goddess Mother Herself.

Ramprasad is fond of symbols. In this song he uses the language and jargons of the court of justice.

[1]This song is a complex amalgam of allegorical reference and Tantric (of the science of Tantra) realization.

The song begins with the poet's realization that the only essence and reality of life is the name of Mother Tara (Goddess Kali).

Looking at the playful sports of the Mother in this living world, the poet is afraid.

Prasad divines in his deepest self,
Mother Tara,—She hides within Herself.

❦ Song 118[1] ❦

You, emissary of Death, better go back,
How oh, what is it I care,—
Owe your wretched Yama's father!
Your Yama, he reckons right and wrong,
He is mere collector of virtues, sins;
My virtue's column, it's zeros all,
Take all my sins through auction call.
The Lord who routs death, His feet
I hold them constantly within my chest,
What fear mine! Sounding trumpet, drum
I will repair to Kailasa Realm.
Ramprasad, oh, his mother Shankari,
Better look at the awesome countenance,

The poet recalls that aggrieved at the wayward ways of Mother sage Vasishtha had been upset. Mother's alphabet is a maze of cryptic letters, which would puzzle her devotee. The poet regrets that, urged by the insane passion of his mind he had spent his time in worshipping the Mother. He has now signed his bond of slavery and therefore there is nothing he can do now.

Mother has taken full advantage and has held him in toils. She has got her false witnesses lined up too.

But then poet knows that she abides in the sixteen petalled lotus within his heart, and the poet vows that he would lift the veil of the Goddess within himself with his unfailing devoutness.

[1]Sage poet Ramprasad habitually talks to Mother Kali.

In this song he dares the father of Yama. Yama is the God of Death. The poet does not care even for Yama's father!

Yama is merely the clerk to record the register of dead men. The Lord God Shiva, he is the Supreme Lord. Ramprasad holds Shiva himself within his bosom. The poet bothers neither about his virtues or his sins. These are for lesser mortal men. Ramprasad holds the key to immortality because his immortal soul is in perpetual communion with the Absolute Divinity. Moreover, the great Goddess Kali is his (poet's) Mother. She is the royal spouse of Lord Shiva. She is dreaded by all including Yama. And then Lord Shiva, His palace portals are guarded by Lord Brahma and Lord Vishnu, the other two great Gods of the Hindu pantheon.

The song is an epitome of Absolute fearlessness of the devout sage. This is the message of Hindu philosophy. Complete devotion elevates the human being beyond the realm of fear of death and the mortal world.

My father, He indeed is Shulapani,
Brahma, Vishnu,—whose portals keep.

❦ Song 119[1] ❦

Oh Death, what use your idle threat;
The grace to whom your office you owe,
She has vouchsafed me immunity;
With just a lease of Her domain
How you dare, show off your esteem!
Oh, tell me, when but one doth burn
The sham image of the doll of reeds
When the owner's there in Her rightful realm?
If I owe Her some on my account
To you, mark it, I would n't give account;
Oh listen, when there's the sovereign King
Does one e'er vouch by the underling!
I dwell in Lord Shiva's domain,
I own my charter from Shiva Himself.
Ramprasad avers, look, in that deed
Brahmamoyee is witness, She Herself.

---

[1]This song (like the earlier one) is the poet's confrontation with the God of Death.

Man is afraid of death. But then the sage knows that man is immortal and the soul of man never dies; he does not care for death of the mortal body.

The poet knows that death is merely an illusion. Death indeed has no powers. He is a mere instrument of the sports of the Almighty Mother. He owes his office to the great Goddess Mahamaya, Kali of whom the poet is a devotee and who is his (poet's) own Mother.

The poet has got a lease of her Domain. That is to say the poet is accountable alone to the Mother. Mother Kali and Her divine consort, Lord Shiva,— they two are the lord of the cosmic world. By the right of his devotion, the poet has earned his immortal place in the divine realm. When the poet has such authority and everlasting possession of light and bliss, what does he care about the useless threat that Death shows to him?

Ramprasad's words are often burning, flowing arrow-straight without any frills or decorations. In this trait and posture Ramprasad is unique even among the great body of Hindu sages. Again and again he claims his rightful place at the feet of the Absolute through his devotion and communion with the Mother Kali.

Song 120[1]

Mother Tara, I'm not one of your timid child,
I'm not afraid should you show red eyes;
My treasure, those two purple feet
Which Lord Shiva holds in His lotus heart;
Oh mother, when I plead my dues
You feint, evade in wild excuse;
My charter sealed, by Lord Shiva signed
I've put it safe in the niche of my heart.
I'd appeal this time before the lord Himself
I'll secure decree with a single shot,
You'll learn what kind of son I am
When in the Court I mount my stand,
While I, in the parade, would exhibit
The evidence, all, by Guru left
Then, in the law-suit between mother and son,
There, Ramprasad avers will be lot of fun;

[1]This song is a rare specimen of the strength of the devotee even against the worshipped Mother. Rights come from love. The child attached to the mother can fight it out with the mother herself.

And then the sage poet Ramprasad is not a dull boy, devoid of wits. He cannot be cheated even by the Goddess Mother Kali. The cosmic world and the qualities of Nature *(sattva, rajas* and *tamas),*—they play hide and seek with the human mind and cause all confusions—attachments, sorrows and miseries. Thus this world is the playground of Mother Kali herself. These pose threats to the human soul seeking spiritual salvation.

But Ramprasad is not afraid. He has his wealth of the vermilion feet of the Mother within his bosom; those two feet that Lord Shiva Himself holds on to His chest. In the Hindu mythology Mother Kali is portrayed as standing on the chest of the supine Lord Shiva under her feet.

Ramprasad will now appeal to the supreme Lord Shiva, consort of Mother Kali against the harassing sports of the Mother. Ramprasad is certain that he will win his plaint before Lord Shiva. Because he has proof by way of a sealed deed, signed and witnessed by the Lord Himself. There will be fun indeed when people will watch a lawsuit between the Son and the Mother in the Supreme Court of Lord Shiva Himself. Ramprasad holds the seed of the most powerful evidence that the Guru has given him.

Finally, of course, the poet is the devoted child of the Mother Herself. He may be angry with the Mother and sue Her in the Supreme Court of Lord Shiva, but his (the poet's) sole purpose and craving, is the sweet and sublime lap of his beloved Goddess Mother Kali.

I'll quieten, oh mother, hold my peace
Alone when you caress me, on your lap of bliss.

⚘ Song 121[1] ⚘

Oh mind, what's your business that you came,
You ne'er learnt your job its very essence!
So you lost what you had and what you gained;
Loading your craft with treasures by guru vouchsafed
How's it you did not do your give and take!
Alas, you kept, oh, evil company
Propelled your craft to sink midstream!
Sri Ramprasad, oh, begs to learn,
Why did you leave that wealth behind?
How will you gain in your commerce then
Oh, you've put your creditor to ruin!

⚘ Song 122[2] ⚘

I've reposed my soul on those fearless feet,

[1] The songs of the poet are very often a conversation. The poet is a spiritual seeker who had attained the highest lore of the occult Tantra Science of Hindu philosophy.

The body of the human being is a citadel of power and bliss. This power is enshrined at sixsome *knots* in the spinal cord, starting from just above the rectum to the apex seat of power in the brain. This infinite power is the reflection of the Absolute in human body.

However, the mind of the man, in combination with the five physical senses plays, truant. The Mahamaya of the Hindu Philosophy is the vast and Infinite Nature Herself. The mind is harassed by worldly matter,— gains and losses, sadness and pleasures and so on; these perceptions are all ephemeral and illusory. That is why the Mind takes the real Self of the man along errant ways.

In this song the poet questions his own mind,—does it know its business? Man has come to the world but what for, and what is the purpose? The mind is innocent of the business and commerce which is its special privilege.

Man is possessed of treasures and the mind as an expert tradesman should know how to make the best of it. All the merchandise is loaded on the craft of life but the mind, ignorant as it is, has allowed it to go all waste. And the mind is in bad company. The companions are the sensuous evils of lust, anger, greed, confusion, vanity and hate and jealousy.

As a result the mind has suffered a total loss in the business of life and has discredited the Principal,—who is the supreme Goddess Kali Herself.

[2] The poet is complacent and fearless. he has no worries now. He is

Have I any longer dread of death?
The bounteous tree of Kali's name
I've planted deep in my bosom's realm,
I've sold my body in this earthly fair,
With that I've bought mother Durga's name.
The one good soul that dwells within
I now abide in his abode, sublime,
I've bethought, this time, as Death doth come,
I'll open my heart and show him in;
Tara's name, the cream of all essence.
I've tied to the tuft of hair on my crown
Ramprasad proclaims, with Durga's name
I've taken leave, tarrying to set out anon.

⚥ Song 123[1] ⚥

That is why I bide under the tree,
With joy in mind and full of bliss;
First, I'll break the leaves and twigs,—
Then I'll rout the branches, fruits.
Rage, malice, greed, others all
I'll banish them to distant lands

untormented by the desires, passions, worries and cravings of the world. He is not afraid of Death.

The devoted sage has submitted his whole being to the refuge of the feet of the Mother. The very name of the Goddess Kali is bountiful and the *horn of plenty*. Therefore the poet has no other cravings. He is fulfilled and liberated.

The poet says that he has made the supreme gainful commerce in the market place of the world. He has sold off his body and soul and, in exchange, has purchased the Sublime Name of Mother Kali. And this treasure he has put safely away into his bosom in the custody of his pure good soul. Just as man has got enemies, foes and predators within himself, so within his inner citadel dwells Divinity Himself. This divine essence, the multiple divinity, that ever resides within man is the perpetual shelter and refuge against all fears and worldly torments.

The poet says, next time Death knocks at his door, he would open up his chest and show him (Death) the immortal treasure,—the name of Mother Tara (Mother Kali) ensconced in his inmost home.

The poet is safe and full of bliss. He has tied Mother Tara's name on to the end of his long plaited hair (usual with Hindu hermits). And he is ready to quit this world of cares and sorrows.

[1] In Hindu philosophy the mundane world is often compared to a magnum Tree. Only, the Cosmic tree has its roots upward into the heaven.

I'll abide, eager, in mellow bliss
In that sea of nectar, swim, fulfilled;
I'll glean the bounty of the quintessence
Of fruits, as then home I return.
You ripen all my errant fruitless ways
Wash away all outcome in deep despair;
What's wrong, oh mind, with you, let's share the bliss,
When two of us work together none is amiss
We'll then drink as one by the self-same breath,
As the sun usurps, drinks up the juice.
Ramprasad declares, my spinal realm
Ablution done with Tara's charm;
That woman doesn't know,—fast, secure
I have bolted, sealed the mind's door.

❦ Song 124[1] ❦

Oh mother, my destiny is to blame,
Indeed it is at fault, oh Anandamoyee;
Mired, drunk in worldly pleasures
I could not make it to Varanasi;

Its branches and foliage hang down towards the earth spreading and sprawling in a wide compass. An earthly tree has its roots inside the earth, where lies its seeds and from where it draws its succour. But the Tree of the World has its origin in the Absolute, which dwells in the high inane. And then, the Cosmic Nature with its wild desires and works and passions and love and all the attributes of mortal life spread downward. The poet knows this. He is happy to sit below this Tree and wear away all the leaves and foliage, that is, all the desires and pleasures of the world. But then behind and beyond these manifestations and wayward expanse of the world, there is a supreme bliss where Divinity lies.

The poet promises that he will take the elixir out of this life and then attain the Supreme Bliss. In this affair, the poet invites his own mind to share and commune with him. When the Mind and the Self of the sage unite in the craving for the ambrosia, then there is no barrier anywhere,— just as the sun usurps the moisture and balmy juice from everywhere in the world.

Ramprasad warns the Mother Nature who as Mahamaya, spreads her elusive toils of the mundane world, that he has shut out all adits into his body and there is no chance for that sorcerer woman to have access to his holy enshrine that is the temple of the human body.

[1]The song is a confession of the poet of his own sins and errors to the Goddess Mother Kali.

Or else, when there's mother Annapurna,
How is it I starve, go hungry so!
To make my living I'm done to death;
I run round, till the soils and this and that;
In mine own floods, all my farming drowned
A lonely furrow that's all I plough.
I have not done any pious deeds
Countless, legion sins, that's all I did
With prickly thorns, my path I've strewn
Having lost my way I bide forlorn,
Being born in the holy Bharata land
Oh mother, what's this all I've done;
My this land is waste, the other lost
In the shoreless sea I drift afloat
Sri Ramprasad bemoans, these worries mine
Beyond endurance, day and night,
Oh mother, when Death will dare torment
I will hang him to death with Durga's name.

☙ Song 125[1] ☙

Is it there, e'er, any fear, pestilence?
Within my body it is here
Mother Tara's own farm land,
Where the Lord of gods as farmer supreme;
Has sown the final seeds of the sublime
Patience as the moorings, Virtue as fence.

> The poet, as common in most of his songs, talks in symbols. Varanasi is holy city of the Hindus. There dwells Mother Annapurna (the same as Goddess Durga or Kali) who is known for her bounty, grace and fulfilment. But then the poet has forgotten to go to that holy place. He is absorbed in useless worldly pursuits in search of illusive pleasures. He is starved of the real sustenance of life which is the spiritual salvation.
>
> He is a diligent farmer but then all the harvest is wasted and drowned in his own sins and foibles. The poet has deserted all righteous work and is drowned in sins. He has careened from the rightful path and has lost, in this holy land of India, both his present life and fulfilment in the life beyond. But then all is not lost. The sage poet has lost his way, he knows that Death will soon come to take him away; but he will tie the knot and cast the charm in the name of Mother, Durga. And then that is how he will escape the trammels of death.
>
> [1]The sage poet is in the midst of worries and torments of this world.

Has confined this body in deep defence;
What can prying Death do now purloin?
Termless Time Himself is saviour.
Watching out, those *oxen six*
Have come out of their secret den,
By the sharp scimitar of Kali's name
Have cut to pieces all sinful reeds;
And then the blessed rain of love, devotion
Day and night is pouring on;
Prasad divines, on Kali's deigning tree
Have blossomed fruits of *four-some bliss.*

❦ Song 126[1] ❦

The mind bethinks it'll go on pilgrimage;
Giving up the bliss of Kali's lotus feet,
It'll dwell in the well for sumptuous eats.
The world's ills of ageing, sins, disease,
Legion ailments there at Neelachal;
When you have fever, Kasi is dire peril,
And a bath at Triveni will augment your ill,
The name of Kali, panacea supreme,—

But then he is not afraid. He has assured his safety from all the evils and foes that work ceaselessly around him. His own body is a domain of Mother Tara (Mother Kali). And then that land and soil (the body) is tilled by no less than Lord Shiva, the Supreme divinity and the unparalleled farmer of the Cosmic creation. He (Lord Shiva) has sown the seeds with the *seed mantra*. The land is safe from the inroads of invading forces. the fencing is so secure. Penance has supplied the manure; piety and righteousness has woven the fence and surrounded this body as a wall of protection. Lord Mahakala (Lord Shiva),—He Himself is the sentinel! What can Kala (Death or Yama) do?

Wary and watchful the sixsome bulls (the sensuous foes) have come out of their pens. All sins and vices have been mown down with the sharp scimitar of Mother Kali's name. And then the sweet showers of devotion and love are raining day and night.

The sage poet has no doubt that the divine Tree of Mother Kali now bears full blossom, all the four supreme missions of human life.

In Hindu philosophy, the aim of life is foursome: *dharma, artha, kama* and *moksha. Dharma* is the end of virtue; *artha* or wealth is the means of virtue; *kama* or ultimate desire is for fulfilment of salvation; and then *moksha* or liberation is the final end of the human being.

[1]This song of the sage poet is rather unconventional. Hindu religion

It is prescribed with deep devotion.
Oh listen, you chant it, drink it,
Your soul then will share the Absolute.
Lord Mrityunjaya, most true, will be there,
You'll soon get well with his boundless care;
Oh harken, all can then befall
You'll get dissolved in supreme All-Soul,
Prasad says, oh my dearest mind
Leaving the refuge of bounty's horn,
Would you, oh, repair to the bush of thorns
To get free from fear of Death's dark doom?

❦ Song 127[1] ❦

Set me free, mother, with waving locks;
In this world I suffer woes and spite,
Ceaseless, day and night, with no respite;
Giving me up to all-consuming Time
Have you forgotten me, oh royal Queen!

commends pilgrimage to the holy shrines of the land of India. There are places of pilgrimage like Varanasi in Uttar Pradesh, Puri in Orissa, Kailasa in the Himalayas, Triveni in West Bengal, Rameshwaram in the southern tip of Tamil Nadu and hundreds of others. Sages and seekers of salvation practise penance and proceed on pilgrimage to the holy sanctified shrines of the land.

Not so with the sage poet Ramprasad to him the lotus feet of Mother Kali is the ultimate of elixir. He warns his mind—what would it do by going on pilgrimage! All the holy shrines do not help the human soul to shed his desires and worries and craving for pleasure. Kashi or Varanasi would enhance his fever and phlegm (the poet plays a pun here because Kashi is a Bengali name for coughing and phlegm and also the name of holy Varanasi). A bath in the holy Ganges in Triveni might also worsen the fever of his physical body. But the ultimate medicine and panacea of all disease is the name of Mother Kali.

The poet enjoins his mind that it should chant and sing that name of the Mother which would cure the inner self of all ills of the world. Lord Shiva himself dwells in this temple and there is no doubt that salvation will be the reward of the sage.

Prasad persuades the mind and declares that there is no point in leaving the cool shade and grace of the Tree of Bounty and moving around under the thorny bushes,—for that would never emancipate the soul from the clutches of death.

[1]Sage poet Ramprasad is unhappy with the worries of the world. He

Tara, how long, when, this mortal tie,
Past enduring, shall snap, unwind?
For, look, holding step-mother on His Crown
Father dwells in the burning ground.

ꕤ Song 128[1] ꕤ

Mother, now I'm vocal in my plaint;
This time be wary, Shyama, how you judge;
Now look there, my 'mind' upholding bail,
Jumping up those sixsome respondents all,
They are ignorant, step-mother's wretched sons,
Those six are 'desire' and others all;
If you and I should tie, unite,
I would banish them from their domain;
The step-mother, she would die of grief
If to those six I should pay no heed.
I dwell so happy in the land of eternal bliss
I ford the wily river of hopes,
Mother, with thy lordship, ferret it out,
The complainant, in person, in attendance;
This treasure earned through worship my own
Is no commonplace that I should disown

has an aching pain day and night immersed in this world of commerce.
    Mother Kali is portrayed in the Hindu pantheon as the Goddess, naked and unrobed, with her flowing hairs cascading round her person.
    Likewise, Prasad prays to Mother Kali that she should free him from the toils of this world. Mother Kali is the queen of Lord Shiva. Prasad complains that Mother, in her royal throne has forgotten her child (the poet himself) and has given him over to the God of Death in this mortal world. The poet pleads with his Mother, when will that time come when she will emancipate him from the stranglehold of this turbulent mortal world!
    Prasad regrets that an appeal to Lord Shiva,—that too is useless for the Lord Father of the Universe (Lord Shiva). He has repaired to the waste of the *burning ghat* (crematorium) with the step-mother on his crown.
    Lord Shiva in the Hindu mythology holds the divine river Ganges (Ganga) on his plaited hair. Mother Ganga, she is the other consort of Lort Shiva and so is the step-mother of the sage poet, whose own mother is the Goddess Kali, the royal queen of Shiva.
    [1]This is a trickly song in the series of symbols. The words and

My Mother primal, knowledge supreme
Father sans beginning, Absolute and One;
Oh mother, thy son step-mother's own
Where have I claim, to whom shall I mourn!
Prasad divines, assured in mind
Father He forsooth no liar none,
Checkmated often, I'm much wiser now,
Is it, I put my foot in trap again!

☙ Song 129[1] ☙

Mother, how so much you dance in war!
Robes sans compare, cascading matted hair,
Bare unrobed on Hara's bosom
How wild so much you dance in war!

ambience are of the Court room where the two sides have filed a suit. The poet is the plaintiff. He has brought his plaint to the Court of Justice where Mother Kali is the supreme judge and arbiter.

The complaint of the poet is against the foes that dwell within himself. These are the forces of ignorance. In Hindu philosophy these foes are six. They are: *kama* (desire and lust); *krodha* (anger and rage); *lobha* (greed and avarice); *moha* (error and confusion); *mada* (ego and vanity); *matsaryya* (hate and jealousy).

These are the creation of the three *gunas*, (the qualities) of Mother Nature. Man goes astray from the path of devotion; he is beset with worries, anxieties, desires, passions and greed because the human mind is tormented by these forces of Nature. This Cosmic Nature, the appearance of Mahamaya is thus the step-mother of the sage poet. If the poet should succeed in banishing the six-some foes, these sham sports of Mahamaya, she is unhappy and resentful.

The sage poet addresses Mother Kali, his own Mother. If Mother should help her child to combat these evil forces then the poet will easily swim in the eternal bliss of Mother's domain. He will cross the turbulent streams of desires and passions.

Therefore, the Mother has now to declare Her decree. Both the plaintiff and defendant are present in Her Court. The poet is ready with his treasures which is his earnings of worship and devotion. This lore and enlightenment is the most sublime. It is a pity that even then the poet should be under the influence of the children of the step-mother, that is, the six-some foes within the body.

But then Prasad does not despair. His father, Lord Shiva himself has assured that devotion to the Mother is the sole route to salvation. Prasad (the poet) will no longer get into the trap set up by wily Nature.

[1]This song is altogether of a different kind. The sage poet Ramprasad

Wreaths of skulls of Diti's sons, just slain,
Waving pendant on charming thighs;
Countless human hands the waist adorn,
Budding ringlets on the lobes of ears.
Lips as ruby curves surpassing plums
Sweet array of teeth as lily flowers
Face bewitching as lotus pure
Loud in laughter alluring wild
Person beguiling as rain-laden cloud
The feet, how charming, crimson with blood;
Prasad proclaims the mind gambols,
Is it, the eyes could hold the grace sublime!

ꕤ Song 130[1] ꕤ

Loose vast hanging tresses
Wreath of human hands the waist laces
The bewitching woman on Hara dwells
The eyes burn as the glorious sun
The moon abides on the gracious face
Tiny corpse, arrow-like under the lobes.
On the left hand the human head and scimitar,
On the right the boon of blessed refuge

was himself a scholar and erudite person versed in Sanskrit and the scriptures. In a number of similar songs Prasad chants Mother Kali's sublime grace and daunting fearsome appearance. Mother Kali in Hindu Pantheon is depicted with a necklace of human skulls and with a sharp scimitar in her hand. She is the extirpator of demons (*daitya dalana*). She stands bare in warring stance on the person of Lord Shiva lying supine at her feet.

The poet is overwhelmed at the fearsome grace of the Mother. her locks are loose and flowing; stark naked, she stands on the chest of Lord Hara (Lord Shiva). She dances with the wreath of skulls of demons (the sons of Diti*)* whom she has slain presently. Around her waist adorns a chain of human hands. On her ears hang rings of budding human forms. Her lips are ruby scarlet and the array of teeth are as white frosty *kunda* flowers. Her complexion is dark like rain-cloud and her lips are smiling like lightning flash. The Mother's feet are drenched with blood trickling from all over her body.

Prasad is enchanted at the appearance of Mother, both gracious and fearsome, in an awful blend of charm and terror.

[1]The song is a description of Mother Kali in her Cosmic human form.

The person dark with grace sublime
The limbs loose as if drunk,
Elixir welling out of the lambent smile
Robed in naught but thine own self,
The voice resounding fearlessness,
In the prime of youth, beloved of Lord Supreme
On Prasad shower thy grace divine
Oh beloved queen of Lord Hara,
Of this worldly ocean I'm so in awe;
This pain of birth, it's thine own pose
In thy feet, Gaya, Ganga, Kasi,—all repose.

♀ Song 131[1] ♀

Home of charmer hopes, dread doom
Of darkness, who's that enchanting woman!
Person awesome as the louring clouds
Brahmas quite some as if therein housed;
Enchanting lass with the moon on her crown
Roaring hairs, denizen in Hara's bosom—
Blazing face, overflowing in elixir,
The homely damsel dances wild;
With sharp swift shifts, the quivering face
She routs by her prowess the demon race

    The rolling rhyme and the choice of words of the song is one distinct type of Ramprasad's composition. Here, there is hardly any symbols. The usual stance of the poet is to mix up ordinary metaphors of life with the sage's occult experience in the path of his abstruse penance.

    Mother Kali in the song is a divine human form, an enchanting woman, her flowing locks cascading down her thighs, Her waistband is of severed hands of human beings. The Woman is awesome and charming; Her eyes burn like the sun and the mellow moon is ensconced on her brow. In Her twin left hands she holds the truncated head of the demon that She has slain and then the dread scimitar.

    Her right palm, upside down is showering grace. Her whole person, hue as the dark rain-cloud, is lambent with the halo of elixir. She is her own costume; robed in open inane. The young maiden proclaims loud assurance from fear and dreaded death.

    Prasad worships the sublime vision of the woman, seeking her grace and emancipation from all fears of the world. Mother should deign and vouchsafe the devoted child the fruits of all worship and pilgrimage.

[1]The words and rhythm of the song are cast in the classical mould.

The jackals howl, can words spell out
She has turned the day to darkest night;
Weak wretched unfortunate
The mind home of nagging wicked thoughts
Ramprasad, what evil has befallen him
The only saviour, Mother Kali's name.

☙ Song 132[1] ☙

Face as the moon without her stain
Ever pleased elixir to drink divine,
Looking at her form graceful slim and lithe
The God of love unsettled himself beside.
Never bethink awry, Oh prince of men,—
He whom you deem as Brahman's form
Lies supine as dead beneath her feet;
That warring woman who is She?
As the young crescent lunar form
Her bewitching smiling lips sublime
Decrying her, alas, how one lives!
The world, radiant, she has illumined;
Bethink yourself well within your mind
The queen of the night the lord of day
In her eyes dwells the god of fire
In her hand flashes the sharp scimitar.

The rhyme and assonance have been blended with Sanskritised sonorous words to describe the Cosmic appearance of Goddess Mother Kali.

The buxom woman is a charmer with a lambent halo round her person that withers all darkness away. The complexion is like the dense dark cloud, spreading out in the vast heavenly realm.

The moon adorns her forehead. Open flowing encompassing locks she stands mounted on the chest of Lord Hara (Lord Shiva) lying supine at her feet. From her glowing face with cascading nectar the maiden woman dances swift in violent turns. The face and neck are waving in marauding rhythm. The woman extirpates the demon hordes; the jackals howl and the day is turned into night,—the awesome appearance of the Mother is overwhelming.

The sage poet knows that he is poor, wretched, immersed in sins and wicked ways but then he is the devoted child of the Mother and the great Goddess Mother Kali must rescue him from all his torments and danger.

[1]This song is a worshipful chant by the sage poet in praise of Goddess

The charming woman, she's supreme!
Blessed the mother of whom she was born
Oh, why, what for she has joined the war
With her uncanny fangs, nails as winnowing fan,
Teeth as radish long, loose the tresses hang,
Dusts on her person, so dreaded dire!
Bard Ramprasad pleads
Thy own page, pray do shield
Who has cried, Mother, in mortal fear;
Were it, mother Shyama
You do not forgive his sin
Oh, "Mother," "Goddess Uma."
Who would call you then!

Song 133[1]

Who is there that ravishing woman,
Flowing locks on a corpse as colossus stand,
The nails, sparkling, sharp array of them
Surpassing the mellow frosty moon,
Person as the dark louring crimson cloud
Face echoing rolling cascading snow
Companions ever changeful weird strange
Mirthful playing with humours of men

Mother Kali.

The moon has its dark spots, but the face of Mother is pure and taintless lambence. She is so beautiful that even the God of Love (the most charming person in Hindu mythology) is charmed and shocked to witness her enchanting beauty.

The lips of the Mother are ever smiling like the crescent moon. One loses oneself as one beholds Her countenance. The world is illuminated by Her light,—as the lunar orb in the night, as the Sun across the day; and the God of Fire himself dazzling from Her eyes.

Who is this supreme maiden, one wonders! Whose daughter is She? And then again how awesome is Her countenance,—nails like the winnowing fan, teeth as the sharp shining radish, locks flowing in torrents, dark all over the person.

Poet Ramprasad divines and craves Mother's forgiveness for he is afraid. But then he is Her own child and if Mother will not forbear and shower Her Grace on Her own son then who else will do it? And then who will call Mother Uma as the divine Mother?

[1] This is a song with sonorous diction.

Laughing dancing loud the woman raves,
The homely maid by fearsome prowess of arms
Danu's mightly sons felled on earth, supine
The gnomes, ghouls, phantoms of the spirit realm
They are spurred by Shyama's warring rhyme
The hands rattle, rap in clapping tune
Babam, bam bam the cheeks play drum
Dhan dhan dhan, gud gud sound the kettledrum
For allaying fears of the earthly realm!
Kabiranjana so overwhelmed, benumbed—
Pray, set him free, thy grace, from the mortal chain!
Hearkening to your gracious deeds
I bethink e'er in my mind indeed
How I escape coming again
Into this dark dismal world!

❦ Song 134[1] ❦

Shyama, the woman of legion charms
On the chest of the slayer of cupid's form,
Roams the woman usurping love's citadel,
Is she a damsel divine or a demon girl;
Or a charmer from the serpent world!
Or, is it, she is a human maid;
The pearl swings from her nostril, lazy pure
The pining bird holds the full moon in her arms

The poet envisions Mother Kali as a dark enchanting woman who is approaching in Her warrior stance.

In Hindu mythology Mother Kali is depicted with Her loose cascading locks overwhelming Her bare naked person. The Mother is mounted, standing on the chest of Lord Hara lying as a corpse supine at Her feet. The finger nails of the Mother surpass the soft mellow moon. Her whole person is smeared in scarlet blood streaming from the severed heads of dead demons which She has slain.

Her companions are wild and wayward, strange fearsome women, denizens of the spirit world. They are all laughing and dancing in war-dance. The mighty warriors of the spirit world are with Her and they are sounding drums and kettledrums as war-accompaniments.

They are making noise from within their swollen cheeks, resounding with the sound of *bam, bam, babam bam*. Such sounding of drums and wild noise from the mouth is part of the mythological worship of Lord Shiva and of his dancing rhythm on the day of annihilation.

[1]This song is in the same tenor as the earlier one.

Swinging languorous all the while
Upon the lips a lambent smile,
Look, in her hand the elephant
Doth she with that the battle mount;
The body slim lithe the youthful frame
Naked unrobed the dame of sweet sixteen,
The blue lotus petals, the face excels,
Lit up by lightning the charming smiles
The twin budding breasts blushing unrevealed
The young crescent moon the forehead adorns.
What fun, what frolics, how sorely I yearn
The charmer woman fresh and young
Bewitching mobile untrammelled;
The sons of Diti all, in fearsome war
Fleeing for refuge into the waters
Who is that who from the mind dispels—
That one—the ocean of travails.
How frightening She, the cause of rout and ruin
Of the last trace of self and the selfish mind!
Ramprasad Das, he chants and sings
Pray, dispel this looming darkness rolls
Abide in the lotus of the inmost heart
Oh mother Shyama, long-haired, constantly;
This world, the next, the laurels mine
They all are trifles, them all I spurn;
The final truth, the god of death forsooth becalmed,
Sublime, as I enter the gracious form.

This is a description of Mother Kali in Her enchanting yet frightening, wild wayward ways. The poet does not know whether the Woman is human, divine, demi-god or demon. She is a young maiden of sweet sixteen, face surpassing the dark blue lotus, with smiles playing around Her lips like the lightning. She wears the nascent moon upon Her brow, yet she is the extirpator of all demoniac forces, marauding in war. She stands on the supine body of Lord Shiva who had burnt to ashes the god of carnal love,—Madana.

The sage poet wonders at the marvel, at the bewitching blend of grace and dread dour might of the young maiden stalking like a terror in the fearsome war.

Mother is grace divine. The bestower of weal and bliss. She dwells ever in the blooming lotus within the heart, lambent in Her glowing light, removing all darkness. Ramprasad is devoted to Her, forswearing all desires of the world. That way he knows, he will overcome the fear of Death and attain his salvation.

Song 135[1]

Lord Shankara beneath her feet
Trampling foes to Her surfeit
Mother, stream of web of hairs,
Thou enchanting face, pure moon-like grace
The person lithe slim sublime.
Surpassing the young *tamala* tree,
The Yoginis legion all
In dour battle, loud turmoil.
With hands clapping measured roll
Mind in rage, above oozing crimson blood,
The eyes drink deep, wide and large.
Dwelling on the portals of time
As worlds come and go in endless turns,
The wheeling universes on her person
The lambent brow reflecting open space
Keeping time,—*ta ta, thai thai*
And drumming tune,—*drimak, drimak—*
Dha dha—the trumpet roars,—
The woman dancing to the loud uproar;
Prasad chants, Oh Shyama of bewitching charm
Do vouchsafe, shield my afterworld
Deign, oh, thy grace, a tiny trace, betimes
On this poor distressed wretched soul

[1] Lord Shiva lies supine under the feet of Mother Kali.
Mother stands on the chest of Her Lord, with one step forward with Her tongue wide out as if in regret, Mother is unrobed. Her clothes are the whole inane. Her long loose hairs flow down to Her knees. Her face is bewitching and mellow like the taintless Moon. Her person is lithe and lissom like a young *tamala* tree. Her companions are warring women versed in occult *yoga*, fighting with the demonic evils in tumultuous war. Her countenance is dread and frightening, blood cascading down her person from the severed heads of demons slain in war.
Her eyes are wide, drinking deep, off the mortal worlds which come and go like bubbles in the sea. Mother Kali in Hindu philosophy is Termless Space who, with her consort Mahakala (Lord Shiva) goes on with her rhythmic dance in eternal time.
The rhythms are tuned to the beat of drums which goes on resounding, reverberating throughout the Cosmic World.
Prasad chants, prays worshipfully to the enchanting Woman that She save him from Death and give him refuge after he quits this mortal world. The poet is poor and wretched and yet the Mother in Her grace should shower Her blessing on Her child giving him safety and bliss from dire devouring Time.

Forfend the mortal looming time.

♀ Song 136[1] ♀

Shyama, that ravishing woman She
Who forsooth, prevades the world;
Her ways are aweful strange awry,
All shame abjured in open war
Buoyant drunk in passion warm
Smiles with swaying facial charm
As if the formless God of Love
Is now incarnate in Her form;
Mandakini, maiden daughter of the Sun,
Saraswati, well-beknown as in-between;
Where all three streams unite
There it is the holiest shrine;
The young Sun, the Moon, they mingle grace,
The rotund moon surpasses the lotus face,
But then as fire's consumed in fire
Fire is extinguished—
Prasad—bard, poet—he sings
The world is image of the Queen Supreme,
Beholding Her for once,
Where is the room for sins, travails?

[1] The song is a hymn of the sage poet to Mother Shyama (Goddess Kali), the enchanting woman that overwhelms the world.

Nature is the Mother's sports. Nature *(prakriti)* is the dual Immortality, The revealed image of the Absolute Brahman who is Lord Shiva himself. The gait and ways of the Mother are in sharp contrast. She is the repository of grace, sublime and bounteous, face smiling, the whole person charming as the enchanting God of Love. But then she is in warring stance, engaged in routing the hordes of demons, the evil forces of the world.

The river Mandakini, the daughter of the Sun-god, and then in the middle the sweet stream, Saraswati they all meet at the confluence of the Mother's person,—the most sacred and sublime.

The nascent Sun, the crescent Moon and then the mellow lunar orb all unite as Fire is extinguished as Fire rushes into Fire in torrents.

The poet Prasad sings and chants extolling the whole of the manifest Universe as the image of Mother Kali; as one beholds it thus where is his sin, worries and torment?

☙ Song 137[1] ☙

That graceful woman Shyama, who is she?
Person balmy dark, face as surface
Of the autumn lambent mellow moon;
The tresses flowing molten long,
In gory crimson roll adorned,
As if the dark nascent cloud
In streak of dazzling lightning coiled;
What is this strange deviant way
She has all shame cast far away,
Look she gorges in her mouth there
Elephant, horse, chariot, charioteer,
The mighty Yama, power of Death,
She has usurped all its fright,—
My mind unhinged hath lost all calm
In harrowing shock is in torment.
Dour enormous power the image of Death,
The foe of the amorous god at her feet,
What is this ravishing woman indeed !
Heaven, mountain, sea—She leaps across
That youthful lass in a twinkle in a trice.

☙ Song 138[2] ☙

The gentle dame, she is naked stark
Flexing in fun in dancing arcs

---

[1] This song has a rich descriptive overtone. The choice of words, the rhythm and rhyme scheme is ornamental
  Mother Shyama is described as a beautiful woman, with dark complexion and flowing wild locks. But then, that enchanting woman is now at war, shedding all her shame and womanly diffidence. She now has taken the image of terror, annihilating all in war. She is the symbol of death.
  The poet wonders how this young buxom woman with Lord Shiva (destroyer of the god of carnal love) beneath her feet could assume such fearful stance. The poet prays to Mother Goddess in his poetic hymns that she shower her grace on him who has taken refuge at her twin feet.
  This song shows the poet not only as a devout ascetic but a scholar and master of rich Bengali (and Sanskrit) poetic language.
[2] This song falls in the same group as the previous one (Song no. 137). The mother is perceived by the poet as an enchanting beautiful woman.

In the prime of her blooming youth,
The damsel slaying Danu's sons
Among dead bodies in the battleground
Tresses molten cascading down
She's loud in dread dour battle roar
Contending, matchless in mortal war,
Robed as turns Madana[1] insane,
Ghosts, ghouls, spirits—companions all
Dancing in fun with Bhairavas[2] in thrall
The charmer Queen with companions
All naked, clothed equal in space
Gorging elephant, chariot, charioteers,
Gods, demons all in harrowing fear
Mobile in war, raging rumbling swift and fast
Wreath of human hands around the waist!
Prasad pleads, oh sustainer of the world
Mother Kali, have mercy grace;
Thou art deigner deliverer guide
Across the sea of the living world
Thou Hara's Queen, vouchsafe heal my agony!

☙ Song 139[3] ☙

As the young lily the enchanting dame
The molten raining tresses loom

She is a maiden of a civil home; but she is now wild and naked. One point in this song is remarkable. In portraying Mother's womanly beauty, grace and the elegance of her naked person,—the poet is not shy or observing what may be called an urbane decency. Sanskrit classical literature does not own obscenity, and then, in the cosmic world of creation which the poet roams—our all flippant concepts of what is decent and what is not, do not arise.

But then, the overwhelming wonder and devotion of the poet for the Mother is loud in the praises of the song. Like the child of the Mother that the poet is, he is free in his warmth and candour of the Mother in her warring posture.

The poet ends with a prayer that the Mother Goddess should vouchsafe her grace and deliver him in this turbulent worldly ocean.

[1] Madana is the god of carnal love whom Lord Shiva had destroyed.
[2] Bhairavas are Tantric worshippers of Mother Kali and Lord Shiva and they dwell and do their penance in the burning ghat where dead bodies are cremated.
[3] This song too is in the same series. The youthful woman i.e., Mother

Encompassing the firmament
She is bare unrobed on the corpse reposed
Lazy, languourous drunk the maid
Sweet sixteen in amorous bloom
Showering grace, candid open,
Young mellow moon upon the brow
Brahma, Vishnu beneath her lobes
Gracious sweet countenance
Honeyed quintessence of love,
Face desired of the moons balmy beam
Dwelling in the blissful solar realm
Worshipped of Mercury, Jupiter
Slayer of all that is mean and sin,
Doey eyes, Hari in her bosom,
Of Lord Hari, Hara, Brahma adored,
He that worships that naked dame
Is one of Hara's blessed ones.

Song 140[1]

Oh mind, is it that you do not know
What peril is soon to come,
When your vital upward wind will swoon
Thorns will spread along your way;
I warn you before it is too late
Now it is your halcyon days,
Oh, to those mother Shyama's feet sublime
In your mind tie, moor yourself;
You have nursed the bird within your cage
Who will keep it behind the bar!
Don't you know within that cage
There are, oh, nine open doors!
It has got companions wretched ill
Six of them, stubborn and evil
Whatever they ask you oblige,

Kali,—she is described in all her bewitching beauty. She has a moon on her brow and Brahma and Vishnu on the lobes of her ears. She is both terror and grace—all in one. She is the destroyer of all worldly pursuits —the object of worship of gods in the heaven. The poet adores this youthful maiden, the supreme image of immanent creation. He knows that the Mother's devotee,—he is beloved of Lord Hara (Shiva) too.

[1]This song is rich in the spiritual analysis of the nature of the mind

Your daring indeed is so strange;
Prasad says, you know, oh mind
What within your heart abides
Shall I open up the secret box
And spill the bean in broad daylight?

♥ Song 141[1] ♥

What justice this, mother, fair play!
One who chants Durga's name night and day
Evil befalls him, that's his destiny;

and the sensuous organs.

The poet warns his own mind that he (the mind) should be careful. A day will come when the mortal body will quit this world. Conscious of this end, the mind should act in time. The vital soul is imprisoned within the body but how can it be kept confined? The body has got nine adits. These are indeed,—the two eyes, the two ears, the two nostrils, the mouth and the two outer passages of elimination.

But then the mind is not careful. It often goes awry. That is becuase the mind is in bad company. These are the six enemies of mankind: *kama* (lust and desire); *krodha* (rage and anger); *lobha* (greed and avarice); *moha* (confusion and ignorance); *mada* (vanity and arrogance); *matsaryya* (hate and jealousy). These evil forces are powers of Nature that taint the mind.

The mind obeys these evils and therefore forgets its salvation. It is only the feet of Mother Shyama to which the mind must hold on, while it is time to save it from disaster.

Prasad warns the mind that unless it behaves, the poet would reveal all its (mind's) shameful propensities.

[1]The sage poet in his songs is used to talking, often to his own errant mind, and then to his beloved Mother Kali. He will often sulk, at times complain to Mother for her neglecting her child, the sage poet himself.

In this song the sage poet complains to Mother about her injustice. The poet, as the Mother's beloved child is ever devoted to her. Yet, all that happens to him is pain, misery and chagrin.

The poet (as he often does) takes to the metaphor of the Court of Law. He is present in the Mother's Court. He has to submit his plaint and petition and it is he again who must argue his case! Witless as he is, how does he do all this, all by himself!

The poet's only hope is the word of Lord Shiva who in the holy shastras, has vouchsafed emancipation to the human soul that is devoted to the supreme Goddess.

The time of quitting this mortal world draws near everyday. The poet is afraid and wants to flee to his mother as the frightened child. His only prayer,—as Death comes, let the name of Durga be on his tongue and let him quit this world on the bank of the holy Ganges!

To his lordship, mother, I've lodged my plaint,
I now keep standing with folded hands
When is't mother, the court will hear,
I'll get released from this peril!
How, oh mother, I plead my plaint
Or how is it I do defend
I have no wits in my wretched head;
My only refuge is Shiva's words,
Renowned for Truth in Vedas, Lores;
Prasad pleads, mother, for fear of Death
I wish I run away in stealth,
Deign, oh, I crave at the time of death
I quit this life chanting Durga's name
On the holy bank of Jahnabi.

Song 142[1]

Why is it, for Kasi I should ask!
Kasi who has enshrined, in his bosom
Reposes mother with flowing locks,
Jagadamba, that mother Goddess,—
There fell off her aural ring,
Since then that place as Manikarni
In the world is well-renowned;

[1] In this song the sage poet describes that Kasi (Varanasi) is one of the holiest shrines of Hindu pilgrimage. Legend has it that when Lord Shiva, wild at the death of His spouse Sati (Goddess Durga), was roaming the world with her (Durga's) dead body on his shoulder in his dire destructive stance, Lord Vishnu, at the request of the divine gods, cut the body of Sati with his famed missile, the Sudarshan wheel.

It happened the divine body of the Goddess was cut to 52 pieces. The ringed lobe of Sati's ear fell on Kasi (Banares). The Sanskrit word for the ear is *karna*. The holiest bathing *ghat* on the Ganges owes its name Manikarnika from this legend.

In this song the sage poet wonders why he need to proceed to Kasi. The presiding Divinity of Kasi is Lord Shiva Himself. Shiva bestows salvation on any one who quit this mortal world in the holy city of Varanasi (Banares). But then Mother Goddess Kali,—She is above and buoyant on the great Lord Shiva himself.

The two rivers of Varanasi,—are Asi and Varuna. Asi is the scimitar (might) of goddess Kali and Varuna is her blessings and grace. The poet is tied with the name of Mother Kali. He has no other craving left for pilgrimage to the shrine of Varanasi.

Asi and Varuna—in between
There lies Varanasi, the pilgrim shrine,
Varuna's flow is Mother's Grace
Asi's stream sharp scimitar,
If in Kasi one should die
Lord Shiva grants him,—"who you are;"
Oh, over that Truth She is supreme
That goddess mother, Mahesha's Queen
Ramprasad affirms, I do not yearn,
Going to Kasi is not my choice,
For oh, mark it around my neck
Of Kali's name she has tied the noose.

Song 143[1]

I abide immune out of bounds
Secured by charm of Kali's name,
Listen, oh Death, I tell you this
I am no child, dud, immature,
Why do I bide, oh, by your word!
It's no cake in the hand of a child
That you'll grab it by feint or wile!
Were you nasty you'll get reprimand
I'll report to Mother do you understand!
She's mother Shyama, subduer of Death
A maid so dread, soon roused to wrath;
Sri Ramprasad so declares,—
By extolling Mother Shyama's name
I'll quit this world by wile and stealth
By throwing dust in the eyes of Death.

[1] Man is afraid of Death. In the Hindu pantheon, Yama (or Kritanta) is the presiding deity of death of the mortal body of man. Death symbolizes darkness, when the departing being is doomed to eternal bondage and the chain of births and rebirths.

Poet Ramprasad warns Death. Let him (Death) not try his tricks with the poet. The sage poet is the devoted child of no less than Mother Goddess Shyama (Goddess Kali). And She is the terror and tormentor of Death himself! And then She is wild and turbulent. Should Death misbehave with the poet and he should report that to his Mother Goddess, then Death would be punished truly and well. Ramprasad has no fears or worries. Death can do nothing to him. He would chant the name of Mother and attain his salvation by throwing dust into the eyes of Death.

♀ Song 144[1] ♀

The way in of Death is now shut out,
Doubts in my mind are all wiped out
Oh listen, the nine doors of my abode,
Shiva's four—they mount guard, vigil,
On one prop the dwelling stands
Tied firm to trinal strings,
On the thousand-petalled lotus
The Being supreme Absolute
Reposes, securing me from harm,
At the portal unfailing Shakti dwells
She has assumed charge as sentinel
By shedding darkness by that Shakti's might
The 'Being' abides, safe, secure,
In the wheel-like realm at 'Muladhar,'
In 'Swadhisthan'—the snowy six-petalled
Lotus in full bloom unfurled,
Again in the region of the throat
Where doth blue sixteen-petalled lotus repose
And then amid the twin eyebrows

[1]The sage poet is now secure, unafraid of Death and repeated wheeling births and deaths in this mortal world.

The sage has reached the zenith of his *sadhana* (ascetic penance). A man has nine adits in his body through which Nature and the world of senses play their pranks with the 'Being.' The nine adits are: the two eyes (the organ of sight); the two ears (the organ and the sense of hearing); the two nostrils (the sense of smell); the mouth (the organ of taste); and then, the anus and the genital for biological health and reproduction. The poet has shut out all these nine windows into the outer world.

The absolute Energy dwells in man, installed in its several seats along the spine. The supreme Divinity dwells within; only this Energy has to be roused.

The song refers to four such seats of Divinity as it successively evolves in man—from bottom upward along the spinal chord. Muladhar at the bottom is the seat of dormant energy, coiled up near the anus. Swadhishthan is the lotus seat in the heart region. Above that near the neck there is the seat of wisdom and light and then, at the centre of the two eye-brows is the luminous seat of Godhead,—transcendent and absolute. Ramprasad has protected himself. Lord Shiva stands sentinel at the four aforesaid portals. The sensuous doors are all closed and no enemies can enter. The supreme Godhead at the crown is his saviour. In this luminous protected House (the body) the poet is safe and calm filled with joy and bliss free from the fear of Death!

Where the bi-petal pastel lotus abides,—
In these four pedestals, ever watchful
Lord Shiva's four images are installed
Mounting guard o'er the nine-some portals all.
Ramprasad says, in this realm of light,
The sun, the moon, they both arise
Oh listen, dark inconscience gloom dispelled
In the heart's temple Mother Tara dwells.

Song 145[1]

Chant Kali, Tara's name oh, ceaselessly,
By which name the fear of Death will flee.
By which name Lord Shiva hermit turned
Made his abode the crematorium,
Brahma, other gods in heaven
Whom, oh, cannot perceive or fathom;
The craft is full, about to sink,
They say, it'll perish there's no chance
E'en so you must try, ne'er give in,
If you can turn Lord Bhola's mind;
I'm so innocent, of mind so dull
I know no worship, cannot extol.
Ramprasad, his lowly obeisance alone
Pray, beneath your feet, a place you deign.

[1]The song is a worshipful submission of the sage poet to his beloved mother goddess Kali.

In the Hindu shastra meditating and chanting the name of the divine goddess is itself a means to emancipation. The name of Mother Kali removes the fear of Death. Real enlightenment dawns when the human being is conscious of the futility of death of the mortal body; the soul of the being is immortal and one with Divinity.

Lord Shiva is the consort of Mother Kali. He is the dweller in the waste crematorium where dead bodies are burnt according to Hindu rites. Mother is infinity. She is the revealed form of the Absolute. She is profound and recondite. Even Lord Brahma cannot fathom Her real essence. The craft of life of the sage poet is about to sink; people say that the end is near. But then, the poet is not afraid. He can still invoke Lord Shiva's blessings. The poet is ignorant, he does not know the rites of worship. He is only craving that the Mother should give him a place at Her feet.

❦ Song 146[1] ❦

It never left me, my evil fate
Alas, oh, me it never left,
Wiles deceit, they ne'er left company
Never left me free alone;
How much I try to sever the tie
The aunt ruined my destiny
All the time in my mind
I crave for happiness and bliss
But the aunt ever intervenes
And causes all the miseries;
The weary attachment of the aunt
Plays with varied wily charms,
It heaps on rubbish, all in vain;
Dwija Ramprasad (twice-born by caste)
Has anxious worries in his heart,
Born on the lap of mother own
I did not dwell in that precious home;
Tasting off the bitter milk
All my body is soiled, it stinks
How long, oh, the infant child

[1] This song is in a different mood.

The own mother of the sage poet Ramprasad is Goddess Kali. The goddess is the supreme being, coequal with the Absolute Brahman. But then, she is also revealed as Mahamaya,—the overwhelming illusion that pervades the whole universe.

This veil or illusion of Mahamaya is the cause of all worldly joys and sorrows, worries and turmoil. This Mahamaya with her three *gunas* (*sattva*, *rajas* and *tamas*) plays with the mind of the human being and leads him awry from the path of supreme devotion to the real Mother Goddess. This Mahamaya is the sister or the other form of the Absolute Godhead. In that sense She is the Aunt of the poet, whose real mother is Goddess Kali. This Aunt Nature is causing all miseries to the poet. The poet is unable to tear away from the fetters and illusions of the veil cast by Mahamaya. The poet laments that he has failed to rest on the lap of his own mother, Goddess Kali. He has been led astray by his aunt all the time and has suffered endless pain and worries. He has been deprived of his own mother's milk (the divine solace and ambrosia) and has drunk off the skimmed milk, which is the sham sport and playfulness of the all-encompassing Aunt, Mahamaya. The poet is unable to live like this any longer.

The song is couched in symbols which is a supreme strength of the sage poet in most of his songs.

Can survive on pale butter-milk!

❦ Song 147[1] ❦

I'm none, no fugitive from law,
What is this threat, oh mother, then
That you hold out, hold me in awe!
Your lease, oh mother, is no worthless plot,
It's no scrap of land that measures short,
I hold the charm of enduring deed
With 'seal' embossed of the 'Word' supreme;
I dwell on mother's own domain,
My right worked out on the whole of land,
By the right of your 'name' this time
I'll hold on to it as freehold land;
Prasad says, due rent unpaid,—
That ne'er happens, not a single coin,—
Should you drown me in the sea of grief
E'en sunk, I'll hold as buoy on to your feet.

❦ Song 148[2] ❦

That's why, oh mind, I tell you so,

[1] This song is typical of Ramprasad.

He often quarrels with the mother for Her neglect of Her child, the sage poet. But then, the poet is never afraid. He dares the Mother to do harm to him and his very strength is his devotion to the Mother. In this song the poet tells Mother Kali that he is not a sinner who pleads justice. Mother cannot frighten him like that. The piece of the world, the poet's own body, is a sacred *field*. This piece of land is meant for sowing. The seeds are the *mantras* whereby the human soul achieves emancipation. The poet is the owner of his plot of land and there is no dispute or deficiency of its measure or title.

The warrant and deed of this treasure is held secure by the poet. He dwells in the Mother's own domain. The land is tax-free and his title to it is sanctified for all times. And then the poet will hold on to it through the strength of Mother's name.

There is no one who can dislodge the poet from his position. Because he has paid all his dues and there is no arrears of tax or toll on the land that he holds. Finally, he warns his Mother that even if She were to drown him in the ocean of pain and grief even then he would hold on to the feet of the Mother even after he has drowned.

[2] The poet is often in a mood when he quarrels with his own mind.

It's often that I remind you
It is so nice a game indeed
That's how you got so enamoured;
The 'self' declares,—my brother own
Do you remember, you were mine!
E'en as brother, on your brother own
You played deceit,—threw him on
To the proffered hand of the God of Doom,
The ambrosial bliss by 'guru' given
That taste your took it away from me,
Oh, in lieu, you fed me on
But with some rubbish, wicked things,
As you led, likewise did I proceed
You tutored, spoiled my ways indeed;
Now with mother I must sort it out
I am no keeper of the garden plot;
Prasad asks,—do you trust, oh mind,
You'll throw me on to the garbage bin!
Oh, don't you know, I've tied to my heart
Dakshina Kali's holy name!

The human being has a 'soul' which, indeed, is 'he,' his own self. This 'real self' of man is parcel of the All-soul, the Absolute Supreme Divinity. God is one in His transcendent Unity and then again He is immanent in His infinite multiplicity. The Divinity in His sub-atomic multiplicity is everywhere.

This "self" of the being is not his mind. The mind is only a subtle sense organ which holds command and sway over his other coarse, physical organs like sight, hearing, sense of smell and touch and so on. It is the Mind that is slave to Nature's playful sports that obsess the self of the being and lead him astray from the unalloyed union with the Mother as the image of the supreme Divinity.

But the Mind when pure and clean, rinsed in *sattva* quality of Nature (*prakriti*) can be the supreme ally of the being; being the own brother of the 'self' of the poet, it has misbehaved and led him astray to the path of ruin and death! The nectar of the *seed mantra*, vouchsafed by guru,— that the poet forgot by the wicked ways of his own mind. The mind has lured him into the sham pleasures of the world forgetful of the bliss and joy of the divine nectar of devotion to the Goddess Mother.

But then the poet is not a fool. He warns his mind, that it cannot bring about his doom and ruination. For, he holds fast, tied in his bosom, the *name* and *image* of supreme Goddess Mother Kali.

❦ Song 149[1] ❦

My mind, how you float on fancy, fun,
Oh mind, you're in frolic and in fun;
You change your ways every now and then
You weep in grief and in fun you dance;
In days of fun all tinsel toys
You bought them at the price of gold
And then when overtaken by grief
You sold your gems and precious things
Threw them away at the price of mud;
Your home of pleasure you built with sham
You sank your mind in that alluring fun
But when that charm will wither, pale
Have you thought of the hideous tale!

❦ Song 150[2] ❦

When is it I would in Kasi dwell,
There, in that garden of joy and bliss
I will banish my melancholy and woe;
I'll worship Lord Vishweshwara

[1] The poet, in this song, mocks at his own mind. The Mind can be both an ally and an enemy of the 'self.' The 'self' or soul of the human being is the reality; the human soul is part and parcel of the Absolute Brahman. The Mind is the bridge between the physical life of the being and his Soul within that is deathless and eternal.

But the Mind often plays truant. It is fickle and wayward. It keeps comapany with the Nature's propensities (*guna*), *rajas* and *tamas*—which, working on the mind lead it astray, mired in the worldly ways of desires, pleasures, endless worries and sham joys and sorrows.

The human life is a treasure when it is spent in devotion and chanting the name of the Mother Goddess Kali. It is gold! And this treasure is being wasted in pursuit of worldly pleasures and fortunes,—which is nothing else but trash and banal playthings. In the bosom there is the seat of the Goddess! But the foolish errant mind has uprooted, banished the divine image, and installed there, instead, the sham tinsel world of chimerical hopes of pleasures and fortunes, enamoured of gains and overwhelmed by pain and sorrows.

[2] The song is the effulgent ambition of the sage poet Ramprasad.

The poet is tired of this world. He pines for the pleasure and bliss of solitude and worshipful ambience of the holy place of Kasi (Banares). The world is full of miseries, pain and sorrow. The garden of joy and bliss is in Kasi where reigns the Lord God Shiva.

With leaves of *bael* and Ganga water;
If I sould die on the water, soil
Of that holy Varanasi shrine
Then, for sure, I'll salvation earn;
Annapurna there, the presiding queen
Of her golden grace I'll take refuge,
And then, Lord Bhola, *baba, bom, bom,*—
So chanting will dance and drum the cheeks.

ꟾ Song 151[1] ꟾ

Oh mother, I am so careworn distraught,
There lies all I own my balance in deposit;
Egged on by foes I forge ahead
Never thought where it all will lead;
There, that Chitragupta, unfailing firm
He has recorded just all I have done
Through termless terms of countless births,
He has carried forward all my debts;
What one has sown that he harvests,
The outcome has come of the fruits of work;
The deposit is thin, expenses mount
How do I escape the King's account?

> The shrine of Varanasi is famous as the pilgrimage where dwells Lord Vishwanatha or Lord Shiva. There also dwells as the presiding Goddess Annapurna or Goddess Durga or Kali.
> The poet is yearning for his sojourn to Varanasi where he will daily bathe in the holy Ganges and sing songs in praise of Lord Shiva by noise and music from inside his swollen cheeks; in the Hindu worshipful rites and practices, such drumming noise as—*bom, bom, bom* in the name of Lord Bhola (Lord Shiva) is a customary accompaniment in the worship of the Lord, and as the devotee sings this tune through his swollen cheeks he dances in joy in wild reckless rhythm.
> [1]The sage poet submits to Mother Kali his plaint and his fears
> It is now eventide. The day of reckoning is drawing near. As he quits this mortal body and passes on all his deeds,—sins and errors in this world will be weighed by the heaven's accountant and record-keeper, Chitragupta. This Chitragupta is infallible, He keeps for every mortal a running balance of his deeds and their effects, across legion births; the poet is anxious that the balance of his debts would far exceed his earnings. He would be dubbed defaulter in the Divine Court of Lord. But then the poet still rests assured. He has the treasure and the supreme asset of Mother Kali's name deep in the recess of his mind.

Within Ramprasad's mind, that (alone)
Is the sole refuge—oh, that Kali's name sublime.

❦ Song 152[1] ❦

In every nook and home there Mother dwells,
Is it that this cream I spill the beans,
Tell it everyone in the market-place!
She's there with *bhairabas* and *bhairabis*
With tiny children there all she is;
She is maiden virgin princess queen;
Like Lakshmana, the youthful prince
With Queen Janaki as e'er companion
She is mother, daughter, beloved spouse
As sister there she is and otherwise,
Ramprasad says, what more do I spell out
You now must guess its ins and outs.

❦ Song 153[2] ❦

I'll take refuge beneath mother's feet;
For where shall I go when time is out,
If at home for me there is no room,
I'll dwell outside, where is the harm,

---

[1] Sage poet Ramprasad is unequalled for his simplicity and symbolism. He has an uncanny way of revealing the profoundest truth through most humdrum homely metaphors of daily life.

This power of the poet stems from his direct vision. He has no need to build and construct elaborate imageries. Truth is ever stark and naked. Only shams and charlatans must be spruced up and draped in costumes. Hindu metaphysics conceive Divinity in His dual form. One is the transcendent Absolute; the other form is His immanence and pervasive presence in infinite multiplicity. This is the form of Mother Kali, in Her manifest omnipresence in every home in every creature in the multitudinous relationships in the human world.

Mother Kali,—She is there with Her companions of the spirit world. She is again in the garb of the child and the young maiden. She is daughter, sister, mother, wife—the woman in every form all at once. She has Her unfailing presence, much as Lakshmana was ever there as the shadow of Janaki his (Lakshmana's) elder brother Rama's consort queen in the *Ramayana*.

[2] This little song is a shining hymn of the poet's utter submission to

Holding fast to Mother's name
I'll stay put fasting, bide my while;
Prasad says, should Uma turn me out,
E'en then I won't quit, I will still hang out,
My two outstretched hands I'll spread out,
Prostrate on those feet my life I'll quit.

❦ Song 154[1] ❦

Who is that woman, whose enchanting love,
Seated on the lotus, by herself, alone!
Smile on the ravishing lips, on the edge
Of her eyes,—flashing lightning streaks;
Never in this life, such a maiden I've kenned
Nor ever heard of her with mine own ears;
She gorges the elephant, vomits it again
That youthful maiden of sweet-sixteen.
(Incomplete)

the Mother Goddess, glistening as the dew drop in the morning sun.

The poet vows to repose himself on the Mother's feet. The time is late and inauspicious and he has nowhere else to go. And he does not care, if he has no place in the Mother's inner chamber or if he must suffer hardship and hunger. He would bide at the Mother's courtyard and would starve holding on to the name of the Mother.

And then that even is not enough. The poet vows even if Mother Uma (Goddess Durga or Kali) were to turn him out he would not take it. He would not leave her. He would cling to her feet and quit his mortal life.

[1]This song seems incomplete but then what scrap of it has remained is eloquent of a typical worshipful stance of the poet.

The Mother dwells alone on the lotus flower (within the bosom). She is a woman of rare grace and charm—face smiling, lightning flashing from the eyes. And she is now in warring stance annihilating and gorging elephants in her wild dance. And yet she is a young maiden in her blooming age of sixteen years.

Ramprasad was a natural poet and composer. He had a resonant tuneful voice and he would often sing his songs, extempore as he composed them. He was a *sadhaka* (spiritual seeker) of the supreme level who never thought or cared to put all his songs in writing. Some he wrote out himself some others lived on through the voice of those who listened in rapt devotion, and who put them down on paper. And so today we have a collection which we seek to preserve between these covers.

Song 155[1]

Oh my mind, I touch your feet, entreat
Call out, listen oh mind, loud, surfeit,
By gracious mother Kali's name,
She is the sole craft on which you voyage
Across the world's ocean's uncharted ways;
The name of Kali is balmy sweet,
Breathe and chant it day and night;
Look oh, should Kali deign her grace
Do I then dread Death's dour face;
Says dwija Ramprasad (twice-born by caste)
Chanting Kali's name I'll get past,
In her compassion to her child
She'll deliver me of this world's ocean wild.

Song 156[2]

Oh my Queen, the metropolis is loud
Clamorous,—let's move, proceed
To where's your beloved daughter, oh;
Let's go receive her, ardently,
With warm welcome love bring her home;
Do, oh, accompany, come with me.

[1] The song is the usual craving of the sage poet for the grace of his beloved mother, goddess Kali. The poet would much like to cling to the sublime feet of the mother goddess, lose himself in her name; but his own mind is an errant foe that betrays him. Often, thus, the poet lambasts his own mind for its crooked ways. and then again, as in this song, he entreats and cajoles and begs of it that it should mend its ways and turn to the Mother and chant her name.

The poet assures the mind, the name of the Mother is ever so sweet. The Mother alone is the sailing craft that will take the soul of the human being across the turbulent sea of the mundane world. Death will flee in her name. The poet feels assured that the gracious Mother will deliver him as he is her own devoted child.

[2] This song is a lyric of the joyous return of the young daughter to her home with the mother from her husband's place.

Uma, the maiden name of Goddess Durga is the daughter of Menaka the Queen of the Mountain Lord, the tall Himalayas. Uma, also called Parvati, did her penance to win the love of Lord Shiva and married the Divine Lord. But Lord Shiva leads the life of a beggarly saint halfclad and totally eccentric in his ways.

Jaya, what words of joy you uttered
You put me in your eternal debt,
What blessed tidings this you brought.
What is there, you I do not owe!
Pray, come close, oh listen, do be here,
With life I'll repay your debt, so dear.
The Queen overwhelmed in tears of love
Hastens fast in her forward move
Her hairs broke loose in droves of cloud.
Whoever near she comes across
Him she asks in anxious voice,—
"How farther still is 'Gouri,' oh?"
As on she hastens, the chariot comes,
She now on Uma's face looks on;
She says,—oh my daughter child,
My child, is it that you have come,
Is it true then, oh, that you have come!
My girl, is it your mother, her.—
Of mother, you lost her remembrance!
Alas, mother says, what words of shame,
I wish I die for all amiss!
From her chariot, climbing down
To her mother she obeisance made,
Shankari her mother consoles
Again and then again;

 Menaka is not pleased at the ways of her son-in-law (Lord Shiva) and pines for her lovely young daughter all the time while she (Uma) is away to her husband's place—at Kailasa the legendary abode of Lord Shiva.
 This song (Song no. 156) is a remarkable scene of joy in the whole palace city of the Kingdom of Queen Menaka. Jaya is the boon companion of Uma (also her other name Gouri). She comes running to mother Menaka and breaks the news that Uma (or Gouri) has come and is on her way home on her approaching chariot.
 Overwhelmed in joy Menaka the loving mother hastens with Jaya and other companions to receive her. Menaka blesses Jaya for bringing her the overwhelming welcome tidings of Gouri's arrival.
 As Uma sees her mother running down to embrace her, she alights from her chariot and in deep love, and reverence touches her mother's feet.
 The song is a charming soulful portrayal of the emotional life of a Bengali home—the pining agony of the mother for her young married daughter, dwelling away at her husband's place and the sweet homecoming of the daughter for a spell of sojourn at her parental home.

Das Shri Kaviranjana sings overwhelmed
Is there a day fairer, else, so benign?

❦ Song 157[1] ❦

I tell you this, oh mind, do worship, chant
Kali, by any rites you will or stance;
Chant *mantra* by guru given all the time
Count beads with the hands all day and night
As you lie bethink it is obeisance,
In sleep her, mother meditate, divine
As oh, you roam ample around the town
Mother, on you right, deem as you move round:
Whatever you hark hear with your ears
They are all Mother's *mantra* know for sure;
Kali, she wears legion uncounted hues
To all forms and colour she lends her name, imbues;
Ramprasad declares in joy supreme
Brahmamoyee,—she dwells in every urn,—
When you take your food remember
It's offerings yours to Shyama Mother.

❦ Song 158[2] ❦

Kasi, Annapurna's blessed land,—

---

[1]The song is the quintessence of Hindu metaphysics. It is also a mark and symbol of the catholicity of the spiritual stance of the sage poet.

Devotion, love and utter submission to the personal God (or Goddess) is all that matters. Rituals are banal and way of worship is of no moment. The poet tells his mind to ever remember the Mother Goddess, contemplate and chant her sweet and sublime Name ceaselessly. The *mantra* (the *seed* sound or words) that the guru has vouchsafed,—that the mind should utter continuously, whether in sleep or wakefulness. As you walk along the streets of the metropolis or do your daily routine,—think and ponder that you are going round the Mother's Image in worshipful submission. All sounds and sights and sensuous forms,—they are all images and abode of the Divine Mother. And then as you take your food, know it as the offering to the Supreme.

The song is the sublime perception of the sage of the immanence of Divinity. That is how the human soul will unite with the absolute at all moments of his mundane life,—in all his actions, thoughts and works even in his mortal life.

[2]This song bears the stamp of the sage poet's scholarship and

Lord Shiva blessed, Kasi blessed
Blest supreme Thou Mother of bliss;
Bhagirathi, holy, there abides
It flows in arch as crescent moon,
River Ganga there is northward bound,
The waters ceaseless flow day and night;
On Lord Shiva's strident Kasi rests,
By Varuna, Asi,—she is begirt;
Amid these as the 'being' departs
In Shiva's person he is dissolved;
Annapurna, how sublime her grace
None goes hungry, starves in her place;
Mother oh, your Ramprasad has naught to eat
He pines, yearning for the dust of thy feet.

❦ Song 159[1] ❦

Oh mind, call out Kali's name,
I beseech you, plead entreat
Do not be remiss, oh mind it's time to quit;
All these treasures, pray, give them up
Kali, Brahmamoyee, do her worship,

command of language. The diction is rich and sonorous. The rhythm and the rhyme flows as easy and facile as the ceaseless flow of waters of the holy river Ganges at Varanasi.

The song is a hymn to the divine shrine of Varanasi (Kasi), the holiest place of pilgrimage of the Hindu spiritual seeker.
Varanasi (Kasi) is blessed by the presence of Mother Goddess, Annapurna (another name and appellation of Mother Durga), who is the presiding goddess of the holy place. Bounty and grace is the image of Annapurna. No one goes hungry in her abode.

The holy river Ganges at Varanasi is a crescent like the half-moon. The river flows northward there, resting as if on the trident of Lord Shiva. The place is embraced by the two other rivers—Varuna and Asi. As one quits this mortal life in the holy place of Kasi (Varanasi), one is liberated dissolving in the person of Lord Shiva, that is in the Absolute.

[1]The song is an expression of the eternal conflict of the spiritual seeker between his worldly desires for gain and wealth and the real emancipation of his soul.

And in this eternal battleground the formidable foe of the human being is within himself. It is his own mind and his own sham 'ego-self.' The mind, as the plaything of Nature's wiles, goes on chasing worldly pleasures and happiness,—oblivious of the shadow of Death that ever watches the mortal house of man.

Oh do in those lotus feet dissolve,
Then the foursome fruits are yours with ease.
The abode in which now you dwell
There Death's emissaries keep vigil.
There's, oh, no chance you escape
Time's eternal noose will tie your nape:
Dwija Ramprasad,—he upholds,
You lost your mission as slave of Time
You'll taste of bitter parched fruit
When the mango season is out and lost.

Song 160[1]

Supreme deliverer of fallen soul,
Goddess, deigner of eternal weal
The warm shade of thy feet in halcyon days

    The poet entreats his own mind to forget this sham futile pursuit of pleasures and to worship the Divine Goddess Mother Kali. Then alone he will get all the fourfold fulfilment of life *dharma* (spiritual salvation), *artha* (wealth and treasures), *kama* (objects of desires), and *moksha* (the final emancipation).
    The poet warns his mind that Death's emissary stands watchful as the sentinel at the door. As time comes he will claim the mortal body of the being. But then man can escape death by his utter submission to the Mother Goddess and ceaseless worship of her feet.
    [1]The song is a hymn to the Mother Goddess Kali.
    This world, to the spiritual seeker is one of sorrows and worries and miseries. As one pursues his craze for worldly riches and fortunes, one is torn by stormy passions and agonies of despair.
    And this futile search for worldly pleasures never ends. Sin and iniquity is the natural product of all these sham pursuits of worldly desires.
    The poet seeks to escape the worries and agonies of the world. His passionate aim is emancipation.
    Mother Tara (Kali) is alone the refuge of the lost soul. She is the deliverer. The devoted worshipper of goddess Kali earns the grace of the Mother. The Divine Mother is the mother of the universe. In her the manifest worlds are born, and by Her grace they are all nursed and nourished. Prasad (the sage poet) is the devoted child of the Mother. He has little virtues and is ignorant of the ways of worship and penance. But he has taken refuge in Mother's sublime feet; and the gracious Mother never lets alone, forsakes her child.
    The poet's prayer to the Mother is that she deliver him from the pain and perils of this mortal world and give him a place in the safe haven of Her feet.

Do thou hold out, oh Shankara's spouse,
Have mercy oh mother in thine own grace
Supreme emancipator thou;
Lowly sinner me, sans virtue
Errant wayward, of worship forfeit;
Me redeem as supreme deliverer
Thou queen mother of the Universe;
For rescue from the world's rolling sea
Thy feet the sailing craft indeed;
On Prasad do thou shed thy grace;
Oh queen mother, Lord Shiva's spouse.

❦ Song 161[1] ❦

Oh my tongue, chant Kali Kali, chant again
Those feet go on musing on
Drink off that elixir of Name
If thou shoulds't dream of deliverance;
Brother friends, beloved wife, sons
And kinsmen—your companion is none;
When the dour lord of Death will tie his noose
Sans those feet no one is none of yours,
For once chant, utter Durga's name
That name alone is treasure that bides with thee
The world is moorless transient, there's no end
Just bethink yourself, it's all inane
Time running out, oh, fast, in vain
There look, louring Death is nigh closing in,

[1]The poet pleads with his tongue that it should utter, chant Mother Goddess Kali's name. The poet tells himself and his own mind, meditation of Mother and drinking off the elixir of her name, is alone the path of emancipation.

Your brother own or dearest friends, the beloved wife, sons or kinsmen all,—no one, none of them is yours. When dour Death comes and fastens its noose round the neck,—Mother alone is your own and no one else. This mortal world is sham and transient; just bethink, nothing in this world is real. All that you cherish and treasure are passing shadows. They vanish into nothingness as yawning Death engulfs everything.

Prasad warns loud and clear,—do take the name of Mother Kali, chant and sing Her songs,—so you may escape death and perils. Time is fast slipping by,—life is wasted, Death is drawing near every moment, do heed, Mother alone is the saviour in this world of storm and turmoil.

Prasad claims, keep chanting Kali's name
Then will flee of death all agony.

☙ Song 162[1] ☙

All merciful! Who calls you all-benign!
In someone's milk (oh Tara) there's honey,—
I'm so wretched, my plate of rice
There, there is no spinach leaves;
You gave some, mother, treasures, chariots;
Oh, tell me, mother, are those, then,—
Your own father's patron saint,
And I'm no one none of yours!
Some abide in palatial homes,
I often long I do the same,
Oh mother, in your ripened field of corn
Did I roll the furrow and all it ruined?
Dwija Ramprasad, sore, laments
It is as if that's my destiny,—
My wretched state as you kenned
Maybe, mother Shyama, you turned to stone!

☙ Song 163[2] ☙

Beyond all knowing, Unborn, Mother Thou!

[1]This is a song in a different strain.
The sage poet has abjured all desires for worldly riches. But then the goddess Mother Kali,—Her another name is Annapurna—the Mother Goddess of bounty.

Ramprasad is poor. He is starving (in real life, Ramprasad indeed suffered from poverty and could not feed his wife and family). Even then the Mother does not care for his wellbeing.

There are people who enjoy life, possess fortunes and pleasures of life. The poet wonders how the Mother is so kind to them and yet so hard on the poet who indeed is Her own child. The poet is angry and scolds Mother on Her conduct. The treasures are enjoyed by the people who are aliens. Why then is the Mother so enamoured of them? Are they someone adored by Her father's family? The poet bitterly asks Mother if he had offended Her in any manner that he is so neglected by Her?

[2]The song is the cream of the Vedanta philosophy. Shiva is the consort of Mother Kali. Lord Shiva is the Infinite Absolute. In Hindu philosophy Mother Kali is the revealed nature who is the dual Infinite of the infinite Brahman who is Lord Shiva. The two are the One and the Same.

The mortal creatures, inconscient blind,
Lord Shiva, His consort thee,—they twosome find,
The two are One, She's the Image of the soul Supreme;
Himself beyond the Eternal Veil,
The confounding veil is He Himself;
He assumes Form as His own symbol
That sages may their mind install;
Thou, deigner of bounty to the wretched men,
Sublime even surpassing the royal Queen.
The garden of bliss is Thy Abode,
It is why "the Deliverer" is Thy name!
Should one remember Thee as he quits this world,
I know, then he in Lord Shiva dwells;
Prasad divines, wretched poor
Sans pious deeds, with sad remorse,—
Deliver Thou, Oh Mother deliverer,
From all three worlds by Thine own Grace sublime!

Song 164[1]

The wretched soul has spread his empty plate
At the portal of the bounteous Queen;
No way you now escape, you shall touch the grain
Of which a morsel I do yearn
That will fulfil my lifelong dream;
That same remains of Queenly grace
Blest with which Lord Shiva dance insane
Opening out heavenward both his arms!

    Mother Kali is immanent in Nature's three *gunas* (*sattva, rajas* and *tamas*), which create the illusion of the phenomenal world. But then it is for the bhakta or worshipper that Mother Kali assumes her form.
    She is the repository of bliss and joy. The sage poet is a devoted worshipper of Mother Kali and that is the way of attainment of liberation from the chain of births.
    The poet knows that he has not earned his right to deliverance, but then the Mother's grace is showered even on the mean and wretched.
    [1]In this song, the poet is seeking the grace of Mother Kali. Mother Kali is the sustainer of the creature world.
    The poet has come and spread his plate at the door of the Mother, seeking food, and rice as the remains after the gracious Mother has partaken of it.

♥ Song 165[1] ♥

Thou hast broken up the fair, Mother Shyama,
In the hour so odd and out of joint,
Tell me, oh Mother, now with what fares,
What with do I go back home?
All I had, alas, is lost and gone
I'm worn wandering aimless woebegone;
The traders in the thick of fair
They're left by now, all one by one;
It's my fault, my wayward ways,
I bided, lost, I'm left behind
With the load of sins upon my head!
Oh look, the Sun is on the waning mount
What, alas, I do in the Fair's this fading round!
Oh Mother, do take me on to your lap,
Do, beseech, vouchsafe this luckless wretch
Thy twin feet as the sole safe sailing craft!

But then, no one is free or permitted to stay away from the Mother's offerings of her food and grace. Mother alone is the deigner of food and grace.

The poet is poor and wretched, not free from the sins of the earth. But Mother's grace is there equally for the saint and the sinner. The poet knows his own yearnings for this grace and he craves for it which will fulfil his life's mission.

Lord Shiva is the consort of Mother Kali. But Shiva, the supreme Godhead, himself rejoices at the grace of Mother and dances in joy with both hands raised high.

The sage poet demands from the Mother the same grace with which even Lord Shiva is blessed.

[1]The song is symbolic. This world is a kind of fair or makret p!ace of Mother Shyama. The poet has to leave the market now very soon because his mortal life is soon to end.

But then what has he collected from the market? He regrets that his life has been a waste. He has not got his emancipation. Those who have gained their life's mission, they have all left the market place and gone home with their wares. The home's the feet of Mother Shyama.

But then, the poet says, that it is all his own fault. He has not done any proper worship. A heavy load of sins is all that he carries on his head. The sun is waning. The horizon of life is darkening. And for the poet the market place will soon be empty. The sage poet now turns to Mother Shyama and prays that she lift him on in her arms. The poet is wretched and hapless. The world is a turbulent sea. Only it is on the safe sailing craft of the Mother's feet that the poet can sail across the stormy world.

☙ Song 166[1] ☙

How longer must I toil round and round
Oh, Kali, as the rolling pitcher of the well?
There's no way of ending ups and downs
In this abysmal well of the world!
My limbs allover, now, are jaded corns
Worn by eight million loops rough-hewn,
And then milled around the neck by stranglehold
Of the cord of confoundment and attachment fond;
I am dying of torment for ages on,
There's no respite, relief,—by no means;
In cold I shiver, I'm drenched in rains,
Like the roasted brinjal I'm singed in the Sun;
When off in illness or by slumber lost
I'm away, I pause as the un-harnessed horse,—
The bell-metal worker, the *vital self*,—that chap
He comes along, Mother,—anon, to weld the breach;
What sin is it, Oh Mother,—I have done,
Why this severe relentless punishment?

[1] It is usual for the sage poet Ramprasad to refer to the pains and misfortunes of the world in terms of symbols and imageries.

In rural India there are deep wells. Water is lifted from the well by a pitcher of brass with a neck around which a loop is fastened at the end of a long rope. Legion people for endless times dip down the pitcher into the water of the well and lift the filled vessel up.

The pitcher of the well thus moves in eternal cycles of ups and downs for nothing. The world is also like the well. The human being comes and goes,—rotates in endless births and deaths, to which there is no end.

The 'rustic wells' have rings of burnt and hardened earthen coils to support the walls. The poet compares each human birth to one such 'ring.' For eight million such births, the poet has come into this world round and round. Chafed by assaults against such rings, his neck is bruised and jaded by rubbing with the coil of rope round the neck.

And this has gone on for ages. He is soaked in rains and burnt in the sun and there is no change.

And then when the poet takes leave of the hazards of the world, during illness or sleep the vital force within the body takes over to revive his weary limbs. This vital life is like the mechanic of bell metal who welds broken parts.

Prasad humbly prays to the Mother,—what sin has he done is deserve this punishment and torture. Let Mother save him from cuts and bruises of the mortal world and lift him on to her feet!

Prasad says,—I beg of Thee, at Thy feet implore
Do not, beseech, so cut and bruise, Mother, any more?

❦ Song 167[1] ❦

How longer must Thou sleep oh Kulakundalini?
Ensconced in Muladhar Thy occult shrine?
Rouse Thyself, wake up within my inner chamber Thou,
Do Thou wake up, blossom, in Sahasrara unfurl!
Putting me to benumbing slumber
How strange, Thou feignest sleep!
Alas, my 'final sleep' is drawing near,
Soon this waking life will end;
The gloom of night overwhelms the day,
What is this, Thy slumber while the day doth shine?
Daughter of the Mountains, Thou,—afraid of Death
I cry aloud,—Prasad, so ardent yearns
Having roamed long eight million rounds,
Deliver me oh Mother with rolls of flowing hairs
Grant Thou, into this world again I do not repair!

[1] In this song sage poet Ramprasad talks the language and idiom of *tantrasadhana* (the penance of rousing the Supreme Energy within the body).

Along the spinal cord of the human body there are six centres of dormant Energy. The supreme Energy, *mahashakti*, lies sleeping coiled like a snake at the bottom of the spine,—at the junction just above the anus. Through *yoga* and *pranayama* (The occult exercise of the inhaling and exhaling breath) this Energy can be roused and then the two arterial passage,—ida and pingala embrace the central channel of sushumna through which the *power of the Absolute* evolves upward, ensconced in various seats, till it becomes stable and immobile in the lotus seat of Sahasrara at the crown of the head.

Mother Kali, the poet divines is asleep in Muladhara, the bottom seat where it has coiled up. The sage poet is urging this Energy of Mahamaya, or Mahashakti to awake.

Mahamaya is the supreme charmer which puts the real self of the human being to sleep. But She, Mother Kali is dormant in pretended sleep. The poet, in distress, calls Mother, the daughter of the mountain Himalayas to wake up and save her child Ramprasad who is immersed in the toils of the world.

The poet's worshipful prayer is that he do not come again into this mortal world but dissolve into the bliss of Mother's supreme feet.

ॐ Song 168[1] ॐ

Look into yourself, oh mind,
Ne'er to others turn;
Whate'er you want, herein you'll ken,
Look for it in your own within;
The touchstone is the treasure-house,
Fortunes legion it can yield;
Such countless gems are scattered around
In the portals of the dancing ring
Of the *crown of contemplation.*
Proceeding to holy shrines,
Running round in hardship, pain,
Oh mind, forbear,—It's all in vain
Worn with cares ne'er bemoan;
Why not, oh mind, in Muladhara,
The trinal confluence of bliss
You bathe and cool yourself in calm supreme?
What is this marvel, sham, you Ramprasad
That you ken in this mortal world,—
You didn't care to know the Queen of marvels
Who dwells within your own mortal frame.

---

[1] In the Hindu Upanishad, the Mantra says, 'Know Thyself *(Atmanam biddhi).*

Hindu philosophy knows that Divinity lies within the 'self' of the human being. The Godhead is both transcendent and immanent. The Absolute Supreme Brahman is beyond the Nature's domain. But then Divinity breaks itself into multiple divinity and suffuses, immanent, every creature in the existential world—moving and immobile and everywhere.

In this song the sage poet urges his mind not to wander here and there or to seek the supreme in shrines and pilgrimage. The treasure of the eternal Mother is well-within his own body. The supreme Mother, the queen of all thoughts, is the origin and fulfilment of all that man seeks and craves. What is the use then of going to Triveni (a place of pilgrimage) to have your ablution, seeking peace and salvation. It is all there, the cool sublime peace of Muladhar itself, the seat of the supreme Mother within the human body.

The poet reminds the mind that everything in this world is illusion, the legerdemain of the sorcerer Mother. The mind should know the Absolute Divine Mother in Her two forms. She is at once the ultimate bliss within your own body; and then again she spreads Her toils across the whole phenomenal world through the play of Her three *gunas* (Nature's qualities),—*sattva, rajas* and *tamas.*

Song 169[1]

Will that day ever be mine
When renouncing this anxious world
With holy Kasi as abode
My life will end in Varanasi shrine?
There, there is no fear of the six-some foes
There will be victory, there, there Lord Shiva dwells;
As if the dawn of the blinding Sun
Will usurp the dark inconscience's sin.
Leaving alone the craze for pleasures,—
Lord Shiva's worship, my craving, desire
there I'll fulfil to my heart's content;
The tongue will chant loud Mother Annapurna,
There will vanish all pain and agony;
Whoever ensconced at the bathing place
Near Jahnavi, Shiva worships, folded hands,—
Ramprasad avers, the news spreads in Kali's realm,
He will attain deliverance in the dire peril.

[1] The song is a craving of the inner soul of the poet.

Sage Ramprasad was a married householder. He had his wife and Mother. It was a poor household and the family led a difficult life,—often wanting minimum food and clothings.

In one or two songs Ramprasad was angry with the Mother Kali. Mother built in the sage poet a deep devotion and a gnawing aversion to all worldly matter—properties and possessions, all that concerns and worries an ordinary man of the world.

Torn by such conflicts. Ramprasad is pining for a life of renunciation. He would much rather give up this world and dwell in the holy seat of Kasi (Banares). There dwells Lord Shiva Himself. The Shrine of Varanasi is the home of Lord Shiva and Mother Annapurna (Goddess Kali or Durga in her bounteous stance).

As the sage poet takes the refuge in the holy city, all foes of the human being—all six passions (*kama*—lust and desire; *krodha*, anger and rage; *lobha*, greed and avarice; *moha*, ignorance and confusion; *mada*, ego and vanity; *matsaryya*, malice and jealousy)—they will all take leave.

Lord Shiva and Mother Kali are the effulgent light. It removes all sins and dark ignorance. The poet would spend his days in worship of Lord Shiva and his tongue would chant the name of Mother Annapurna. He would sit by the holy river Ganges and all his worries and agonies would end.

Poet Ramprasad declares, everyone knows that whoever does his penance and worship in the holy city, is freed from all sorrows and perils.

Song 170[1]

Do not wake her up my Jaya girl,
Abhaya, thou innocent soul,
Uma, She is just asleep after what travail!
As my little 'mother', once, is roused from sleep.
To put her back to slumber is a task uphill!
She, my girl, by nature, is e'er so fickle mobile.
It was dusk last day when Uma came home
Below the *bael* tree how she was, to me unknown;
Parvati, as beneath the *bael* tree she abode
Wide awake the night how she passed;
Uma, she cannot escape the distress calls.
The whole day she roams round the homes of all;
She fell asleep, tired numb, as the evening fell,—
The betel leaf in 'mother's' mouth,
Absent, lost, remained where it was;
Shoulds't thou, Jaya, with Uma sport and play,
Play with her, oh Jaya, when the blessed girl's awake!
Radhika, twice-born, proclaims clear and loud,
Oh, if Uma does not wake
Who ever will awake, tell me, all the world?

[1] This song is in a different mood of the poet.

Goddess Durga is the lovely young daughter of Mother Menaka, who is the queen consort of the great Himalayas. The other name of Goddess Durga is Uma. this is Her sweet homely name that Her Mother loves to call Her by.

Uma has come from Her husband's place to Her mother's home in the Himalayas. She is sleeping, tired with the journey, and peaceful at Her own mother's home.

Uma's husband is Lord Shiva who is wayward and portrayed, in Hindu annals, as a vagabond.

Uma goes round everywhere as people crave for Her presence. The metaphor is the overwhelming worship that Goddess Durga (Uma) receives from every home in the world. And She cannot disappoint Her worshippers.

Thus in the evening, the young daughter, Uma, of Mother Menaka is so tired that she falls asleep early in the evening. Mother Menaka tells Jaya, friend and companion of Uma that she should not wake Her up but wait for Her to come out of sleep when they should play together.

The song is a sweet symbol of the loving mother of the Indian family; the great Goddess Durga is also the young charming daughter of Mother Menaka. To the loving mother she is merely the affectionate young girl, given out in marriage to an errant husband (Lord Shiva).

Song 171[1]

Oh listen, that One He,—He is my groom;
The Bull is his mount, He's half insane
The absent, naked, Lord Supreme
Through leaves of *bael*, I've searched, I've failed,
Round Hara's neck I've hung my bridal wreath.
Then, why Mother, why again,
In vain you offer me as bride!
With Him, of mind unsound
Me too, insane, I'd abide
Happily ever as man and wife.

Song 172[2]

Should'st my mind be amiss, or err,
Then on the bed of sands, pray chant
Kali's name into the pit of ear;
This body, it's none, not my own,
With sworn enemies it travels on;
Do thou (Lord) Bhola, I beseech,
Do bring,—where is my *lace of beads*?
So I'm afloat on the holy Ganges water!
Ramakrishna in utter fears
Invokes (Lord) Bhola, worn with cares,
What's good for me I hardly ken,
Of what's my fate, I'm least aware.

[1]This a singular song which sings young Uma's great love for Her husband Lord Shiva albeit His errant nature and insane way of life.

The song is a remonstration of Uma with Her Mother Menaka. Menaka is unhappy with Her son-in-law, Lord Shiva, who in Hindu mythology is wild and wayward. His mount is the bull. He is forgetful and careless of the household. But then Uma tells Her mother that She has married that mad person out of love and her own choice. She would much like to live with Him as His wife,—and she would much rather share His madness and wild ways.

Mother Menaka should not think of giving Her in marriage again.

Uma here is portrayed as the loving chaste wife of Her Lord. This echoes the divine tradition of Hindu mythology and society.

[2]Ramprasad addresses this song to Bhola, which is another name of Lord Shiva.

The poet's prayer is that as he quits this world and his dead body is laid on the dusty floor, someone should chant the name of Kali into his ears.

♀ Song 173¹ ♀

Alone I came, I'll quit alone
What cares have I for others here!
Trudging weary this worldly fair
I'm thin and worn in my skin and bones.
Leave alone this world of pain,
Brahman's Image install in thy heart;—
Then will vanish your all torments,
In chasing ends of your lust, desires,
Then alone, showers of peace sublime
Will fill your heart, ceaseless and serene.

♀ Song 174² ♀

No more, my child,—grieve, sulk resent,
Do forgive, Oh Shankari, I entreat;
The twin eyes in streaming tears
Me, Mother Thine, how could I it bear?

---

¹The poet does not trust his mind to do this service. The mind is often wayward and the enemy of the poet. His own body and the physical organs are not his own. They keep company with the foes dwelling within the human being. These six-some foes are *kama* (desire and lust), *krodha* (anger and rage), *lobha* (greed and avarice), *moha* (error and confusion), *mada* (vanity and ego), *matsaryya* (jealousy and hatred).

These are born of the two qualities of Nature, i.e., *rajas* and *tamas*. The poet wants that he should chant the name of Mother Kali and count beads before his death. He is seeking the grace of Lord Shiva in helping him to bring the string of beads, for, the poet is innocent of his own welfare.

With these preparations the poet craves that his body should be thrown into the holy Ganges for final salvation.

¹The poet Ramprasad is conscious of the illusion of the this world. Son and wife and kith and kin,—they indeed are none of yours.

Every man or woman comes into this world alone; and then when he or she quits this world, he or she is alone again.

But then Ramprasad is not worried or afraid. He has ensconced the image of Mother Kali, the emblem of Brahman itself and his liberation is assured. He will no longer return to this world of pain and sorrow. He is tired and worn out in his sojourn in this mortal earth, but then, he knows, he will attain eternal peace, serene and sublime with the grace of Mother Kali.

²This tiny song is a picture of Mother Menaka who is so sad at the

Thou art no common, slight little girl,
Thou, the spouse divine of Shiva Supreme
Adored, worshipped of the trinal worlds
I bide here for Thee alone
Watchful of the way you come.

❦ Song 175[1] ❦

I do not shut my eyes for fear of that,
Lest I should lose her, Mother Tara
Should mine eyes be shut;
When I lie upon my cot
With that same fear I am beset,
Lest I lost her out of sight
I fall asleep with open eyes.

❦ Song 176[2] ❦

Turn me insane, oh Mother (Brahmamoyee)
I've need no more of learned lores;
Make me drunk with the wine of Thy love divine!
In devotion let me lose my mind,
Do drown me, Mother, in Thy sea of love!

melancholy of her daughter Shankari. Shankari is another name of Goddess Durga.

The young daughter somehow is emotionally injured and is sad and sulking. The Mother Menaka cannot bear the sorrow of her daughter. The Mother knows that her daughter is not an ordinary girl. She is the supreme Goddess of the Universe.

The daughter is also the consort of Lord Shiva. She is angry with the Mother and is not returning to Her Mother's place. Anxious and pining the Mother is watching at the portal of her palace waiting for her daughter's return from Her husband's place.

[1]This song touches on the borderline of modern poetic diction. The message is unrevealed and must be guessed or divined by the reader from half-spoken symbols. The poet is afraid to close his eyes. That way the 'pupil' of his eye will be lost from his eyes. The Bengali word for pupil is 'Tara,' which is also another name of Goddess Mother Kali. The poet is anxious in his sleep. He is awake, lest his beloved Mother should be lost from his sight.

The poet has got a solution. He now sleeps with his eyes wide open.

[2]The poet sings here of love and devotion as the highest form of bliss.

In this Thine House of souls insane
Some wildly laugh, some loudly moan;
Isa, Musa, Srichaitanya,—oh Mother,—Thou,
They all lost their senses in Thy love;
Alas, oh Mother, when is it
I'll be blest, dissolve as One?
The heaven, it is full of souls insane,
As the Guru is, so are his followers same,—
Who knows the pranks, the ways of love?
In love, Mother Thou, Thou art raving rank,
Among all crazy souls Thou'rt the gem on the crown!
In Thy love's treasure-trove, Mother, do Thou make me rich
This slave of Thy love, poor wretched, this I do beseech!

❦ Song 177[1] ❦

Put 'Her' in the niche of your bosom—caressing warm,
Mother Shyama,—the dearest, most beloved One;
Thou be'est wise to it, hearken, I too ken,
Let no other know it, we two, my dearest friend;
Playing truant to foes like lust, ire, desire
Dost Thou come, let's balmy, cool, bless our eyes:
We would keep the rolling tongue in company
Just he, too, should join chanting Mother's Name;
Dark Inconscience,—he is evil minister vile,
Do not let him approach, draw near-while,
Post *consciousness* at the portal as sentinel,
Do be cautious, most wary, vigilant;
My friend, Kamalakanta opens his mind,
Just one little thought, a mere submission, mine.

All philosophies,—Hindu or Christian,—have discoursed on divinity. All metaphysical literature teems with profound analysis and discrimination. To the sage poet Ramprasad, all that is futile. He wants to go insane, completely forgetting himself in supreme love for Goddess Kali.

Such madness and insanity is very common in the paradise as well. The supreme Lord Shiva, He himself is half mad, unconcerned with any affairs of the cosmic world. Mother Kali, the consort of Shiva, She too is wild in Her ways and diverse stance. The poet wants to dissolve and be one with that madness of joy and devotion.

[1]Sage poet Ramprasad's relations with Mother Kali is intensely personal. In Hindu philosophy there are three ways of worship. One is through

Even the meanest poor, should he treasure come by
With it does he ever part, put it somewhere away?

❦ Song 178[1] ❦

I am not that dud moronic son of Thine,
I am not afraid should'st Thou show thine eyes;
Having brought me on to the world's rocking quay
In the truant stream Thou art throwing me away,
I'm lost overwhelmed in the turbulence
By the helmsman's errant words wayward awry;
The quarrels, Mother, 'tween mother and son,—
'Deliver me'—implores the devout sagely one;
I've clasped Thy feet, Mother, firm, I won't relent,
I swear, I won't retreat to step-mother's tent.

complete renunciation of the world of works. The world is an illusion. all works are tainted. the ascetic *(sannyasin)* must renounce all works.

The other way of worship is to work without desires, ego and attachment. The *Srimadbhagavat Geeta* has given this way of worship the most sublime status.

But the third way is utter devotion. In this form of worship the devotee has a deep personal relation with the God or Goddess. Sage poet Ramprasad, Sri Chaitanya, Sri Ramakrishna,—they were devotees of their personal God or Goddess.

In this song Ramprasad wants to install Mother Shyama in his own bosom with great love. He invites his mind that he and his mind should alone witness the gracious Mother. The sensuous foes like desire and others should be shut out. Only he would keep his tongue with him so that it should chant the name of Mother. But Prasad (Kamalakanta) will take all cautions. He would keep *ignorance* out of the way, for, he is a bad counsellor. And then, he will post enlightenment and consciousness as sentinels so that no undesirable intruders should enter the holy union with the Mother.

Ramprasad has secured his treasures. He would not part with it nor give anyone else its custody.

[1]The poet is in a mock quarrel with his Mother, Goddess Kali.

Like every child the poet is often amiss. Naturally, the Mother is angry and scolds the child. But the sage poet is not a fool. He does not sulk. He is not afraid of the Mother even when she is annoyed and angry with him.

The poet charges the Mother that, indeed, She is to blame. She has put the child on the shore of the tempestuous worldly sea. and then, instead of giving refuge to the child, She is pushing him into the waters.

☙ Song 179[1] ❧

Come, Mother, let's have duel in the 'penance-ring,
I'll see, who loses,—is't Mother or the son?
I'll mount the chariot of 'Kali-worship' in war,
The twin prying chargers,—penance, meditation,—
Then, the two—them, I'll harness there;
Tanging at the string taut, tempered tense
Of the bow of conscious light supreme
I've taken post, set the sharpest shaft
Of Brahma—devout to let it fly sanguine;
Mother, I'll test Thee in battle, of Death I've no fear.
I'd sound alarm to seize deliverance's treasure;
The tongue will join in battle-drum
Roaring loud Kali's Name,
Who dares me, in battle, to contend?
Thou art vanquisher of demon hordes
Again and then again in tormenting war;—
Now, come, Thou Queen Brahmamoyee,
I dare Thee, contend me in duel fair;
Rasikchandra, the soul devout,—he declares,
Mother, Thou, I'll conquer Thee
By Thine own puissance nonpareil!

    Symbolically, the poet tells the Mother that it is She who ordains everything. This world is like a stormy ocean, full of worries, pain, sorrows and chagrins. The poet is tormented in this rough waters of the world. That is how the Mother throws the child into the sea. And then the mind of the poet, again a creature of Mother, is in error. The mind steers the craft wrong and errant.
    But then the poet knows that this quarrel between the son and the Mother is an internal misgiving. Ramprasad knows that if he should weep and crave to the Mother for his rescue then She will not spurn him. The poet has firmly held on to the feet of the Mother and he refuses to go over to the step-mother.
    The step-mother is the elusive image of Mother Kali Herself as the Cosmic Nature. Ramprasad is aware of this illusion and will not be caught by its bewitching charm.
    [1]This song is rich in mystic poetry.
    Hindu philosophy is unique in its avowal of the power of the *yogin*. The devout soul is fearless. He dares death and is careless of the powers of the evil and torment of this mundane world. But then what is the

☙ Song 180[1] ☙

How now, today oh Queen Kali
You're beneath the *kadamba* tree?
Where have you veiled your *wreath of human skulls*?
Who has 'dorned your neck with wild floral lace?
The *dakinis* and *yoginis*,—
The lurid girls of the spirit realm,
Your boon companions in frolics, fun
Where have you put them all away?
In your left-hand the scimitar,
Shyama, glowing in flowing hair,
The *lute with loud alluring crown*
Calls the tune of Radha's name!

---

source of this strength of the *yogin* who has immersed himself, united with the Absolute Divinity?

This strength is the absolute freedom from fear of the *yogin* who has reached the realm of eternal bliss. Mother Kali is supreme in her power and puissance. She is dread, dour in war, the slayer of demons. But the dvout sage poet is not afraid; he dares the Goddess Mother in the war of penance. And what are the weapons of the sage poet in this spiritual battle with Mother? The weapon is none other than the strength of the poet of his devotion of the Mother herself.

The poet has no doubt that in such a war and spiritual contest the poet will win over his supreme Mother by the invincible power of his devotion and love for the Mother herself.

[1]The song throws light into an occult corner of Hindu religion and metaphysics. It is commonly perceived by the people of other faiths that the Hindus are idol-worshippers and they are partial and parochial about their chosen personal deity. In practice too there are factions and schisms among Hindu sects. The Shaivites (followers of Lord Shiva) quarrel with Vaishnavites (worshippers of Lord Vishnu) and the devotee of Mother Kali is jealous and hostile to one who worships Lord Krishna. And it is alas with all religions: factions fester, Shias fight Sunnis, Catholics against Protestants, and the Hinayanists mock at the Mahayanists.

But the genuine spiritual seeker along the path of Hinduism has no such illusions or ineptitude. He knows that Divinity is One and Absolute. Lord Sri Ramakrishna avowed,—"There are as many ways as there are creeds." And all such 'ways' and 'creeds'—are the path to the same supreme godhead.

The present song has a sweet allusion to a well-known Vaishnava annal. Sri Radha was the married wife of Ayan Ghosh who was a devotee of Mother Kali, but Sri Radha was in overwhelming love of Lord Krishna.

❦ Song 181[1] ❦

The daughter of the mountain king,—her metropolis
It is the verdant land of joy and bliss;
The mind whispering calls,—why oh mind,
Here thou dost not dwell?
The realm is the same as holy Kasi,
Or else it echoes sacred Puri *dham;*
Oh mind, do listen, chant and sing, hymns
Of Primal Brahman, Lord Supreme;
Oh mind, just and fair, then why not sing,
Songs and poems, extol the great God, Lord Shiva's Name?
Where flows Ganga's holy, emancipation's stream
Be it gods, men or sages,—chant unfailing Hara's name!
Queen Mother of worlds, Oh, primal friend.
Deliver me from the toils of the mortal world!
As the end arrives let Lord Shiva, Shambhu, awake in front
Before my ken,—hymns and songs in my ears do chant;
The Royal King in tiger-skin,
Queen Bhabani along with him,
Sonorous, sounds the kettledrum
The horn blows in loud alarm;
Tulasidasa entreats, oh mind, chant, extol and sing
The Name of Lord Mahadeva,
The paeans of Kali, Mother Queen,—
Then, oh mind, you'll attain
The supreme divine feet, sublime!

News was taken to Ayan that his wife, Radha was doing her love and worship to Krishna away from home. Ayan, mad in anger, went right then to where Radha was doing her worship to Lord Krishna. Radha saw her husband coming with her hostile sisters in law. But then as Ayan reached the cottage he saw Mother Goddess Kali, dread and smiling as Radha was worshipping her. He went back so pleased and angry with his sisters who (he thought) carried canards about his devoted wife, Radha.

In the present song, the poet perceives Mother Kali in the image of Lord Krishna!

[1] The song is yet another symbol of the catholic nature of Hindu theology and spiritualism.

The sage poet is suffused with the universal presence of Divinity. In his wonted way the poet pleads and remonstrates with his mind on

Song 182[1]

My fond desire has gone in vain
My hopes are lost bygone,
Mother, oh, all is waste and wan;
I call you, Mother, as life's last and final call
Oh, do come, Mother, to your lap, pray, take me on;
No one of this earth does, indeed, do love
This earth ne'er does know the way of love,
I yearn, so, Mother, to there move on
Where there's love requited by love alone;
All longings I have renounced
Smitten by most aching wounds,
I have withdrawn from all desires
Singed by hurting burning pain,
I have wept long and bitterly
I can, oh mother, weep no more;
My heart is broken, oh Mother
It splits in pain and agony!

Song 183[2]

The day's no longer far away
When burnt to ashes, you'll be no more,
When all and one will let you go,

---

the sacred nature of the sublime realm of holy Kasi (Varanasi). it is there that Lord Shiva dwells and then over it doth preside divine Goddess Durga or Annapurna, the queen of Lord Shiva.

[1]This song is the poet's disillusionment with this world's sham and transient relations.

As the poet came into this world he had many desires, dreams and aspirations. Many years have gone by and life is ebbing. The poet's desires have remained all unfulfilled. The poet feels lonely and forsaken. Like the forlorn child the poet calls the Mother to lift him on to Her lap.

The poet has loved his kith and kin, wife and friends. His love has remained unrequited. The poet now knows, this mundane earth has no real love, no one here knows how to love. The poet now pines for the world where there is love alone,—compassion and taintless bliss! The poet has been mortally wounded. He has been bruised all over and his heart bleeds. He has wept long and bitterly. He is now waiting for the Mother to call him back into Her lap.

[2]In this tiny song the poet reminds himself that world is sham and

Father, mother or brother yours;
That day when your home and all,
Should they perish, burn away
You'll not look behind even in error or for once;
That day, when you'll know discern
All so meaningless and sham
That's why, oh, contemplate,
Mother Shyama's feet bethink!

Song 184[1]

What shame is it, oh, how obscene!
The woman mounted on the man,
Down below her feet, supine—
Lies a *yogin* awful strange!
Lord Shiva, he doesn't even open his eyes
To look, as a dead corpse he lies,
What kind this awful maiden dread
Shorn of modesty and shame!

futile. All things here are transient and meaningless,—with rise and fall as melting bubbles.

As one quits this world, the body that is so dear and precious to the person is burnt to ashes. All the nearest relations,—parents, brothers and friends, they all let you leave, pass away! Man is worrying all the time about his family and his concerns in the world. But then, when death comes, he leaves this world forgetting all his possessions, kith and kin, as if they had never been! Even if his house should burn and all the human possessions perish, he would never lift an eyebrow or look back from the other world. Why then all this constant anxieties, pain and passions for something that will soon vanish into the void and will be forgotten, lost for ever.

[1]This song, a mere scrap of some thoughts of the poet, is altogether on a different pattern.

The sage poet, Ramprasad often takes, liberty in his familiar utterances to the Mother. He is the devout son of the Goddess Mother. But even then he often puzzles, lost over the way of the Mother in Her image in the human world. Mother Kali is all naked and then she stands, thighs wide apart, on the body of Lord Shiva, Her divine spouse. By worldly conduct and decent manners this stance of the Goddess Mother is strange and awkward. As the poet looks at the Mother in her shameful stance, he is totally perplexed. The woman, without a shred of clothes on her person stands on the strange *yogin* who lies prostrate under Her feet. Lord Shiva lies as a corpse. What kind of shameless woman the Mother is, who has shed her good manners and shame!

Song 185[1]

Mother Kali, I've lost my caste;
That fellow 'Jata' in my home,
Mother, dread, into my ears,
He's the one, that one's put in
Hari's name; round my neck
He has tied the wreath of tulasi beads;
With the sack of twigs of *neem* he has me bedecked,
He has painted me all o'er my limbs with holy arabesque
And then he has got me to don
The scarf overlaid with Hari's name,
I yearn to worship Thy twin feet
With bunch of *tulasi* twigs and leaves,—
Why not discard your Lord, insane,
Assume Lord Krishna's grace in Brajaland?

[1]This song carries the cream of catholicity of Hindu religion.

The poet Ramprasad is a devout worshipper of Mother Shyama. He is a follower of the Shakti cult, a well-known branch or path of worship of the Hindu religion. But then, the sage poet is conscious that Divinity is One and Absolute. The same Mother who appears in Her image of Goddess Kali, is also Lord Krishna, the divine personal God of the Vaishnava cult. The Absolute One Supreme appears in many forms. The Absolute is One and the Same. But then, it is the error of the worshippers that they quarrel, they suffer rivalries between followers of one sect and the other.

In this song the poet confesses to the Mother Kali that he has lost his caste. He is a worshipper of Goddess Shakti, but then, the name of Lord Krishna (Lord Hari) has been put into his ears. He has now taken to the worshipful way of the Vaishnavites. He has worn the necklace of *tulasi* beads and has taken the begging bag which is customary for the Vaishnava hermit, He has painted all over his body the sandal mark of the Vaishnavas and has taken a wrapper, printed all over with the name of Hari.

And all this has happened because Lord Shiva has put him into this new way of worship. But then it doesn't matter. The poet prays to the Mother, why not he worship her with the leaves of *tulasi*, as it is the practice in worshipping Lord Hari. Why can't the Mother give up her wild stance and appear in the image of Lord Krishna of Vrindavana (known as Vrajadham in Hindu Vaishnava mythology)!

❦ Song 186[1] ❦

Mother Tara, Thou art the queen of thoughts,
Hast Thou ever thought of me?
Thy *name* is the 'conscious soul' of the worlds,
Yet, in Thy ways that's not what I see;
Thy gift is worldly worries at the break of dawn,
By noon it is anxious thoughts of livelihood,
When I go to bed Thou deignest cares, concern!
Tell me, Mother, when is it I chant Thy name?
Thou maiden, thyself beyond all cares,
The crowning gem that Thou hast in store
Of Meditation sublime,—Thou art lost serene
Eluding this humble page,—beyond his ken.

Song 187[2]

I've known, oh Kali, now Thy mental stance
Being beloved of Lord Ashutosh,
Thou art so miserly and mean;

---

[1] This song carries the essence of enlightenment in the simplest of words as is wont with the poet.

The highest metaphysics of Hindu spiritual thought is that the human being is merely an instrument. Everything that he thinks or does or desires,—is ordained by the universal power, the supreme Divinity. Mother Tara (Goddess Kali). She is the ordainer of all thoughts and waves of emotions that arise in the human mind. The poet here complains to the Mother. It is She who creates all his errant thoughts. She is the queen of the constant vibrations which rise and fall in the human mind. Even then, She has not thought anything about her beloved son, the sage poet Ramprasad. The poet finds that in Her conduct and Her ways with the poet, She does not seem to have any thought of the poet himself.

The poet complains that in the morning of each day the Mother makes him think of his worldly matter; as noon arrives he is worried about his food and sustenance and then as he retires in the night all kinds of worldly thoughts and worries absorb his mind. These thoughts are all Mother's creation; they are all Her wishes. But then, what is the result? The poet has no time to think of the Mother. And the Mother is careless. She is the queen of the world of thoughts and She has got, in Lord Shiva, the ultimate of Her desire. That is why, She is so indifferent and careless and She has cheated Shambhuchand, that is the sage poet Ramprasad himself.

[2] In this song the poet is in a fair combat with the Mother. He is

Thou art Lord Ashutosh's spouse
Yet hast Thou taken to Thy father's ways?
That's why, meseems Lord Shiva's words
Mother Tara's lost, amiss!
The lotus is beset with thorns,—
Lest Thy purple feet should singe,
Is it, that's why Thy twin tender feet
Thou dost sulk, forbear to deign!

☙ Song 188[1] ☙

When, alas but when,
Thou Hara's beloved queen,—
Would'st Thou reveal, appear before my ken?
My days of sport upon this world,
Mother, are now about to end,
The day now wanes, dusk descends,—
As days go by the limbs are thin
With passing days the eyes grow dim;
If it's now Thou dost not come,
Later could I, oh Mother Shyama,
Know discern Thy countenance?
Oh Mother, Thou,—Thou hast fed me, clothed me,
Nursed me with such love and grace,

unhappy with Her. The Mother is known as bounteous, gracious and open in Her showering of grace and kindness.

Moreover, She is the queen consort of Lord Shiva. Who is known as Ashutosh. The word *ashutosh* in Sanskrit or Bengali means one who is easily contented and pleased! But then, She is difficult to please—apparently compassionless and unkind. Why is it that She is not kind to Her own beloved son Ramprasad although he is so devoted to the Mother.

The poet wonders, is it that She has got the nature of Her father's family? The father of Durga of Kali, in Hindu mythology, is the Himalayas. And the Himalayan mountains are stone. The way of Her Father's clan is thus naturally stony-hearted, compassionless.

The poet divines that, that must be reason why She has fallen off the compassionate way of Her Lord and is so hard-hearted and compassionless.

Or is it, there are thorns in the lotus and Her golden lotus feet may be hurt and that is why she is afraid to let anyone have Her twin gracious feet!

[1]This song is the agonising cry of the sage poet Ramprasad. He has

Yet I only hear Thy name, Tara,
I never know how is Thy face!
This veil, it is but Thine own charm
Oh Kali, before the eyes of Thine own son;
As I divine, my limbs with time turn so blue and pale,—
To come and see for Thyself, Oh Mother.
Why is it that Thou dost fail?

❦ Song 189[1] ❦

I'm most wretched, the meanest of the mean;
If Thou woulds't not deliver, oh Tara,
Then, Tara, who, tell me, would deliver me?
Mother Tara, Tara, Tara Mother,
Do not, I pray, torment me any more.
Thou hast pained, punished me now,
True, all that was my destined lot,—
Do, pray, no more torment me, Mother,
Smite no more,—why punish, yet, anymore!
Ramachandra,—heir of Shiva Lord
He is so humble, wretched, mean,—
He calls loud ceaselessly—oh listen,
Hark, Saviour Thee, Oh Mother, mine!

---

worshipped and searched for Goddess Kali all his life. Now the worldly life is coming to an end. The eyes are dim and the body is weak. Even then Mother Kali does not appear before the eyes of the devout soul.

The poet is impatient. Time is wearing away. He knows mother Goddess through her constant association with everything that he does or thinks or chants or worships. But he has not yet seen her image in person. The poet knows that the mother wears a veil. It is the mask that She wears as symbol of her own legerdemain. The poet asks that the Mother should shower Her grace on Her lonely son and lift the veil on Her own.

The poet is pining to see Her in person before his eyes.

[1]The mood of this song is one of surrender and craving for mercy. The sage poet Ramprasad knows that he has earned no virtue. He does not deserve the Mother's grace. But then, he is the devout son of mother Kali. It is the grace of the Mother to deliver her own child from the worries and agonies of the world. The poet himself is wretched, mean and pursuing all errant ways. But then, he is all the time seeking Mother's compassion and love. It is the poet's prayer that She do no longer torment Her son and deliver him of all the pains of this world.

❦ Song 190[1] ❦

Should I come by a rupee one crore purse
Listen, I would tell you, oh Mother Tara
What I would do with that, how disburse;
I'd adorn the land with foliage, fruits
I'd build a temple of marble white
An image of Thine then I'd sculpt
In touchstone of dark basalt,
And then in the bank of the Ganges Thee install!
At the end of worship, offerings done,
Serving up the poor divine,
Then partaking of what remains
Beneath Thy feet I'd bide my time
In supreme joy and bliss divine.
As the dusk would loom I'd light the lamp
I'd do my vespers with perfume incense,
And then seated at the temple portals
Chant and sing to my heart's content;
Would e'er this longing, Mother, be fulfilled?
Or else bide, dark in the mind frozen stilled?
Suryakanta entreats, Mother Shyama,
Grant, beseech this prayer be fulfilled
Reveal Thyself as he quits this mortal world!

[1]This song is in the mood of the poet where he exults at the legion ways in which he would serve and worship Mother Goddess.

People of this world pursue wealth and prosperity relentlessly. The poet is a human being who is fond of wealth and riches as well. But then, what he would do with such wealth, is somewhat different.

The poet tells the Mother, if he would get one crore rupees (in Ramprasad's days Rs. 1 crore would be many billions today) what he would do with it. He would build a temple of marble stone and install Her image in black granite, on the bank of the holy river Ganges. He would worship the Mother and then he would feed all hungry creatures of Lord Shiva to their heart's content. Then he would partake of the small remains of the offerings to the Mother. Then, as the evening would come he would adorn the temple and the image of Mother Kali with light, incense and music. He would sing and chant Mother's name ceaseless in utter bliss.

Ramprasad was poor himself. He had little means to feed his own family and to carry on his wishes of worshipping Mother and give away food and riches to the million poor. The song embodies the craving of the devout soul. It is a contrast between what the ordinary wealthy man does or would do with his riches and what the sage poet would long to do with it.

❦ Song 191[1] ❦

Today, Mother Kali, Thou hast assumed, as if,
   all-devouring form
Erazing the moon and stars,
Swift ceaseless oft Thou rushest with the lightning flash;
The night spells dark dismal doom,
Letting out roaring thunderous boom,
As if with a loud lurid laughter in the gaping yawning mouth,
Thou dost stalk ravenous to swallow up the earth!
With deep loud resounding howl!
As one with reverberating thunder peal,
Thou robed in dread, dire, horrid image
Dost rock the earth with roaring thunderous rage;
Thy tempest breath doth curl and swirl
Churning trees and homes as in a grinding mill;
Raising dense, dark louring mass of clouds
Thou art as if breaking down the inane aloud;
Sweats stream unceasing in cascade,
Rivers, streams,—they rush all in floods;
The worlds to Thee are all revealed
In the vision of the oft-quivering lightning flash;
Meseems, Mother Thou, now dost roam
Set on bringing down the final doom;—
Suryakanta wonders how Thou should'st thus destroy
These worlds of marvel Thou had'st carved
With Thine own hands in joy!

[1] This song is a portrait of Mother Kali in her most turbulent, annihilating stance.

    The Mother is full of grace and charm and sublime beauty. But she is also the slayer of demons and all that is dark and sinful. The image of Mother Kali, in Hindu mythology, is dread, dour countenance with scimitar in hand, and necklace of severed human skulls around Her neck. In this Her image, She is the annihilator of the created worlds. The poet is face to face with this fearsome appearance of the Mother. The sun and the moon have all vanished in Her raging storm. The vast open mouth of the Mother, as if, She is swallowing all the world. The frightening roar of Her voice is reverberating as thunder in which the earth is quaking and the winds are fleeing in terror and torment. The trees are all wearing down in great noise, the rivers and waters of the world are all in floods inundating all creations.

    To the poet it looks like that the Mother is entrusted with the cosmic task of annihilation of this phenomenal worlds.

❦ Song 192[1] ❦

Oh Tara, you Queen of thoughts—
Who but knows what you think;
You just do what you will
With someone that you would sink
And then someone else whom
You take safe across the stream.
Once as he uttered your 'Durga' name
Kalaketu did your feet attain,
And then someone doing Yoga, trance,
Yet, never, Thee kens across the aeons;
Srimanta, to him you did appear
Revealed yourself in the lotus-lair;
Then you sent him to the burning place;
Again, in a twinkle by your grace
You deigned him niche at you queenly feet;
By your wink the worlds move on,
My own desire,—that's a mere pittance;
I'll offer myself to your feet sublime,
On the last day of my life's reunion.

❦ Song 193[2] ❦

Deliverance is her 'Name';
Thy 'Name,' Oh Shyama, alone, is my chance.

---

[1] In this song the personal devotion of the sage poet and the supreme power of the Mother are portrayed.

Man is powerless in this creature world. He is merely an instrument in the domain of Mother Kali. She is the creator and she is the ordainer of whatever happens in the universe,—from the tiniest movement of the eyelid to the vastest annihilation of the galaxies. Nothing is, or ever can be, nothing happens, no thoughts can be thought or 'will' can be willed without the gracious nod of the Mother. The poet knows this mystery and this is the simple truth. There are no saints or sinners to the Mother. In million births deliverance does not come but the most wretched human being can be emancipated in a twinkle of time with the grace of the Mother.

The poet concludes that the Mother's 'wishes' are vast and pervasive; but the poet has only one small desire. that is, that he secures the gracious feet of the Mother as he quits this world.

[2] This song is the essence of worship that is the highest and the most sublime in the Hindu metaphysics.

What use tokens of worshipful acts,
Sham rituals empty artefacts,
Thy 'Name' alone snaps mortal toils
That's what the matted-hair Lord's announced;
Me, the porter of that plaited Lord.
To whom else to bow could I afford?
Let whate'er come out of it, I'd take the 'Name,'
Why this sham worry for nothingness!
I've taken Shiva as mine own Lord,
All that's true in Lord Shiva's words.

♀ Song 194[1] ♀

Wake up, arise Thou gracious queen,
Open, unbar Thy cottage door!
In dense darkness I cannot ken
My heart quails in constant fear,
I call Thy 'name' shrill and loud,
Tara oft and endless times;—

    In the scripture worship is ordained through *yajnas* and varied forms of rituals. But the poet knows that these are all superfluous, meaningless. The 'name' of the Mother alone is enough. Contemplating Her name chanting Her name and singing joyously of the image of the Mother,— this is the last and final worship.
    The poet no longer worries about his own ignorance about the varied Mantras and the elaborate ways of worship. He is content to dissolve in the name of the Mother and constantly chant and sing Her name in utter joy and bliss.
    [1]The poet laments to the gracious Mother. Like the wayward child the poet had wandered here and there and lost in the world. He forgot his Mother, who dwells all the time within with her overwhelming grace.
    Now the night has fallen. The days are coming to an end. Life is ebbing. The lost child is frightened in the darkness. He is calling his Mother, loud and anxious, but the Mother is not responding. She is still inside veiled and unrevealed to the anxious call of Her devout son. Is it that the Mother was annoyed and unhappy at the wicked ways of the son? The poet is ignorant. He has lost his time in meaningless sham pursuits of the world. He now prays to the Mother that She forgive Her child and lift Her face to his pleadings. He promises that never again he will go awry, wandering astray into this world. After all she is the Mother of the universe. It does not behove that She not have mercy on Her child. However wretched her son, the Mother must have compassion and lift the child out of his miseries.

Being the Queen of love and grace
What is this stance, I ken, is't Thy face?
Shutting out the son outside
Thou art asleep in Thy niche inside;
Calling out mother, mother mine,
I am lean and thin mere bones and skin,
Is it that I was drunk and spoilt in sports
That's why Thou dost so resent?
Do Mother, look up for once, I pray
I swear, I won't go again for play!
This wretched Rama avers, oh Mother
To whom else Mother, I should repair?
Who else than Mother would take him in fold
This wretched mean and lowly soul?

❦ Song 195[1] ❦

Tell me oh Uma, my little child,
How did you abide in an alien home?
All kinds of tales people tell,—
As I hear I'm dead with concern.
A mother's heart, can it shed its qualms,
The son-in-law (they say), he lives on alms
This time as he comes to take you home
I'll tell him, my Uma, she's not at home.

[1]This song is a lyric of lament by the queen Menaka, mother of the great Goddess Uma or Durga or Kali. Queen Menaka the consort of the great Himalayas, is not happy with Lord Shiva, the husband of her daughter, Uma. Lord Shiva in the Hindu annals lives like a mendicant, half clad in tiger skin, with ashes smeared all over the body. He is portrayed as half mad and then he goes on begging and seeking alms.

Uma has now come home to Her mother's palace. The Queen wonders how her little daughter Uma had spent Her days in Her husband's place. The son-in-law, Lord Shiva, is not the proper princely groom, fit for her daughter.

Menaka declares, she would not send her daughter back to her husband's place again. When the son-in-law would come to take Uma home, she (Menaka) would tell Him that Uma was not home.

This song is one of a series where the love of the mother Menaka for her little daughter Uma, finds sweet and sad expressions. In the Bengali home, the daughter after her marriage leaves her parents' home and goes away to reside in the house of her husband. This parting of the daughter at her marriage is always melancholy for the mother. And then,

Song 196[1]

Come mother, welcome Uma, little child,
Say no more, pray, 'let me go,' 'let me go'
Haimavati mother, to mother Thine
Such words of parting never behove;
As the year does end, do come again,
Do not forget mother, thine,
Oh, beloved daughter own;
Lest I should miss that sweetest call,—
'Mother,'—from thy face as the moon!
Oh neighbours, ye all, who in the city dwell
Do come, sound with your tongues—joyous music rolls.
Uma, She is the priceless gem
At home such treasure,—there is none!
Yet, conscious enlightenment sounds the call,—
'Oh Queen of the Mountains,—tall,—
Hara's Queen,—that's how to all she's proclaimed,—
Shut thy eyes, and in your bosom ken,—
Thy Uma,—oh, she is nowhere seen!

when the husband is beggarly and poor and the daughter is the princess of the Royal Lord, the mother is sad indeed. The divine Lord Shiva or the Goddess Durga, they are all painted in their human forms with all the emotions, joys and sorrows, of the ordinary worldly household.

[1] This is another song in the same series. Uma or Goddess Durga is worshipped in the Bengali home (and in fact all over the Hindu society) for four days in the year. These four days of Durga-*puja* (worship of Mother Goddess Durga) is the homecoming of the Mother. For the rest of the year, Durga dwells in Her husband's place at Kailas,—in the remote recess of the Himalayas according to Hindu mythology.

Uma has come back to Her mother for a brief four days time. As the day of Navami ends, then arrives the Dasami day (the tenth day of the waxing moon) when Goddess Durga must come back to Her Lord. Menaka pleads with her daughter, that this time after she has come home, she must not utter a word of leaving her parents' place. She comes only once in the whole year and She must remember to come again. The Mother pleads that She do not forget Her mother and her own home. The mother asks all in the metropolis to rejoice and celebrate the return of her daughter Uma.

But then, mother Menaka is not ignorant. She knows that her daughter Uma is not an ordinary girl. She knows in her mind that the Goddess Durga is everywhere and all the time. As soon as she should close her eyes, she would find Uma vanished in her physical form, and pervading the phenomenal worlds.

♀ Song 197[1] ♀

Is it that, oh Brahmamoyee,
Yet, it's not to your heart's content?
What torment, pain, deceit, Mother—
You shower on your lowly son!
You coiled the spring of life on earth,
Of earthly possessions served me gall;
The more I burn of earthly poison
'Durga,' 'Durga,' the more I call!
You gave me the treasure of conscience's light
You took it away as a debt of plight;
Mother Tara, do reckon count,
How much of pain is still unpaid!

♀ Song 198[2] ♀

What is this game, oh Kali,
I am at a loss to ken
As I go on calling 'Durga,' 'Durga,'
My agony yet never ends;
Unceasing you I contemplate,—
If misfortune doesn't end, yet then
Lord Shiva will sure a liar become
And then no one will listen to Him;

This song is a sweet blend of the homely scene of the return of the married daughter to her parents' home and consciousness of universality of the great Goddess Durga.

[1] This song is a loud lament of the sage poet Ramprasad. The poet is the child of the Mother Goddess Kali. Goddess Kali is the supreme ordainer of the Universe. She is the Absolute Divinity. It is She who decides the ways and thoughts of every creature. If the poet has lost himself, immersed in the poisonous world of desires and wealth, She alone is responsible for all that. How is it then that the poet is to blame? The poet now is worn with all the miseries of the world. He is suffering from gall and poison of the worldly desires. He is now calling Her loud and ceaselessly that She save him. The Mother, of course, had given her child the light of consciousness, but then again it is She who had veiled it with ignorance and confusion. The poet has suffered a lot. Is it that he is not yet quits? The poet asks the Mother to reckon whether he has not repaid by now his sins and defaults by all his sufferings or is it that there is more of miseries for him in his Account.

[2] This song is in the usual mood of the sage poet.

The child is wayward often errant
All mothers yet must bear with him,
She scolds yet takes him in her lap
She cannot ever give him up;
If the wretched beggar must beg to live
Where is, Mother, there the harm?
Dvija Sambhuchandra,—his evil days
Will they never pass away?
Is it that better days will never come?

ꕤ Song 199[1] ꕤ

This time I will sure go mad;
The singeing fire of this world
Burns smouldering within my head,
How longer must I bear with it?
Passion, lust, pursuit of wealth
Me, oh Tara, has made purblind;
I'm ruined, I work myself to death
Bearing no-man's burden on my head;

    The poet knows that he is at fault. He is the child of the Mother Goddess, full of devotion. But he has been wicked and wayward. Sent into this world by the Mother, the child has gone astray, ignorant and simple, immersed in the fruitless pursuits of desires and riches in this mundane world. But then, the poet is miserable, suffering from pain and anxieties.
    The poet tells the mother that he is calling Her grace all the time. But why even then, his agonies and pain still persist! It is said in the shastras, which are the words of Lord Shiva himself, the worshipper and the devotee of Mother Kali is freed from all pain and misfortunes, attaining the realm of bliss.
    The poet finds that this is not happening in his case. Is it then that the words of Lord Shiva (the shastras) are not true? And if this happens that would be a great misfortune. Because, no one then would listen to the words of Lord Shiva enshrined in the shastras.
    The poet tells the Mother that the child is always prone to mischief. He is wicked and wayward and errant. But then, mother has to be patient. She cannot forswear her child. She may scold him, admonish and reprimand him but then she takes him back on to her lap. Will it not happen so with the sage poet (Shambhuchandra) and gracious days return?
    [1]This song spells out the essence of the hurdles that confront a spiritual seeker.

(Oh Mother), if the mind with great travail
Be in Thee somehow installed
(There) it does not lie tranquil,
It runs amuck with the craze of the world;
(Oh Mother), this beggar slave care-worn bewails,
Oh, he has no one else in all three worlds;
He has one prayer, Mother, to those feet
Let him not for ever be lost!

❦ Song 200[1] ❦

Come, oh Mother, in my bosom dwell;
Oh Mother, endlessly and then again
Thee, loud, I call, bewail!
I'm ignorant, alas of worship's ways
I'm so naive in penance profound,—
How is it, oh Thee, I do adore,—
If Thou shoulds't know my agony,
Do not, I pray, so tie me down
To the toils of this tormenting world!

The mind is fickle, ever playing sports with the *gunas* (*sattva, rajas* and *tamas*). As the sage meditates and contemplates the image of Divinity the mind goes astray again and again. In the *Srimadbhagavad Geeta* Lord Krishna has elaborate message for the *yogin* on the ways of concentrating his whole being on the Absolute. In the chapter on the Yoga of Practices (Abhyasa Yoga), Lord Krishna warns his spiritual seeker that the mind would ever play truant and still he must not relent; he should never give up. Again and again the mind will be disturbed. Desires and worries will intrude his world of contemplation. But he should bring back his errant mind repeatedly and continue his efforts ceaselessly.

In this song the poet laments that he is harassed and tormented by worldly desires. greed and lust and all the evils of the world. He goes on working and worrying, carrying the burden of his earthly life. With all his thankless jobs and meaningless pursuits if he is still able to instal his mind on the great Goddess Mother, the peace and calm is all too soon disturbed. From nowhere worries and desires of the world assail the inner world and tear asunder his meditation.

But then, the poet submits to the Mother, whatever happens, She should not forget that he has no one or nothing in the three worlds except the gracious feet of the Mother. The Mother must grant him the lost refuge in those two feet so that he is never lost for ever.

[1]This song is a scrap of prayer by the sage poet to his Goddess Mother Kali.

⚵ Song 201[1] ⚵

It's now betimes, oh Tara, my prayer I submit
So, worthless wretched that I am,
Me, in the end, you do not cheat,—
When the *scion of the Sun-God* (Yama) will come,
When he will send his own emissary,
The *five-some elements*, they'll all flee
At the sight of the awesome appariton!

⚵ Song 202[2] ⚵

It's time, oh mind, you better call
The Mother dark and blue sublime,

The songs of the sage poet are mostly his dialogues, prayers and conversations with the Mother. He often talks to his own mind and then again to the Goddess Mother. And his dialogues and prayers are not merely hymns and worships in very simple and often in rustic words and humdrum imageries, but he blends the most sublime spiritual truth with his life in the ordinary world. The experiences of the spiritual worshippers (*sadhakas*) in their occult overtones, interspersed in symbols in his simple tunes—is what marks out Ramprasad's songs as a unique literature in poetry and spiritualism, all in one!

In this song the prayer of the poet is simple. He pleads with the Mother that she should come and dwell in his bosom. The poet is not proficient in the ways of worship, in the varied rituals as laid down in the shastras. He is innocent and ignorant. His only possession is the great love and devotion for the Mother. The Mother should understand all this and take pity on him. And if She so accepts his worship in Her own grace then She should ordain that the poet is not tied down with the ceaseless toils and miseries of the world.

[1]This song is a matter of fact appeal by the sage poet to his Mother Goddess Kali.

Ramprasad's songs are remarkable for their familiar tones. The sage poet is a great devotee. Many of his songs are dialogues and prayers to the Mother. But the language and the manner of the dialogue is like the homely conversation of a child with his personal mother. There is no devotional architecture or high spiritual ambience.

The present scrap of song is just that the sage poet tells the Mother that she do not let him down because he is wretched and worthless. The poet knows that when the emissary of Death, comes to collect the mortal body of the poet the earthly elements will all flee in fear and despair.

[2]The poet talks to his mind. The mind is urged to think and contemplate the Mother Goddess Kali of dark blue complexion. The mind should

Dire Death, he is itching you to summon—
Any time he'll lift you off the auction room;
When Eternal Time calls the auction bid
Who dares name a price to him overbid!
And then when Death lifts you off the auction mart,
What profit then calling Mother, alas, too late!
Calling friends, all kith and kin
A shroud o'er the dead body drawn
They would all lament and moan,
Yet no one's call will get response;
Hairs have gone grey now
The teeth have fallen away
The destined years are pretty near their term;
Look, the summons is waiting there,
That's why I urge concern!

☙ Song 203[1] ☙

Oh, it is not that wine I drink,
I savour elixir in joyous toast to Kali's Name;
The mind as it's drunk turns one insane,
The one that's drunk with wine is out of mind;

hurry up because time is running out. Very soon death will come and then he will take the poet away. Already he is ageing. And as he would quit this world, the friends and kinsmen will all lament but they would cover the body with a white piece of cloth (as is the Hindu custom) and send it away to the burning *ghat*.

It is then that it would be too late. The mind should better at once turn to the Mother.

[1] The sage poet Ramprasad was worshipper of Goddess Kali on the creed of Tantrashastra. In the Tantric method, drinking and certain other rituals are ordained. Often people comment on such sages because taking alcoholic drink as part of worship is not in common acceptance in Hindu religious systems.

But then, the sage poet explains that the drink that the sage takes is not the ordinary alcohol with which a normal person gets drunk. The sage is not touched by mundane properties of alcohol. It is so purified in the name and touch of the Goddess Mother Kali and by the *seed mantra*, that it becomes elixir. In the high level of penance and worship all conventional perceptions of good and bad, or right or wrong vanish. Ramprasad assures the ordinary people when drinks are taken as such pure elixir with the grace of the Mother, it leads one to total fulfilment.

With the sweet syrup by Guru given
Adding spices, Mother, of the mind's yearning,
My brewer consciousness ferments the pot,
And drinks off it my mind, insane;
The *seed mantra* fills out the limbs,
I cleanse it, calling Mother Tara's Name;
Ramprasad divines, as one drinks such wine
Life's foursome missions are all attained!

☙ Song 204[1] ☙

Oh mind,—
Do I' gainst you, lodge a plaint!
You can utter 'S' and pronounce 'V,'
Yet Durga, Shiva, you cannot 'lip!'
You have relished hot *jalebi*
Savoured tasty sweets, *luchi*,
Oh, it is all at the end
You will face the fun
As you quit the world
When the time will come;
The senses five, each one thrives,
They cherish each its own sweet will
How is it with them I dwell!
Oh mind, should you swindle steal
Your punishment will be just, equal!

[1] In this song too the poet talks to his own mind.

In the Hindu religion and spiritual literature the mind is compared to a wild horse in the world of Nature. That way comes all illusions and errors, the sense of duality, the distinction between right and wrong and sorrow and pleasures and so on.

The poet tells his mind that it can utter the letters and syllables all right. But then, it is reluctant to utter the name of Durga or Shiva.

The poet warns his mind that it is immersed in the passions and joys of the world. It is so happy with useless pleasures and fortunes. That is because he is slave to the five senses and obeys their urges. But then, when death comes, all his allies will vanish and he (the mind) will be truly punished.

♀ Song 205[1] ♀

Do thou get up, oh Uma, leave thy bed,
The night has retired, the day has dawned,
Invoking weal with lamp and chiming bells will now begin,
Arise, thou Mother,—thou weal and bliss of all the realms.
The night is worn and gone
The Lord of the Day is on the mount,
How long, languorous, will you sleep?
Do call 'mother,'—mother, Oh
Sweet and loud, oh, 'face as the moon!'
Brahma and the deities all
They keep awake as sentinels
That they may adore those gracious feet,—
With hibiscus, leaves of *bael* in hands,
Holding Thee for just three days
In my arms in warm embrace
My life's cravings I so fulfil;
Thou would'st proceed, mother, to Kailasa realm
To this meanest slave what'll happen then;
In Neelkantha's twelve-some months
The twelve-some foes, they hold their reign!

♀ Song 206[2] ♀

Oh thou Mother Kali, ever ceaselessly
You robed me in this world of sham,

[1]Mother Menaka is waking up her daughter Uma.
In Hindu mythology maiden name of Goddess Durga or Kali is Uma. She is the daughter of the Mountain Lord, the Himalayas and Mother Menaka, the queen of the Mountain king. Uma has come back from Kailasa, the place of Her husband, Lord Shiva. She is now with Her mother in the palace of the Himalayas.

Uma, as the universal Goddess Mother has to roam extensively because everyone calls Her in distress and peril. She is tired and sleeping. But then the Sun is up and the day has dawned. Already Brahma and the other gods and everyone in the world are ready to worship Her as the morning *puja*. She now must wake up to receive the worship and offerings of the devotees.

And then, the mother cannot forget that she is there at her mother's place only three days in the year. As the period ends she would go back to her husband's place in Kailasa.

[2]The diction of this song is a linguistic marvel of rustic Bengali

In the mantle of the clown;
There's no fun in playing the clown
Inside, it hurts in aching pain,—
Oft deep in the waters of the main
You fashion me in diverse forms;
I have wandered endless realms,
Countless costumes I've worn
Even then there is no end to it,—
Oh Mother, how, I thee extol!
But then the devout soul in me,—he says,—
My mind,—'you are so wicked' knave
That's why to lure you succumb so;
Or else, would your tricks and ploy
Have worked so oft and repeatedly!

☙ Song 207[1] ☙

Oh Mother Kali with wreath of skulls,
You showed me what this countenance!
Oh Mother, you taught me 'Mother' call,

vernacular language.
    Ramprasad himself was a scholar. His spiritual range and experiences were the highest in the path of *sadhana* (penance and practices); on top of this he was master of the simple rhetorics of puns and alliteration. The same little sounds, the same small words turning and twisting with different meanings to enrich the song. And, yet, with all these tricks of the language the bottomless depth of the spiritual message is unharmed. The style is cheeky but the message is profound.
    In this song Ramprasad complains to the Mother. In this world man performs a pantomime. His mind is a chameleon. He takes forms and shapes like the clown in the circus. Often crazy, seldom silent and peaceful, at times taking postures, practising charlatanism, in varied mood and gaits, he is a hybrid animal.
    And all these happen because the Mother is such a sorceress. She plays and sports with the human mind through Her mischievous *gunas* (*sattva, rajas* and *tamas*). These qualities of Mother's Nature are the sporting ground of the Mother who toys with Her children, and enjoys their frolics till at last the tired despairing child turns to the Mother seeking refuge and bliss.
    But sage poet Prasad knows all the Mother's tricks. He promises that he won't be deceived by all these playful magic. He knows his own mind and his wickedness. And he is not afraid.

    [1]Sage Poet Ramprasad had not renounced the world. He was not a

Then Mother's name to drink, extol;
How is it, oh, Mother Tara,
Where, oh, tell me, did you get
Your 'Name' so full of elixir?
The people of the creature world
As they look at me and ken,
They only call me love-lorn, insane;
The kinsmen own who are at home
It's they alone that will call me name,
But then, is it, oh Mother Shyama
At their wayward words do I careen?
Let whoever say what they will
Kali, Kali, I'd ever chant!
Honour or shame, they're all the same,—
Fond love and longings, forsaking all
I've taken to those crimson feet,
By worldly words do I err again?

☙ Song 208[1] ☙

(Oh) you must go,—to tarry there's little time,
How long would you be left behind?

sannyasin in the conventional sense. He had his wife and mother. He had to look after his family. But then, he got his spiritual message and the craving for Mother Goddess Kali. And that made him wild and careless. He forgot all about the so-called worldly wisdom and conventional sense of gain and loss. Such a person will be dubbed by friends and relations as someone insane and idiotic.

People would acknowledge his devotion to the Mother but then, often when he would forget worldly duties and get completely mad in the joy of his relation with the Mother, they would call him names.

But Ramprasad is careless of so-called fame, applause, slander or disgrace. He knows that all these conventional words and perceptions are meaningless. The ultimate bliss and joy,—the emancipation of the human being lies in his devotion to the great Goddess Mother Kali. Ramprasad vows that he is no longer to be misled by the words and advice of his near and dear ones and the people of the world. He has taken refuge of the gracious vermilion feet of the Mother and he has no worries at all.

[1]Ramprasad is talking to himself.

He tells his own being that this world must be quit very soon. A man's life in this world is a little span. We come here, born in to a family. We

Companions yours, they're all left and gone;
The sports of the world all done, do come,
Look, there's looming darkness all around,
Looking behind every now and then
For whom, my friend do you pine and ken;
To this world's fair for sports you came
With new companions an alien game,
Now come away, oh, leave this place
Or else they'll pelt you with stones missiles!
Your life's burden, put it down
Come straight, oh, on to another realm
There anew you will build your home
And play there another novel game.

❦ Song 209[1] ❦

Why not, oh Mother Tara, I so beseech,
Yield the right of worship's occult reach,—
Then I would test the six-some foes,
I'd see what they can do to me?
With devotion's cord I'd fasten the mind,

have relations,—parents, brothers and sisters. As we grow we collect friends familiar men and then enemies. We get mixed up in the storm and turmoil of the world and go on with the sports. We often despair, sometimes exult in our gains and success. But then, all these sports are like bubbles, transient ephemeral.

Ramprasad reminds himself that the people in this world whom you call your own,—they are only play mates and companions for a short while. Man's home is elsewhere. There it is eternal. All these people, relations and friends, of this world must be deserted as one quits this world. It is no point forgetting the real home of man for this brief interlude of sports, joys and sorrows, love and hate in this passing world. The poet calls and invites his own self to get freed from the meaningless sports of this world and get ready to proceed to man's real and eternal home. There too, there will be sports but then, that is all peace and bliss sublime.

[1]Sage poet Ramprasad often words his songs in symbols.

The poet had worked for a time in a zamindar's office. He got familiar with the language of the Court,—and the various drills and procedures that the Court officials have to discharge in a Court of law.

In this song the poet mixes his language of the Court with spiritual experiences. He prays to the Mother that She deign him the access to the world of spiritual penance. Once he gets to know the methods and

I'd bring him along to your presence divine,—
Pray, oh Mother, shut him in
Promptly to your prison feet!
The mace in hand of Kali's name
The six-some foes I'll put to shame,
The conscience then will take account,
The design of Yama to contend;
The bailiff of 'songs of praise'
Will collect virtues for royal cess,—
With this, oh, take this humble page
Across the world's vast open sea.

❦ Song 210[1] ❦

I wonder how oft you dwell in diverse moods,
Oh, Shyama, cascading stream of Elixir!
Mother, Your brow is the marvel's gossamer veil,
You wear the wreath of princes' crowns;

the tricks of *sadhana* (penance and worship), he would easily control the six foes that dwell within. These foes are the property of the man's mind and his ego-self. These are: *kama* (passion); *krodha* (rage and anger); *lobha* (greed); *moha* (confusion and error); *mada* (vain ego); and *matsaryya* (hate and jealousy). These enemies of the human soul, they take man astray, away from the path of spiritual peace. They play with the Nature's Qualities (*sattva, rajas* and *tamas*),—constantly harass man in this world's maze. But once Mother Kali gives the poet the message and the way of spiritual worship, these foes will be fettered in no time and this he will do with the power of his devotion. He will tie these six foes up and present them in the Court of the Mother. And then, he pleads with the Mother that She, as the Surpeme Judge, at once put them into prison, which is none other than under Her gracious feet.

The poet will take the baton of Kali's name and with that would punish those six enemies. Yama, the God of Death, his ambitions too would be curbed by his own conscience. In the Hindu mythology, the God of Death is supposed to take charge of man as he quits this world. But then, a devoted sage who has surrendered to Goddess Mother, he is beyond the reach of Yama himself.

Finally, the poet assures the queen Mother that his own devotion and chanting of Mother's name,—will work as the bailiff and he would collect all the dues of the Mother. and what are these dues? These are virtues and devotions. With all these promises of the poet all that Mother should do is to take him safely across this turbulent ocean of the world.

[1]This song is the cream of the sage poet's perception of the absolute

Often the earth rocks and trembles
As you dance insane in turbulence,
Crimson scimitar in hand, face in frown;
And then sometimes in rolling limbs
In wavy curves of luring dreams,
With winks and lustful look askance
The God of sensuous love you put to shame;—
Thou goddess sublime beyond all reach of thoughts
Beyond words,—of the *gunas home*, and Mother Thee;
Oft Thou dwells't in the *gunas* three pervading all three worlds,
Tara, dread, horrid,—consort of Eternal Time;
Do Thou assuage the cravings of the seeker Thine
In Thy varied legion forms divine;
Then again, Thou art installed in the lotus heart
As the Primal Brahman Absolute!

divinity of the Mother Goddess Shyama (Kali).

In the Hindu metaphysics the Absolute Brahman or Purushottama is revealed in two forms. One is the Absolute still Divinity. He is beyond all revelation, transcending the manifest world of Nature. The other form is *Prakriti* or Nature herself, ever moving, ever changing, as the mother and the repository of the phenomenal worlds.

Mother Kali is the Dual Infinity. She appears in diverse shapes and forms. In her revealed image she is veiled in hypnotic illusions. Her image is that of a warring damsel,—adorned with the necklace of human skulls, with the gait of the warrior woman. Her dark tresses and awesome appearance is frightening. She wears the scimitar with which She destroys all evils and dark forces of the universe.

But then, Her gracious form and appearance carries charms which surpass the God of sensuous love.

Mother Goddess is beyond all thoughts and beyond all revelation. She is the home of the three everlasting, ever changing *gunas* of Nature, *sattva*, *rajas* and *tamas*. She is the Queen of the Absolute Brahma.

Her various moods overwhelm the trinal worlds. She is the Queen of Lord Shiva, the all-consuming Eternal Time. Her own appearance is frightening. But, She is also the gracious Mother of the devoted sage.

The sage poet craves that the Mother, in all her diverse moods and forms, She vouchsafe the desires of the poet. She is the dweller in the thousand-petalled full blown lotus, which is the seat of the Eternal *Brahman* himself.

❦ Song 211[1] ❦

My Mother, She is the sea of joy supreme,
Why then must I so suffer pain!
Knowing, in her unfathomed ocean of bliss
There's deep cool tranquil peace;
The image of Shyama (how gracious sweet,
Hue as the dark nimbus cloud),
Fills the eyes as with a shroud,—
That is why tears flow streaming by,—
I cannot tell who so nigh, all these are
I know now, they all dissolve in Her;
These worldy ties, they are all in vain,—
Who must be here, let them remain;
This page proceeds where's Tara Mother,
Oh, heed this essence as you retire!

❦ Song 212[2] ❦

Oh mind, what is this error on which you err,
This error, won't you, even in error shirk?
Lest in error you should miss the prime

---

[1] The sage poet Ramprasad is a true *sannyasin*. *Sannyasa* does not consist in the renunciation of the world. *Sannyasin* can do his worldly work as the instrument of the supreme divinity without himself being involved in the outcome of work, and with no desire or attachment of his own.

The poet is such a sage who worships Mother Goddess Kali. He reached his emancipation without leaving the world as such,—his home and family. Mother, as the supreme divinity, is the epitome of joy and bliss. Why then it is that he, the sage poet should be in misery! The grace of the Mother is unparalleled. Her complexion is as the rain-laden cloud,which becharms the eye.

The poet has seen and shared this Supreme bliss, that is in the image of the Mother. That is why his own people in the world,—friends and relations, have become so meaningless and unimportant. He may dwell in this world among his people but then he is ever united with the ocean of elixir of the Mother's grace.

The poet knows that all attachments in this world, they are trivial and fragile. The poet is ready to proceed to the abode of the Mother,—careless of whoever else remains behind in this world of worries and sorrows.

[2] This song of the sage poet Ramprasad is a strange amalgam of modern science and ancient Hindu metaphysics.

Search for the primal root sublime!
Father, friends, wife and son,
Wherever they are your all kinsmen,—
Of whomsoever you are most fond,
Divine in him the Mother's form;
The primal thing is the element
From which all things and forms are born,—
When it is one with rack and ruins,
Just think of it, who is your own?
Shri Ramdulal,—he avers
You wander, errant, here and there,—
Brahmamoyee is everywhere
Bethink yourself,—that's the end!

Song 213[1]

Tell me, oh hibiscus flower, how,
By which way of worship, was it thou,
Dids't attain Shyama Mother's feet?
Severing shackles of sham mirage tree
You fell headlong on Mother's feet—prostrate;
Free from bond, you blossomed full

The poet, in his usual stance, talks to his own mind. He warns the mind that it should make no mistake. The world is wayward luring its denizens to errant ways. The error is the omission of the fundamental. The Absolute is the ultimate of all created worlds. Friends, relations, brothers, wife and children,—they are all there. One is most fond of his own kinsmen. But these are the mere shadow and elusion of the Supreme Mother, who is the creator of the fundamental element. As you love mother, all your mundane love is fulfilled.

Something same is what science tells us. Modern Physics has found out that the tiniest element behind all visible worlds is a mere vibration. Quark mechanics or particle physics have lost track of matter, in its ultimate tiniest unit into absolute and formless energy. Matter melts into energy to where it owes its origin.

Ramprasad tells his mind to bethink of the truth and the root of the material world. No one in the world really exists and no one is one's real own. They all wear away in time and dissolve in the infinity. Mother Goddess Supreme,—Brahmamoyee—She is everywhere; all forms only reveal this Supreme in her physical image. It is then that all confusions, joys and sorrows, love and worries,—melt away.

[1]This is a famous song of the sage poet. The song is the culmination of devotion and poetry.

Overwhelmed, drunk, with joy and bliss!
Oh mother, teach me thou that worship thine
Let this my life fulfil its dream!
Legion loud fragrant flowers bloom,
Charmers of the sylvan realm,—
How is it thou, hibiscus, by what charm,
Dids't attain, strange dark Mother's feet?
Like thine own, to crimson Mother's feet
When is't me'll be offerings floral
Roused in scarlet vermilion flame,
By touch of Mother's rosy russet feet,
Thou woulds't be set aroused aflame
When, like thine, will shine the ruby glow
Of my mind's pale petals in floral bloom?

☙ Song 214[1] ☙

Being mother thou, oh Mother Tara,
Thine own son you so torment;
Thou art, oh Mother, so stony-hearted,

    The poet takes the hibiscus flower as the symbol of utter submission and surrender. In the *puja* of Goddess Mother Kali, the hibiscus flower is the most favourite and indispensable offerings. That way the flower hibiscus some how has earned the everlasting right to the feet of the Mother Goddess. The poet too is doing his worship and penance for gaining the golden feet of the Mother. But then, he has yet not succeeded. The poet addresses the hibiscus flower to find out what holy worship and penance it must have done to have attained the Mother's feet almost as its heritage and birth-right. The *jaba* (hibiscus flower) grows on a plant. The plant is the bondage that ties the flower to its mundane roots. But then, suddenly the flower is picked and offered as worship to the Mother's feet. All its bonds are severed and it gains eternal bliss with no seeming efforts.
    The poet is jealous. There are millions of flowers in the forest. How is it that the blood-red *jaba* (hibiscus) alone got the supreme right of the Mother's feet.
    Is it that the crimson, vermilion colour of the flower is the symbol of its radiant devotion to the Mother? Would *jaba* tell the poet, what is the mystery? How the poet could also be rinsed in the radiant ray of the Mother's feet and would offer himself to Her in absolute surrender!
    [1]The sage poet Ramprasad here is his usual child self. Goddess Kali is his mother. Ramprasad is Her own son. The mother is supposed to give all grace and love to Her son.

It is sham Thy Name is 'Deliverer!'
Mother's name thou hast put to shame,
Daughter of mountains, thy heart is stoned;
Thou hast slain thy son with thine own hands
Is that, Oh Mother, mother's wont?
I can't call you 'Mother,'—no longer hence,
Father, He,—I'll call Him, now on;
He won't be home, shut in, all the time,
His ears are e'er watchful for his son;
Markandeya,—he attained life divine,
His own mission he accomplished;
Now Mother, show Mother's marvel's ways,
Me, too, won't be reborn, thou Immanent One
Surya, he now beseeches bowing low,
This time, now, proceeding Fathers' ways,
Taking Lord Shankara with Him alone,
Save me, thou deliverer of the worlds
From dread, dire, Death's peril!

    But then, Ramprasad is in agony. He searches for the Mother, weeping for her in his peril in this world,—but the Mother does not respond. She is hard-hearted. She belies her name,—She is known as 'the saviour and emancipator.' But her indifference to her son Ramprasad is most ungracious. She has thus put a stain on her own name. Of course she is made of stone; she is the daughter of the mountain Himalayas. She has lost all her love and kindness and withdrawn into her own stony heart. She has tied her son to the bonds of this world with her own hands. That is so because of the charms and sham attachment of this world which is all but her own creation.
    In sadness and regret Ramprasad declares that he would no longer call 'Mother.' Henceforth he would turn to Lord Shiva and call him the Father. Lord Shiva is not unkind like Her. Lord Shiva is known as the Supreme Divinity who is easily won with love. He is happy and contented with the smallest of offerings. His attention is always alive to his children. Many sages like Markandeya have got emancipation through worship of Lord Shiva. Mother, too should reveal her grace like the Supreme Father;— She is none else than Lord Shiva's own consort. The poet prays that She should ordain that he (poet) too is emancipated and freed from the chain of repeated births. Along with Lord Shiva She should rescue him from the clutches of Death.

Song 215[1]

I pray, oh mind, why not thou dost blossom
On Mother's feet, as the vermilion hibiscus bloom!
Never mind, she lacks fragrance,
Whatever she has, of her own,
It is, sure, not sham ornament!
I know, jasmine, hawthorn redolent, they bloom
They shower sweet aroma all around
Yet, the same is treasure not their own,
They give it away, barter it to aliens,—
Oh, listen thou, they do not own
Like thee, between Mother and son,
The give and take and then the lien.
That is why fear lurks in my mind's recess
Should'st thou err trapped in temptation's mesh,
Oh mind, then beware, Mother ne'er forget
She's Mother divine, suffused in grace;
Oh, on her twin lotus feet sanguine
All taints and sins lie prostrate supine;
That's why, oh mind, I urge,—do come

[1]This poem is a conversation between the poet and his own mind.

The poet is often unhappy with his mind for its errant ways. The mind is proverbially fickle. It plays to Nature's *gunas*. Nature's propensities,— *sattva, rajas* and *tamas*, are unstable and wayward. They toil up the human mind in the attachments in the world. Joys and sorrows and worries, greed, love and hate,—all these dualities are but sham creation of the Nature's *gunas* sporting with the human mind and the ego self.

The poet here tells the mind to be like the hibiscus flower. The simple hibiscus flower, in its dark crimson hue is an offering to the Goddess Mother. The hibiscus flower has no fragrance. But, the mind should know that what the flower has is not a mean possession.

The poet knows that flowers such as jasmine, hawthorn and others,— they are redolent with fragrance and perfume. But then, the possessions of such flowers are not their own; they are used for the pleasure and happiness of others. These flowers have no such kinship with Mother as hibiscus has.

The poet is afraid. He too may be entrapped. He may become involved in the joys and pleasures of the world forgetting the gracious Mother. Those golden vermilion feet,—they wipe away all stains, sins and darkness. Therefore, the poet urges the mind that like the hibiscus flower let it (his mind) surrender absolutely as the *jaba* (hibiscus) flower to the Mother's precious radiant feet.

Let's surrender to those two vermilion feet;
Oh mind, as the hibiscus flower at Mother's feet
Do, pray, unfurl thyself in full bloom!

🌺 Song 216[1] 🌺

Durga Mother, be'est thou with Durga's page
In the dire days of his peril,
Queen of marvels, with thy grace
Vouchsafe the refuge of thy feet;
When in the midst of dread peril!
Bethink the haven of thy feet sublime,
Then as the saviour Mother thou,—
"No fears, have no fears,"—do call out!
I proud, proclaim to all of them
Mother abides by my side
This proud stance should it perchance
Get hurt,—that is my aching pain!
Sambhuchandra, he, twice-born,
Oh Queen of Shiva, he divines
Lord Shiva's words shouldn't go in vain;
Should I gain my cherished end—
Oh Mother, then, I dare Death to come!

🌺 Song 217[2] 🌺

When the child's in tears crying, 'mother,'
Can the mother stay aloof!

[1] This is a prayer of the poet to the Goddess Mother Durga. The poet appeals to the Mother that he is the humble slave to her,—her own devoted child. Mother should be with him as saviour in his perils. When the poet is tormented by the turmoil of this world, the Mother Goddess should come to his rescue and remove his fear. The poet as a devoted son of the Mother, often acclaims to people that the great Goddess Mother is on his side, is saviour in all his perils. The poet is now afraid that he may not be let down; that his boastful talks to people should not prove worthless. Lord Shiva himself has said that one who surrenders to Goddess Mother, has no fear; he is emancipated. The Mother should take note of Lord Shiva's assurances and be with the poet in all his miseries and worries. And then the poet is not afraid of Death when he comes at the time of his (poet's) quitting the world.

[2] The mood of the poet is one of complaint.

She comes and takes him in her lap
And tells him sweetest words in caress love;
That is, oh, the way of mother's lore,
Oh Tara, Mother thou art than mother more;
I call weeping, so, without reply,
My heart quakes with qualms and frights,
Is it, Mother, then, I'm not thy son?
I weep and cry till I'm done and worn;
Unceasing thou dost make me weep,
It is not right indeed, becoming thee;
I've wept careworn prone on earth
I'm crying battered by the thorny world;
Then I would cry the cry of death,
And then must return to cry again;
I'm so weak, mother, I'm so worn
I've no strength, nor refuge none
I'd go on weeping till I reach thy home;
Lift me, oh mother, this wretched one,
To the sailing craft of thy feet sublime
This time, pray, let me not cry
Roaming alone in the wilderness!

When the child weeps, cries in sore agony, it is natural for the mother to respond. No mother can bear the grieving sorrow of the child. She takes the weeping child on her lap and treats him with warmth and caress.

But then, how is it Ramprasad does not get answer from his great Mother Goddess when he too weeps for her, he shivers with fright and worries; even then, Mother does not lift him to Her lap. And then, Mother Goddess she is even more loving and gracious than any earthly mother.

The poet complains that it is She, Mother Goddess, who has set him on to the miseries of the world. It is She that makes him weep. Is it right for the Mother?

The poet submits that he is weeping all the way. He sheds tears at the pains and worries of the world. When death comes, then too, he will have to weep. And even after death he has to return to this mortal world for another spell of weeping and agony. The child poet Ramprasad is weak and has no refuge. He promises that even as he weeps he will proceed and take refuge in the Mother's feet. The poet's last prayer is that Mother lift him up, her wretched son, and put him on the sailing craft of Her sublime feet. Let him not go on crying in the wilderness in unceasing grief and misery.

❦ Song 218[1] ❦

Kali ever immersed in joy expansive vast,
Thou art, oh Mother, enchanting nonpareil,
Thou swims't in joy within thyself
And dance of thine own sweet will,—
And then absent, amused, clap Thy hands;
Thou art primal immanent Queen,
The moon on the brow, thy form is the vast inane;
When the phenomenal worlds,—they weren't there,
How did'st thou get the wreath of skull from where?
Thou art alone, of all, the counsellor
Me, I'm but the tool that obeys thy will,
The way thou dost ordain decide
The same I be and abide,
The way thou wills't so do I speak,
Kamalakanta,—tormented, harassed
He speaks out in words so naive,—
This time, thou devourer of all
In hand the open scimitar at call
Thou gorgest the two some twin,—virtue and sin!

---

[1] This song is the sage poet Ramprasad's perception of the great Mother Kali in her image of infinity. Goddess Kali is ever cheerful, in blissful joy. The supreme Goddess is beyond all grief and worries, transient pleasures and happiness. Her image is one eternal blissful peace. The Mother is the supreme charmer. The varied sports of the phenomenal world are her creation. She dances in Her own joy and She claps in her own fulfilment.

The Mother is the primal being, eternal, denizen of the vast inane. She wears the moon on her brow. The poet puzzles, where the Mother had got the necklace of human skull, because She was there sans beginning, even before the phenomenal worlds were born. She is alone the ordainer. The poet is mere instrument, proceeding by the rules of shastras. He abides as she bids at her pleasure, he converses as she desires and prompts.

The poet is now restless. And he tells the Mother bluntly. The all-devouring woman now has taken up the falchion, and is now bent on swallowing up both virtue and vice.

In fact, the Mother, as the image of Supreme Brahman is beyond all dualities, virtue and vice,—none exists in the realm of the Absolute. Therefore, the Mother has devoured, destroyed all dualities including vice and virtue.

❦ Song 219[1] ❦

My Father, He is unvaried full of joy,
My Mother, Tara, she is the sea of bliss—
Me alone,—I'm ever cheerless,
It's me who is amiss;
I cannot call, loud,
The way the call is due
Tara, Mother, you didn't listen,
That perhaps is why,
Were it, She had hearkened
She would have come and picked me up,
She is gracious Mother mine,
She is not at all who'd let me down!

❦ Song 220[2] ❦

My heart's in aching pain
It dims but never ends
Tell me, Mother, what I do
What is there that I should do?
Having left my home, I dwell here as alien;
My mind ever mourns and joy
Has left, leaving me alone!
I suffer torment e'er since I was born
The sorrow, mother, ne'er ends even then;
I do not know why wherefore, to what ends
I weep so, Mother, in torment, aching pain?
At the winter's end arrives the spring

---

[1] In this small scrap of song, the sage poet Ramprasad owns his own sins and shortcomings.

The father of the poet is Lord Shiva. He is ever cheerful, full of joy and bliss. The Mother, Goddess Kali is the queen consort of the Father, Lord Shiva.

If that is so, Ramprasad laments why it is that he alone is one who is always in misery? He knows that it is but his own faults. He cannot call Mother the way She must be invoked. That must be the reason why Mother Tara cannot hear and respond to his calls. If it were that Mother could hear his ardent calls, she would have at once taken him into Her lap. She is all grace and love. It could not be otherwise.

[2] This song is a lament of the poet's consciousness of life on the world and the eternal life beyond.

The morning shines as the night is gone
As the life ends, the new life is born,—
The cycle roams as thou dost ordain;
Happiness and grief, they turn wheeling up and down
That's the way the world moves on,
Yet this wretched soul is fated else,
After grief, it's grief that e'er returns!

❦ Song 221[1] ❦

Who bethinks of Tara's feet,
Where those feet do dwell!
Those feet Lord Shiva has preserved
On His lotus heart as cool, tranquil;
Or else He would not be alive
When He *drank poison as burning flame;*

    The poet knows that his real home is elsewhere. Yet, he has abjured his own home and has made his abode in this earthly resort. That is why he is not happy. There is always some sense of loss and melancholy void.
    He is suffering worries and miseries ever since his birth in this earthly home. There is no end to his miseries. The poet does not know why this unceasing weeping and agony, and why all these sorrows?
    The laws of nature are otherwise. After the cold winter spring comes. After night there comes the dawn and the glorious sun. At the life's end another life is born. All these are as Mother has designed. Joy and sorrow they move in a wheel, like in a merry-go-round. This is the universal law.
    But then, it is the other way in the poet's destiny; in his case, even after misery only more misery comes.
    The song leaves the message that the poet has no pleasure in the so-called worldly joys and happiness. He is conscious of the eternal bliss. And so long as he does not attain that eternal realm of joys and bliss, his agony and sorrow does not desert him.
    [1]In this small song the poet is alluding to the cool bliss that dwells in the Goddess Mother Kali's feet.
    The poet ever bethinks of the mother's feet. But where are these feet? Lord Shiva, He has put those feet on his own chest. The reference is to the image of Mother Kali standing naked with Her two feet on the chest of Lord Shiva, who lies supine below the Mother's feet. And why has Lord Shiva placed the twin Mother's feet on His chest? This is because the Mother's feet are cool, balmy, giving solace and peace to where they lie. Lord Shiva had swallowed the hemlock and his chest must be burning! That is why he clings on to those balmy feet.

Such treasure lost (alas) your name 'poor lot,'
You whiled away your days
Forgetful, absent, lost!
(Oh you) call Mother
With mind single still,
Then let her do, vouchsafe
Whatever She may will!

♀ Song 222[1] ♀

Let's go, oh mind, we two together
We would go a-hunting for Shyama mother
Mother Kali, She is crafty, full of wiles,
Is it that, we could, oh, Her beguile?
Should we succeed, oh mind, in reaching out to there
Then my friend, the two of us, ever,
Will not come back to this home again
I have heard it somewhere said, oh mind,

This refers to another annals in the Hindu mythology. The ocean was being churned for elixir a taste of which would make one immortal. Contestants were the gods and the demons. From the churning, a jar of hemlock came up. It was bitter poison which must be fatal to whoever takes it. The demons claimed that the gods must swallow and the gods would not oblige. A battle was about to rage. Then Lord Shiva came forward and swallowed the whole can of poison Himself! But the poison was deadly and must not be consumed. Therefore, Shiva swallowed it but imprisoned it within his throat without letting it pass into the body. That is why Lord Shiva's throat is blue (Lord Shiva is known as Nilkantha i.e., the blue-necked God).

Shiva therefore must have been in pain, burning with the bitterness of the gall. To assuage his pain, Lord Shiva put the Mother's two cool, and balmy feet on His chest.

The poet Ramprasad knows all these, and he has lost those two feet, being bemused with the world's charms and illusion. But then he should chant and contemplate, call Mother with ardent devotion, then Mother will respond as She would deem fit.

[1]The human mind stands as the bridge between the mundane and the spiritual. The mind is the seat and citadel of all worldly desire and passions. Thoughts arise in the mind ceaselessly. And the mind is in constant play with Nature's sports. Nature is the dual Infinity of the Absolute Brahman. She is the repository of all thoughts and movements. She is the creator and the annihilator of the phenomenal world. And She does so, through her three *gunas* (*sattva*, *rajas* and *tamas*) which are sporting with the human mind in playful chameleon colours.

Should you to Shyama's feet hold on
No longer then you need to come
To this world again and then again!

❦ Song 223[1] ❦

Is it for nought that my soul so weeps!
The band of foes, e'er so vile,
The child thine own they shame and snipe
Even thou art, mother, present while;
In Thy own realm, in this sea of bliss

In this way, the mind and the ego-self of man are nature's playthings. Such a mind is ever disturbed, swaying in ripples with its attachment to the world. But then, the same mind, when calm and tranquil, is the path of spiritual progress. *Srimadbhagavad Geeta* never tires of repeating that work as such is not the cause of bondage. It is the desires behind the work, man's worries and aspirations, that cause the bondage and his eternal cyclic incarnations into this mortal world.

It follows that, to the spiritual seeker, the mind can be either a foe or the most valuable friend. That is why in song after song, the sage poet Ramprasad talks to his mind, threatens his mind and cajoles his mind,— to be with him, the human soul, in his spiritual endeavours. Ramprasad wants to attain the Goddess Mother Shyama (Kali) and dissolve in Her sublime feet. And he wants to take his mind along with these efforts of him.

In this song, the poet tells the mind, the two of them, the poet's being (the human soul) and his mind,—should proceed together to get hold of Mother Shyama. But the Mother is a sorcerer, full of tricks and sham elusions. But Ramprasad does not despair. If he and his own mind make a joint effort then they can catch hold of the Mother's feet. And the reward of such success is eternal emancipation. In that case, the mortal being is freed from the chain of his works. He is no longer reborn into this world.

The poet tempts his mind with this precious prize for its friendly cooperation.

[1] This song is rich in profound lyric and devotional charm.
The sage poet Ramprasad is appealing to the Mother. He tells Her that he wears melancholy in his soul all the time. And why must this happen in her own world of bliss and peace?

Ramprasad is the dear son of the Mother. Even then, the enemies of man, dwelling within himself, all the time torment him,—the being within the man. It is the Mother's world. The world is full of peace and joy. But then, the six-some foes *(kama, krodha, lobha, moha, mada* and *matsaryya),*—they seem to have no fear of the Mother. They constantly enter the citadel of the human being and harass him, as if there was no protection of the Mother. They treat Ramprasad casually like an orphan.

How do they, the foes gain access,
And threaten, grind me unremiss
As if I were an orphan child, oh, mother-less;
Oh Mother, yet I am, oh, thine own son
Thou, day and night my haven lone,
Thou art my sole refuge alone.
I know none other barring thee
Thou art my peace, sublimest bliss.
Then, why in this world I roam and rave,
Of the hordes of foes as bonded slave?
Why I suffer ceaseless pain, torment
In thy own presence, how's it ordained?

❦ Song 224[1] ❦

If the world is full of grief and pain
Then why is't thee, (Mother) I call in vain
Chasing pleasure night and day
I carry heaps of grief, dismay;
With who should I share this agony,
Who is but there save, Mother, thee?

Ramprasad pleads to the Mother that he is Her own son. He does not know anyone else. He has taken total refuge in her. The Mother is all his happiness and peace and his inmost soul. Then, why is it he still suffers confusion. He seems to act as a slave to the foes and move in the world in blind disorder.

The poet submits to the Mother that this is not fair. He should not be toyed with and harassed by the enemies of the human being in the very presence of the Mother.

[1]The sage poet Ramprasad was a spiritual seeker of the highest order. But unlike other great sages and holy persons like Kabir, Sri Ramakrishna and other emancipated souls, he was also a scholar. He was a natural poet and composer of songs. As he would bide his daily worldly life (Ramprasad was married and had a family), he would ceaselessly alloy himself with the Mother. He did penance and most arduous worship of the Mother, seated on the same *aasana* (seat) for days and nights.

But then, his songs would come to him naturally, as he would be walking the paths of the village or taking his bath in the river Ganges that flows by Halishahar (North 24-Parganas, West Bengal) where Ramprasad had his home.

That is why his songs have great literary value as well. And the unique quality of his composition is the rhythm and tune in which words and symbols, subtle messages of the spiritual world blend as in a rainbow, with simple mundane experiences.

(I hear it said) should the child so weep
Can Mother, ever, bear with it?
This time, Mother, having come to thy realm
Not a day in joy I dwell or roam;
My counted days in a flash have fled,
Even at the end would'st thou play the trick?
(Oh, Mother), I've heard thy name,—'Deliverer
Of grief' that's why so long, Mother Tara,
I call thee, (is't a living corpse I am),
I'm dark what's there, yet, in the life to come!

Song 225[1]

Is it, oh Mother, thou wouldst send thy son—
Thy very own to an alien home unknown?
Oh, they all heap scorns, throw missiles and stones
As they spot the sack of the beggar's mean
Lowly I have bowed my head;—
The One behind whom I proceed and tend

In this song, Ramprasad tells Mother, if this world is full of miseries then why is it that he goes on day and night in the pursuit of pleasures. In chasing happiness the poet is never happy and suffers pain and worries ceaselessly. His only aspiration is his Mother's feet, the final emancipation. But then, there is no one with whom the poet can share his sadness and cravings. One hears that when the child weeps and suffers pain, the Mother cannot remain indifferent. How does Mother then forget Her son Ramprasad?

The world is the very own creation of the Mother. Where the Mother dwells, there must be bliss. But then, while Ramprasad has come into this world, there has never been one day when he was happy and in peace. His numbered days of life are fast waning. Is it that the Mother should still deceive Her son? Another name of the Mother is 'the supreme deliverer.' Then how is it that even while Ramprasad constantly invokes Her and chants Her name, no salvation comes to him?

The poet wonders if he is a walking corpse. What will then happen to him in the next world!

[1]This song is an expression of sage poet's loyalty and love to his own Mother.

This world is Mother's own. Ramprasad is Her son and he dwells in the Mother's world. But then another image of the Mother is the sham elusion that pervades the world and takes the human being into wrong paths. Ramprasad tells Mother, that is it that he should go to other one, who tempts him all the time as the deceitful step-mother.

If that One should spurn perchance
Turn me away, oh, with no pittance;—
Yet, what do I do here where I dwell
Leaving alone my Mother's grace?
'Of power I've none, not a touch or trace',—
That's for sure, thy words, a lie,
Four hundred million sons, they're still alive,—
Our puissance own our own devotion
Upon thy feet we will unfurl;
Then I'll crave with the begging-bowl
Whate'er is there in the house I dwell,
And spread out the fringe of my overall
Then as thine eternal seat.
Our christened name and our soul
There, and there it is—they dwell,
And there is where we pour out heart.

♀ Song 226[1] ♀

I call thee, Shyama, often and then again
Where art thou, Mother, quick as the chameleon;
Deliver me, Mother Kali saviour Thou
Oh, where art Thou, deigner of all bliss!
To this mortal realm you sent me down

    This Image of Nature promises pleasures and happiness and seeks to wean him away into Her fold. Ramprasad is unwilling to go there with a begging bowl. He does not mind if he is to live frugally and suffer penury. He will never agree to go to an alien home,—however bright or prosperous that may seem. Then, Prasad knows that Mother is all powerful. If She would plead that She has not much to offer to Her son that indeed is a lie. Mother has a billion sons. all Her children will surrender all their powers and devotions to the Mother's feet. Her children would be happy to collect whatever little grains that may be there in the Mother's home. They will collect it and offer it all to the Mother's lap. Indeed, that is where the poet's heart and soul and all his self-respect eternally lie.
    [1]This is a strip of a song.
    The sage poet is in peril. He suffers miseries and agony and weeps in terrible fear. He calls out for the Mother Shyama. Where is Mother, he wonders. Her dear son is in agony. She is all gracious and the queen of bliss. The poet calls loud by Her name and pleads that she come and deliver Her own child. The poet has been bruised and hurt by the worries and enmity of the world. Where has his Mother gone? Why does She not cast a look behind and lift Her son from his miseries?

Then never looked back, alas, again;
Who would but know, it'd happen so,
The world so full of pain, chagrin!

☙ Song 227[1] ☙

You must save me, oh, thou saviour mine
If thou dost not deliver, Mother,
What will happen to this wretched mean?
The one who knows worship, hymns,
He sails safe across of his own,
But the one who's poor in worship, chant
How, oh tell me, is he then destined?

☙ Song 228[2] ☙

That naked girl, her laurels care
Is swelled by that Fellow with plaited hair;

[1]This scrap of a song is the pleading of the sage poet Ramprasad to his dear Mother Goddess Kali. In the Hindu spiritual lore, devotion has been given the highest of place. The Hindu scriptures, the Vedas, have gone into great detail about the rituals and methods of worship. But then, the *Srimadbhagavad Geeta* has dwelt on the several ways of worship. Renunciation of the world and meditation by the sage in deep lone solitude is one such path. It is the Jnanayoga—the path of enlightenment. Then, there is the path of *karma*—of unattached work. Here the *yogin* goes on doing his worldly works but without desire, attachment or expectation of the reward of work. This is the way that the spiritual householder should abide in the world.

But most profound of all is the Bhaktiyoga—the path of devotion. The sage and the seeker here holds on to his image of divinity, almost in a personal way. Ramprasad is devoted to Mother Kali through the path of devotion. She is the Mother and he is Her child. He is all in agony for getting back to the Mother for eternal bliss. He does not know the various ways and rituals of worship. He has earned no virtues by observing rules of scriptures. One may think therefore that he has not earned his right to deliverance. But then, the sage poet pleads with the Mother that She must deliver him as her devoted child. Her name is 'Mother Deliverer.' He pleads to the Mother that a person like Ramprasad who has only unalloyed devotion as his weapon has no other means to deliverance unless Mother Goddess should shower Her grace and take him back to Her lap.

[2]The song is a singular example of the use of words with complex nuance of spiritual truth and poetic pun and rhythm.

How else, is it, her, one must so cajole
Calling 'Mother,' oh 'Mother' in piteous rolls?
Lord Rama, he is guru of the Creature world
That Fellow with matted locks,—He is his Lord;
He never knew Who, whence, He was
And fell supine below the woman's feet;
The One with matted hair, He is stark insane,
The burning ground's His lasting haunt;
But then how dauntless daring is that woman,—
She put her feet on the chest of the matted One!

☥ Song 229[1] ☥

Shyama, oh, who is that, below thy feet, supine!
Oh, how strange today, your stance that I divine!
Round thy neck rolls the wreath of human skulls,
Whose daughter She, the dancing girl?

Lord Shiva has plaited hairs. He is a half-clad *yogin*. He is the Supreme Lord. Lord Sri Ramachandra,—he is another incarnation of Divinity. Even he, Sri Ramachandra was worshipper of Lord Shiva. But then, that great Lord Shiva, he has raised the ego and status of Mother Goddess. How has he done it? In the Hindu annals and mythology Goddess Mother Kali is portrayed as the image of a dark charming woman standing naked on the chest of Lord Shiva, lying supine at her feet.

The poet thus reflects that, that is why the Mother Kali is so difficult to attain! And that perhaps is because she has grown in her swollen vanity. She has the cheek that She stands on the great Lord Shiva himself,—who is the Supreme Lord of the universe. And that is why when the sage poet cries ceaselessly for the Mother, calls Her all the time, She is dumb and has no time to respond.

The song is an example of the poet's intimacy with the Mother and the great liberties that he can take with Her.

[1]The image of Mother Kali in the Hindu mythology is an awful portrait. She stands naked with Her flowing locks all over Her bare body. And then, amazingly the great God Shiva lies supine at Her feet.

The Mother has complexion like the dark rain-laden cloud. She wears falchion in Her hand as if in war with the forces of evils, of the demonic world. Around Her neck is a necklace of human heads cut from the neck and with this frightening awful stance the Mother dances. Who knows who is the maiden, this great Goddess? And who knows Her sports in this trinal world?

But Ramprasad knows that She is the Mother of the universe, She is the sole refuge and the deliverer, that is why the poet chants Her name and calls Her day and night for a place in Her sublime twin feet.

Who knows thy sports, oh Mother, in this trinal worlds
Thou art mother of the moving worlds
Of thee they all are born—Thou art deliverer
Nonpareil of all fears, ills, perils.
That is why I call Thee, Mother,
For a place on Thy feet, Oh Saviour!

❦ Song 230[1] ❦

The worlds dwell in Thee;—in thy marvel
Bemused all men in the trinal worlds;
The sun, the moon, the stellar worlds
To Thy oracles, they are all slaves,
They obey, ever, what Thou dost ordain;
With sons and wife, the worldly toys
With them, Mother, thou hast charmed the ways,—
Confounding all,—that's why the unconcern
For the immortal truth and the real thing!
Of the realm of thoughts Thou art the Queen,
What Thou dost will all that is done
Who is it who knows, Mother, Thee,
Thy marvels, splendours fathom?

[1] This song is an expression of the ultimate consciousness of the spiritual seeker.

There is the Supreme Being as the primal source and seed of the universe. He is still and immobile. He is sans beginning, uneroding, termless and infinite.

The Mother Goddess Kali is the dual infinity. She reveals Herself as the cosmic phenomenal world. Through Her three qualities or *gunas*,—*sattva, raja,* and *tamas*—She plays sports with all creatures of the world. Man's mind and his ego-self are held in toils by the illusions and forces of Mother Nature.

She pervades the world. It is Her veil and chimera that holds the whole world in thrall, in confusion and confoundment.

All things of the world, wife and children are playthings. The Mother has bewitched Her children with these toys. That is why they forget the ultimate truth. Mother commands the realm of thoughts. Man has no 'will' and desire of his own. These are all born of the Mother. That is why She is beyond knowing. She leads man to ways which are destined by Her.

Ramprasad is an enlightened sage. He is conscious of the ultimate truth. That is why he seeks the feet of the Mother for his emancipation from the labyrinth and confusions of the world.

Whichever way Thou dost lead
I merely follow, Mother, without care or heed;—
The whole of the world purblind recoils
Bemused in thy confoundment's toils.

☙ Song 231[1] ☙

I have got it, Mother, thy wily wish;
By your crafty marvel, splendour's trick
You'd put me into the sea of grief
So I should forget Durga's name
By your feint cunning and counterfeit;
However you put me so to grief and pain
Durga's name I won't forget, all the same,—
Is it that Mother doesn't scold the child
Yet,—'oh Mother, that is how it cries wild.
I do not want wealth and fortunes,
Fortune, that is dire peril
My heart yearns for the safe haven
Of thy feet, so it there may fearless dwell!

☙ Song 232[2] ☙

This life, for ever it will not last,—
Then why is it, you confounded fool
With worries, cares you're so overcast!
No one knows when Death will strike

[1] Sage poet Ramprasad is almost in a spirit of challenge to the Mother. He tells Mother that he is not afraid of the worries and sorrows, the utter agony of this world. He knows that these are all for sending Her child awry from the path of seeking Her sublime feet. But Ramprasad will not be led astray. Whatever sufferings Mother may destine he will take Her name. The Mother may scold the child and punish him but the child still weeps for her.

The poet vows that the worldly treasures—riches and wealth, these are causes of peril. His whole being seeks the refuge of the Mother's feet which alone can free him of all fears of this world.

[2] Hindu spiritualism accepts the eternity of the human soul.
The cosmic system is the product of a vast system of energy, of which the beginning is the Absolute. The concept of Brahman or the Absolute Supreme is that He is unborn, uneroding infinity. But then, this Being, itself calm and still is yet the source of universal energy, and can transform

He has no time that is odd, betimes,
To sever confoundment's wily toils
Wait no longer, lose no time!
Listen, thou, oh mind, bewildered lost,
For so long you have your strength
Contemplate Kali's feet sublime!

⚘ Song 233[1] ⚘

Oh Mother,
What kind of mother, thou, no one knows!
Oh Mother, I cry 'mother,'—howsomuch
And howsolong,—yet, it does not touch,
Oh Mother, does not hurt your inner cord,—
This time now I'll call Father's name.
Let me see if you aren't hurt and put to shame,—
Should my soul so call the tune!
Stone-hearted carved in stone

itself into kinetic or mobile energy. The Absolute Brahman is formless and transcendent. But the moment it is muted into mobile energy it assumes form, shape and revelation. This Supreme Energy in its mobile form is Mother Goddess Kali,—the Queen and progenitor of the phenomenal world. Since Mother Goddess Kali is the muted form of the Absolute Brahman, She too is as eternal as Brahman Himself. She is the Dual infinity.

And this Nature or Mother Goddess Kali, as the revealed infinity is pervasive and immanent. She dwells everywhere and in every creature. The Supreme energy is a vast invisible infinite ocean, but it breaks itself into its tiniest form and dwells in every creature of the phenomenal world—living or inert. This tiny spark of the Supreme energy is the human soul. Since any part of infinity, however tiny, is also infinity, the human soul is eternal; it never dies. What dies is the physical elements that make up the body of the human being which houses his soul.

Ramprasad is conscious of this existence of marvel. He knows that the coarse and physical body will die away. Why is it then that one is worried so much about his mundane life,—which vanishes with the death of the body. Just as the body is ephemeral so are the worries and anxieties of the world, sham and meaningless. The human soul, the tiny spark of Supreme energy, melts and dissolves into the infinity. Goddess Mother Kali is the image of this infinity. Therefore the human being should meditate the Mother ceaselessly, forgetting his worries of the world and that is the way to spiritual salvation.

[1]This song is in the usual mood of the poet. The sage poet Ramprasad is an ardent devotee of Mother Goddess Kali. All the time he is seeking

Mountain's daughter maiden queen
She never once looks even askance
She dances wild with ugly sprites.

♀ Song 234[1] ♀

Thou Mountain Lord,—Ganesh mine,
He is deigner of weal and bliss,
If one bethinks and takes his name
Then his will is accomplished;
When he arrives, Lord Shiva's spouse,
The gracious queen she comes home along.
Down beneath the *bilva* tree
His invocation I would chant,
To bless Ganesha, her own son
Mother Gouri would descend.
As mother Chandi will come home
We would all listen to Chandi hymns,—
With their *holy staff* countless saints
Yogins, matted-haired sannyasins
They would all in legion come.

his Mother, chanting Her name and dwelling on Her sublime feet. But even then, Mother does not seem to respond.

The devoted sage is sad and angry with the Mother. Like the beloved child, he warns the Mother that if She should remain dumb and quiet, then he would no longer call Her and chant Mother's name. He would now seek his Father. His Father is Lord Shiva, who is the royal consort of Goddess Mother Kali. In Hindu spiritual thought Lord Shiva is the Supreme Brahman and Queen Mother Goddess Kali is His phenomenal manifestation.

The poet reminds the Mother that She is cruel and hard-hearted. She is like the stubborn stone and this is no wonder. For, She is the daughter of the Himalayas (in Hindu legend),—the mountain of stones. And the Mother has a very awful way of life. She does not bother about her child. She only roams the desolate burning ghats with all kinds of companions who are ugly sprites, dancing with them.

[1]This little song is in the words of queen Menaka, the consort of the great Himalayas. Goddess Durga is the daughter of mother Menaka and father, the Himalayas. Goddess Durga is married to Lord Shiva. Ganesh is Her elder son along with Kartikeya, the younger brother and the two sisters, Laxmi and Saraswati.

In the Hindu way of worship, Ganesh is the Lord of success and fulfilment. Ganesh is worshipped in the home of every one who seeks success, specially the world of business and profession.

❦ Song 235[1] ❦

Oh Mountain Lord, my Gouri, she did come,—
She was there to wake me up in dream,
Then she, the image of conscious light,
Where was it she vanished out of sight?
So said alas, the Mountain Queen.
What do I do, oh Mountain King,
I'm so staid, oh, immobile;—
Frozen, motionless inert.
Like her, agile evanescent
Life too is fickle, so fleet,—
The gem of my life was mine and lost;
Why is it this her chameleon lair
Why is it then she did appear;
She the marvel's queen supreme
For mother she has no love, concern,—
But then, I bethink, oh Mountain King,
What sin is it of the Saviour queen,
It's her father's way, she's built of stone.

 Menaka tells her husband, the Himalayas that the little grandson Ganesh is the bringer of weal. And when Ganesh comes then Mother Uma (Goddess Durga) follows. That is why Menaka welcomes the arrival of Ganesh and with him Her own daughter Gouri (another name for Goddess Durga). Another image of Gouri or Durga is Goddess Chandi. Chandi is the warrior form of Durga. Goddess Durga is the symbol of prowess and Supreme might. The forces of evil—the demonic powers of the universe—are vanquished in the war in which Goddess Durga in the image of Goddess Chandi, is the slayer and extirpator. And then, there is a shastra or Book of Hymns by the name of *Sree Sree Chandi*. As Goddess Durga or Chandi should come home mother Menaka should love to listen to the hymns in the book of *Chandi*. And when that holy recitation takes place, countless yogins, sannyasins and sages with plaited hairs and holy staff, they too would come and grace the home with their sublime presence.

 [1] Mother Menaka has a dual consciousness. She is the mother of Goddess Durga, who is the conscious Queen Mother, the sublime infinite Goddess of the created universe. Menaka knows that her daughter is not only her own child but the Mother of all creatures of the phenomenal world.

 Goddess Mother Durga is the enlightenment in the human soul. Menaka has dreamt of her in her inner consciousness. But then,—she (Goddess Durga) vanished in a while. Menaka laments, that she saw her child within herself but then she had disappeared as the mobile energy of the universe.

Song 236[1]

Aloft oh lift your limbs oh Mountain King
Take your girl warm upon your lap,
Oh Chandi you discourse from the holy Chandi lores.
Look, Chandi, she is home here
She is, remember, yours.
Do thou holy worship chant
The gracious girl, her welcome home
All ills and omens will flee
As you take her in your bosom warm
Tara, her, as I adored
Tara, she, is my own
Tara, that gracious girl
Most sublime in all three realms
The twin eyes of mine,—they forswear
All grief, at her balmy sight becalmed.

Song 237[2]

The dark dense cloud, in the inner firmament,—
  it loomed
The peacock-mind, it danced and roamed
  in wild joy serene,

Menaka knows that everything in this world is so fickle and transient. But then, Durga, the daughter child of Menaka, should have some affection for the mother. She is hard-hearted towards her mother. But as Menaka addresses her royal consort, the Himalayas, she tells Him that it is not her fault. The Himalayas, he himself is built up in stones. Uma or Goddess Durga is the daughter of this Himalayas. It is natural that She should also be hard-hearted as Her stony father.

[1]This song is also a plea of mother Menaka to her Lord the Great Himalayas. The Himalayas are immobile, not easily moved or discomposed. His daughter, Chandi (Goddess Durga) has come home. Menaka urges her Lord that he should wake up and receive his daughter with all grace, love and worshipful chanting, Goddess Durga or Chandi is the queen of bliss. She is the deliverer from all miseries and bondage. Through Her ardent penance and worship Menaka has got Chandi or Durga as their own daughter. But then she is the Goddess Queen of the Universe. That is why the father Himalayas and the whole house should break into joys and hymns when their own daughter, the universal Goddess is back home.

[2]This song is a poetic portrait of the dark cloud in the sky and the joy of the peacock at the sight of the blue clouds.

The sound 'Mother' roared rumbled resounding
   in all three realms
In that love's lightning flash
   of lambent smile adorned,
Ceaseless cascading tears from the eyes,
   termless rolled
In that the yearning arid soul's fears and thirst
   were quenched
Beyond this life and the life beyond;
   and then legion lives beyond
Prasad divines, no longer more there'll be life
   in the womb again!

❦ Song 238[1] ❦

Kali, how long like this time will lapse,
That one He, He never cares
If it's morning, eve or time to spare
Or hour so well or inauspicious
He moves along with eternal Time
In his voyage along the stream of Time
In his hand the dour deathly Mace,

   Mother Shyama (Goddess Kali) is conceived in the image of a dark woman with complexion of the nimbus cloud. The mind of the poet is like the dancing peacock.
   The peacock dances at the tune of thunder. The lightning flashes and the peacock joins it in equal laughter. The poet's mind responds likewise to the Mother's presence. There is loud chanting of Mother's name, which is like the thunder of the rain cloud. Mother's beaming face is like the charm and glow of the lightning flashes.
   Then, rains come from the pregnant clouds. So do tears flow from the eyes of the poet. The soul of the sage poet is like the *chataka* bird. The bird is known for its nature that it assuages its thirst only from fresh falling rains. The poet's soul is like the *chataka* bird. As tears flow from his eyes the soul drinks off it and quenches its thirst.
   The poet Ramprasad avows that one who has tasted of the Mother' bliss, he is freed from the cycle of births.
   [1]The sage poet appeals to the Mother Goddess Kali. He is restless and impatient. Man has a short life span. The time is wasted pursuing trivial things of the world. When the poet was in the Mother's womb, he had hopes that he would spend the life in worship and penance. But as he was born to this world the wicked foes within took charge and he was overwhelmed by ignorance and attachments.

For so long I was in mother's womb
I had hopes, in the world as I was born
In worship chant I would spend my time,
But then again, the foes they all aligned.
In ignorance, arid the childhood went.
The youth went by I whiled my time
With charming maidens in frolics, fun
As age overtook my time was gone
In disease and woes of age infirm.

❦ Song 239[1] ❦

What is the treasure I can offer Thee;
As I closed my eyes the vision came
The trinal worlds, they're all thy realm;
What is that jewelled robe I give,
The treasure of treasures all,
That one he, he is thy slave;
Thou dwell'st in golden Kasi realm,
Of rolling bounty thou art the queen;
Who says, Lord Hara, he's beggar mean
In whose home is treasurer supreme,
Kuvera, the Lord of fortunes, means;

> His childhood was spent in plays and sports. Youth was wasted in dallying and sporting with women. And now that age has taken over disease and pain takes away his time.
> The poet craves to the Mother that She must deliver him from these miseries and hostile forces of the world.
> [1]In Hindu worshipful rituals it is usual to pay offerings to the divine god. Some offer *yajnas* and sacrifices. Fruits, flowers and all kinds of wealth are offered in the *puja*.
> But then, the sage poet Ramprasad knows better. As he closes his eyes he knows that the Mother is the queen of the universe. All wealth and possessions of the earth are her domain. What then is it that the poet can offer to the Mother in his worship?
> It is a fiction that Lord Shiva, consort of Mother Kali, is a beggar Goddess Kali is the queen of bounty and grace. She dwells in Kasi (Banares or Varanasi). Kasi is also the place of Lord Shiva, there the God of Wealth, Kubera is the treasurer of the queen Mother. Even Lord Vishnu and Brahma are anxious to secure Her sublime feet. With this knowledge, the poet knows that the queen Mother and Lord Shiva can only be pleased with devotion; there is no other wealth or treasure or offerings which will do the trick.

Prasad divines,—at whose portals
Brahma, Vishnu,—beggars all
Of her twin queenly feet sublime!

❦ Song 240[1] ❦

That woman as the dark sombre night,—
in battlefield,—who's She
Stark naked, mass of floating hairs
scimitar in the left hand unsheathed
Routing demons loud full of joy;
Beneath her feet, the mother earth
Fearful trembles as one lost,
Beholding that Lord Pashupati
Fallen supine at her warring feet;
Ramprasad, so mean and poor,—he avers,
Then who is there, whom else to fear?
Effortless, Yama, he is trounced
In life and death and battlefront.

❦ Song 241[2] ❦

What is thy 'name,' Mother by which thee I call!
Sometimes, Lord Shankara, on his left thou art,

[1] This song is a vision of the poet of the Mother in Her warring image.
  The Mother is a woman with complexion as a dark night. She is now dancing in war with the demons. She is naked and unrobed with flowing tresses all around Her person.
  The earthquakes under Her feet. It is shivering in fear and consternation. Watching these Lord Shiva is afraid about the safety of the creation. That is why he has fallen at Her feet, seeking to restore Her peace and grace.
  The sage poet therefore has no reason to fear. If that woman is his own Mother, he is safe from all perils.
[2] This song is a marvel of the sage's awareness of the immanence of the Mother.
  Mother is the Supreme Divinity, She is the mobile kinetic dual form of the Supreme Brahman. It is She who takes various images. Her sports are infinite. The poet is confused as to how, in what image of Her, he should worship Her?
  Often Goddess Mother Kali is on the left of Lord Shiva. She is the queen of Lord Shankara (Shiva). The queen consort takes Her place on the left of the Lord. That is the Hindu way of imaging the husband and the wife. But then, She is sometimes standing on the chest of Shankara who lies supine at Her feet.

Often thou dwell'st, aloft upon his heart;
At times thy image in the vastest worlds
Then oft thou art the woman bare unrobed,
Sometimes Shyama's beloved queen
And then at Radha's feet, how strange!
Then oft thou art Mother of all three worlds
And then thy home is the five-some seeds,—
On the four-petalled leaf of *bael*, again
Thou'rt the *coiled Energy* supreme!
Prasad avows,—'I won't listen,' care,
The name, 'Mother,' it's beyond compare;
That is why I call thee Mother, by thy 'Mother' name
So, thy twin saviour feet I may attain!

♥ Song 242[1] ♥

How could you my little mother

Then, the Mother appears as the whole of the phenomenal nature. That is the universal manifest image of Goddess Kali.

But then, again she is the enchanting woman, unrobed and naked in the open space, waging war with the forces of evils. Mother is also the gracious queen so beloved of Lord Krishna (Shyama).

But then, She also took the image as Lord Krishna, assuaging the annoyance of Radha by holding Her feet. This is a token from the Hindu annals of the love of Lord Krishna and Radha.

The annals have still another tale. The divinity as Lord Krishna was worshipped by Radha. Radha's husband Ayan Ghosh was a staunch follower of Goddess Mother Kali. He thoroughly disapproved of his wife Radha worshipping Lord Krishna. Once it happened that Ayan Ghosh, on tips from his sisters, wanted to catch Radha red-handed, worshipping Lord Krishna. As Radha saw him coming from his cottage in the woods, she pleaded to Lord Krishna to assume the image of Mother Kali. When Ayan Ghosh reached the place, he found Goddess Kali in Her dour image, standing before Radha, who was worshipping Her. Divinity is One. The Supreme Brahman is the eternal energy. It is often still and unrevealed. But then, in its manifestation, it assumes different forms and images who are worshipped as personal gods by devotees according to his/her desire.

Then, the poet perceives that the Mother dwells in all the elements of the world; and then again as the puissant energy in Her seat in the spinal cord of man.

But even then, Prasad is not reconciled. He would rather stick to her Mother's image. He would call Her Mother, chant her name as Mother, and worship Her as such, whatever others may say or do.

[1]The little daughter Uma, she has returned to her father's place, in

Forget thy mother sad and poor!
Thou daughter of the stony mountain
Is it thou hast the heart of stone?
The full year was past and gone
I missed you so,—forlorn alone
How I wept, mother, how I tell in agony?
There was no pleasure in rest and sleep.
Face all the time sad melancholy
How I suffered, long days and weary nights!
As I saw the moon in the firmament
I bethought your face as the lambent moon;
Awake, sleepless throughout the night
I would weep, alas, how I moaned,—
I would sometimes behold in dream,
My little girl, oh mother Uma,—slim
Dark pale shadow veiled the face
Weak emaciated with hunger's lace,—
Then I would wake up with a start,
Run out of home upon the street
Would tell someone out of turn,—
Pray, bring her, my Uma,—to me return!

❦ Song 243[1] ❦

Come, mother, thou Lord Bhola's spouse
On to my lap,—oh, light of my eyes!

the abode of the Himalayas. Uma (goddess Durga) is the queen consort of Lord Shiva. Once each year, for four days, she returns to her parents from her husband's place in Kailasa, where (according to Hindu Mythology) dwells Lord Shiva.

Uma's mother is Menaka, the queen of the Himalayas. She cannot forget that Uma's sojourn with her mother is so shortlived. She has spent the whole year pining for her little daughter. The song is a rare poetic image of the mother's melancholy for her married daughter specially in the home in Bengal. And then the daughter (of mother Menaka) is no other than the great Goddess Uma, the Queen Mother of all three worlds —the supreme Goddess Durga of the Hindu pantheon!

[1]This is a typical song of the sage poet Ramprasad. Queen Goddess Durga,—she is the consort of the supreme Absolute, in the image of Lord Shiva. But she is also the beloved little daughter of mother Menaka, the queen of the great Himalayas. In the Hindu mythology, Parvati, or Uma, the maiden name of Goddess Durga is the daughter of the father, the Himalayas and mother, Menaka. Menaka's love for her little daughter,

The pupil of my eye, I have lost,—
Those that seek mother Tara, is't that
They are, like me, forlorn and lost?
I'll beseech, mother, Divinity
I'll never again your mother be,
This time born as daughter thine
I'll show how mother's love,—it pines!

❦ Song 244[1] ❦

She came just only yesterday
(Yet) my Uma wants to leave today;
What I do, alas, you tell me all,
With what heart as fond mother,—
Uma, daughter, my only treasure,
Her, do I so bid farewell?
I had felt so happy, so full of joy,
At her words my heart split in dismay!
I so beseech, ye, all of you,
You plead and have a word with her,
So she bethink and change her mind,—
My Uma, more than life She's dear!
Let it not be long six months or nine
Yet, shouldn't she stay for ten days as mine?
Mother, alas, if that ten be the tenth day, adieu,
What's there then in my destiny?
Uma, she now is mother of beloved child

Uma, is utterly human,—echoing the passionate love of the mother in a Hindu home of Bengal. It transcends the divine image of the great Goddess Durga,—who indeed is no other than Uma,—who is the queen consort of Lord Shiva,—and the Mother Goddess of the phenomenal worlds.

Uma is away to her husband's place, most of the year. The lonely mother, Menaka, suffers utter agony in her little daughter's absence. She knows, Uma is adored by the whole world as the supreme Divine Mother. She divines whoever loves Uma (Mother Durga) must be suffering as she herself; for pining agony goes with the supreme devotion of the devotee for his (or her) divine Queen Goddess! Menaka promises she won't be mother again to her divine daughter. She would much rather be born as the daughter of the divine queen; then alone, Uma (the Queen Goddess) would know the pain and sorrow of the mother who so loves and misses her daughter.

[1]Uma has just come to her mother, Menaka's place from her husband's home in Kailasa. But her sojourn is short. She must leave almost

She hasn't fathomed mother's woe so wild;
The son-in-law, he is an alien's son,
What cares has he if my heart should mourn!

❊ Song 245[1] ❊

As tomorrow, Bhola comes,
I'll tell him, Uma, she's not at home,
How do I, my image of gold
Send her away to an alien home!
Let them say what they will
I won't care that he is son-in-law,
Should he leave abrupt, let him go
I will see what happens when time comes.
Is't that for someone's father's money
My daughter I've bartered her away!
If Uma should leave then but with whom
Would I, weeping, bide my time?
The little girl, she clasps my scarf
Lest she should wake up starting from sleep;
Does she know the husband's place, what's it like?
There's so much left for her to learn in life!

immediately the very next day. In Hindu symbolism, Uma is Goddess Durga, who is Goddess Mother of the whole of the world of creatures. Everyone invokes her, in every home people do her worship. Her domain is large and universal. She, the great goddess, indeed has no respite. Her visit to her parents' home must be a short sojourn!

But then, mother Menaka is so sad and melancholy. To the mother, the great goddess Uma is still her beloved little daughter! She cannot bear her separation! Uma's Lord husband is the supreme Lord Shiva. Uma herself is now mother. She has her own children. Even then, is it that she does not know the mother's pain and sorrow for her child!

The song is a portrait of the homely pangs and sorrows of the mother of the human world; so common with a loving mother in a home in Bengal.

[1]Uma, the little daughter of mother Menaka, the queen of the Himalayas, has come to her mother. Uma is grown up. She is married to the great Lord Shiva. Indeed, She herself is Goddess Durga, the supreme immanent Queen Goddess of all creations. Lord Shiva leads the life of a mendicant. His another name is Bhola,—which, in Bengali, means 'the forgetful, absent-minded one.'

Menaka is a queen. She is unhappy with her beggarly son-in-law, Lord Shiva, and his wayward way of life. But in Hindu society the husband has complete mastery over the wife.

❦ Song 246[1] ❦

To this slave what grace, thou gracious Queen,
Could'st thou but offer deign?
The treasure that is thy ruby feet,—
That too is pledged to Lord Hara's place;
Even should I thee attain in Yoga stance
Having taken poison Shiva stands ever wakeful sentinel;
He has banished sleep to watch his treasures
He has put to sleep the bull, his mount.

❦ Song 247[2] ❦

Take me on to thy lap, oh, Mother Kali,
Don't leave me alone in the womb of Eternal Time!

Uma has but a short sojourn every year to her parents' home. Soon, Lord Shiva calls to take her back to his place. Then, Menaka has to send her daughter away with her husband.

This song is the mother's pang at the departure of her daughter soon when Lord Shiva comes to take her away. But then, this time she will do a subterfuge. She will tell Shiva that Uma is not home. If the son-in-law (Lord Shiva) should get wild and angry, let him! Menaka will not care. If others would shame her for her unusual conduct, she would ignore it! Sure, she won't let her daughter go away. She can't bear to live without her, can't let her daughter pine away in an alien home!

[1]This little song is unique as a mystic complaint of the sage poet to the divine mother goddess Kali.

The poet worships the Mother for her divine grace. That is the supreme treasure to which the human soul aspires. This treasure is the vermilion twin feet of the Mother. But then, how does the Mother vouchsafe these her gracious feet to her devoted child Ramprasad! She has already pawned them, in perpetual bondage, to her Lord, the great God Shiva. Reference is to the Hindu image of Goddess Kali standing on the chest of Lord Shiva, who lies supine at her feet.

The poet has tried another way of accessing this treasure of her twin feet. That is through *yoga* and meditation. Even there he has failed. For Lord Shiva, as he lies supine at her feet, is ever wakeful. He has put to sleep, sleep herself. And He is sleepless because he has consumed poison that has taken all sleep away. The allusion is to the legend. When the ocean was being churned for 'elixir,' a vase of poison came up. The gods and the demons fought for the elixir but some one had to take the poison as well. Lord Shiva resolved the quarrel by swallowing the mortal poison himself; but he let it suspended within his throat which turned permanently blue. That is why Lord Shiva is also known as Nilakantha, the blue-necked God.

[2]The song is a call of the poet sage for liberation and relief from this harassing world.

I suffer, oh Mother, in aching pain and agony
Let me quit, Mother oh, with 'glory be to Kali,' call
You sent me on to this world to cry and moan,
I've wept long, oh Kali, I'm now pale and singed!
I've done with all I cherished in this mortal world,
In the life hence, upon thy feet, do let me dwell!

⚥ Song 248[1] ⚥

Oh Kali, do this thou when Death doth come
When Eternal Time at an opportune time,—
When he looms around
Do thou appear in the lotus-seat
Then within my heart;
Let not my mind as it kens
The louring god of doom,
Of the treasures lose remembrance,
By the guru deigned, divine!
Taradas, he avers
As life should come to end,
Let the tongue in Ganga waters
Chant Kali, Kali's name!

The poet is the child of Goddess Mother Kali. In this world of sports of the Mother Goddess, the poet has been sent for a life of sorrow and weeping. Like the sad weary child the poet cries for the mother' lap. All his desires in this mortal world have worn thin. He now seeks to go back home to Mother for his eternal bliss. Let Mother take her own child back to her refuge; let him not be left at the mercy of Eternal all-eroding Time, caught in the endless chain of births and deaths in this mortal world.

[1] In this typical way the sage poet Ramprasad talks to his mother Goddess Kali as his own dearest human mother. He has complete liberties with her,—as her own child, often in a stance of challenge, even of contest. In this tiny song, he pleads with Mother that She remember to grant him a few things when Death will come at his opportune moment.
   She should appear then in the lotus seat of the poet's heart. And then She should make sure that the poet does not forget the *seed mantra*, that he has learnt from his guru, for fear at the sight of Death. And finally, when he will be taken to the bank of the sacred Ganges river (as is wont for a sagely person before his quitting this life) his tongue should remember to chant the name of Mother Kali!
   The song is the cream of yearnings that fill the heart of the sage at the summit of his spiritual level.

꠶ Song 249[1] ꠶

There's no son so wretched as I,
Because, mother, thou art 'mother'
You bear with so much, that is why!
Like offsprings of crabs, as they gnaw away
    at the mother's breast
While on the mother's breast itself
    they dwell and rest,
That's how I hurt you ceaselessly
Even while I in you bosom abide,
By the way of crabs, mother, thou hast shown
Mother's love it's nonpareil,
And by their offsprings' ways thou hast revealed
The gracious way of the precious son!

꠶ Song 250[2] ꠶

It is my fault I have cried and moaned
Mother, she has so suffered wound,
Mother calls,—"come child my own, on to my lap,"
Wiping off my tears with warm embrace;
I have found, kenned saviour Mother

---

[1] The song is the poet's regret and surrender to the Mother.

The whole of the phenomenal world is the Mother's bosom. The human being is born and he abides in Nature which is the Mother's breast. Even then, he is so ungrateful that he behaves and commits sins that so hurt and cause pain to the Mother. He is like the crab-child. Even when it is in the mother's womb it pinches and gnaws away at its mother's tender breast. Yet, the mother-crab is all love and patience. It bears and nurses the young crab till it is born into the light of day.

The poet confesses to the Mother his own wicked nature and perverse ways throughout his life. He is like the young of the crab, wounding and saddening the Mother right from the womb. And the mother has revealed her love and patience for the child by the example of the crab-mother.

[2] This song is a scrap of the wailing cry of the devoted child.

The sage poet has long wept for Mother. She has been distressed at the pain and sorrow of the child. She has taken him on her lap in love and concern.

Now that the poet has attained the saviour feet of the Mother, he is no longer afraid of any one. He will now hold on to the sublime feet of the mother.

Whom else, oh, do I now fear,
I will hence hold on to her, so dear
With eyes e'er on her feet installed!

❦ Song 251[1] ❦

Let us set out, oh conscious mind,
Proceed, Mother's feet to ken;
My mind so yearning, aching keen,
To witness Mother's feet divine;
Oh mind, let's go, pray repair
Where mother of all three worlds—she's there,
The soul will be so balmy cool
To have a glimpse of Mother supreme,—
As you ken Mother's twin lotus feet
You get dissolved, you sink in it
You then no longer need to come
Into this mortal world again!

❦ Song 252[2] ❦

Whose dark swarthy maiden there,
She (Oh!) so dances loud in war;
Enchanting languorous she rolls and swings

---

[1] The poet often talks to his own mind. He spends long hours in meditation of his beloved Goddess Mother's image. And then he is immersed in her thoughts.

The mind is often errant. The mind keeps company of the wayward Nature's forces—the three ever-wavering *gunas* (qualities) of Nature—*sattva, rajas,* and *tamas*. But the poet knows better. He is constantly leading his mind to the sublime feet of the Mother. There, in her feet, there is peace and calm. It is balmy, cool. As one attains the mother's feet there is no more worldly pain, woes and chagrin. Then it is that the soul is freed from nature's bondage. It is emancipated from the chain of works,—from the eternal cycle of births and deaths into this mortal world.

[2] Songs like these (a mere scrap of a few lines) establish sage Ramprasad's place in Bengali poetic literature. Unlike some other great saints and sagely souls of ancient and medieval India Ramprasad Sen was a scholar and a linguist. He was a natural composer and his songs are no less great poetry than landmarks in the highest spiritual revelations of the supreme sage. The rhythm of the language of his songs and poems, the rich imageries—often occult, often so mundane and humdrum

Drunken deep with elixir;
Limbs lissom lithe as flowing stream,
On that, crimson blood sanguine,
It is as if in the waters dark
Of Kalindi, the hibiscus swims!

❦ Song 253[1] ❦

I have drawn the fence with Kali's name,
Secure I dwell there within;
Oh Death, should'st thou be rude
Thou would'st for sure receive thy due
I will report to Mother, all the same;
She, Shyama—She's stern tormentor of doom,
She is a maiden wild insane,
Listen, oh Death, what I tell you
I'm no dud, for sure, you know
It's no cake in the hands of a kid
That you would snatch by doing some trick!

—culled from the everyday life of human experience—is an awful mosaic unequalled in Bengali poetic and devotional literature. Ramprasad's works are of lasting interest not only to the sages, saints and spiritual seekers of all times but to the lover of poetry and literature. Like many others, Ramprasad's works is still a much neglected corner of the strange treasure house of Indian poetry and devotional literature.

Mother Kali's image is dark and sombre. The charming bewitching maiden is in a wild and warring stance. Her limbs are like the dark flowing waters of the swollen river, lithe and licking in the demonic battle with the evils of the world.

The Mother Goddess' person is all crimson with the blood of her enemies in war. Her image reminds the poet of the dark waters of the legendary Kalindi river,—with scarlet hibiscus flowers floating all over.

[1] The poet sage is here in a challenging posture. He dares Death on his face!

The Hindu philosophy believes in the immortality of the soul. The creature soul is parcel of the Infinite Absolute. And the tiniest part of Infinity is itself infinity. Death is feared by all mortals. yet, what can death do? It only destroys the mortal physical body of the Being built up of the five coarser elements of phenomenal Nature: (i) the earth, (ii) the water, (iii) the fire, (iv) the wind, and (v) the space. But the 'being,' the human soul is beyond and transcendent.

The enlightened 'being' knows this truth. The poet is the devoted child of goddess mother Kali. He cannot be touched by the crude and sham hands of Death. The name of Mother Kali is the fencing. The poet

꣸ Song 254[1] ꣸

What do I offer thee as worship
Do tell me what is it I own?
Thou art Queen, oh, of the limitless worlds
Whatever's there, Mother, all is thine.
With urges yearnings legion calls
I have amassed all wherewithals
As I bethink, they are none of mine
I have no title or command;
To bethink (oh Mother), they're all my own
Is a sham wayward way of mind,
Offering thee what is thy own
The mind's unwilling to be content,
That is why, oh Mother Tara Thou,
As I think I'm lost, I do not know
With what do I worship thy feet sublime;
Yet, that's not true! Devotion, it's mine,
That's what I'd offer thee, oh Mother, divine!
What would I ask or seek indeed,—

abides in the protected arena immune from Death. Death should not take chances with him. If he (Death) should misbehave he would be properly punished. Mother Kali,—She is dreaded by Death himself. Ramprasad is a conscious enlightened soul. He is not a child,—a fool or an idiot. Death should take note of it. He should not toy with the poet who is mother Kali's very own beloved child.

[1]The poet, as he worships his beloved Mother Goddess Kali, is lost and confused. He would pay homage and offerings to Mother. But then, what is it he would offer? Has he got anything that he could call his own? Mother is the queen of the universe. She is immanent. Everything is She and She is everything. The poet is loath to worship the divine mother with an offering that is Mother's own. It is dark ignorance to think that one can give or offer something to the divine Absolute!

But then the poet suddenly remembers. Yes, there is a thing that is all his own. Something that he can offer to the Mother Goddess. And that is his devotion and ardent love. The poet is so happy at this flash of enlightenment.

But then what is his prayer to the Mother? What boon would he ask? The poet wonders! Does he know what is good for him? What he should covet and seek of the gracious Mother? He does not know. But the poet knows that Mother is the best judge. She knows all and She is all that is to know. and She is the deigner of weal, the repository of universal bliss. Therefore, the poet decides to leave that, too, to her will and judgement.

I'd erring ask what I do not need,
What is good and what's but harm
Do I know it or discern?
Thou art the Image of bliss supreme,
Thou art the deigner of cosmic weal,—
Do thou, Mother, what thou should'st 'will,'
I leave it all to thy feet divine!
But (then), should'st thou heed my words
Light up, then, the darkness of my mind!

❦ Song 255[1] ❦

Where art thou, the world's deliverer
Saviour thou of all miseries,
How long, when is it thy grace will rain?
When would'st thou thy face reveal?
Balming all my anguish, pain,
Take me on into thy arms?
In the din of toil of Mother's domain
Of the twin gracious feet I've lost the ken;
Consciousness and careless unconcern
Should'st thou, Mother, fail to deign,
Would this confoundment, error travail
Will they ever flee lift their veil?

Finally he finds he has a desire. Let Mother judge and if She should so decide, let her grant this last boon to her devoted child. Prasad's prayer,—let her dispel the dark inconscience from his mind,—let Her decide if She should grant that boon to the sage poet!

[1] The song is a pining wail of the spiritual seeker. This world is sham full of toil and worries. The human being has no respite. Desires. passions and worldly pursuits elude ceaselessly the errant mind. Peace, calm and salvation that dwell on the Goddess Mother's sublime feet,—it is all forgotten.

The sagely soul cries, impatient, for Mother's grace. The human life is short. Death comes all too soon. The lonely human soul is lost in peril, buffeted in the storm-tossed sea of life. It is only Mother's grace that will lift the veil of ignorance and illusion. then only the glowing sun of enlightenment will dawn on the spiritual seeker. Mother's feet, her compassion and grace, this alone is the sailing craft that will take the lost weary soul across the turbulent sea of life.

The sage child of the divine Goddess Tara (Goddess Kali), weeps in agony for the Mother's refuge. He urges her to come soon as the poet's span of life is waning and he is in utter pain and misery.

The sun of my hours of life,—
It is now well-nigh on the wane
Where art thou, oh Brahmamoyee
Do, hasten, oh, thou racing come!
Deliver thou, thy son, oh Mother
In this dread dire peril
Who is there but thee sublime
Who would sail him across the main!

♥ Song 256[1] ♥

What dread have I of dreaded Death,—
Oh Death, tormentor Kali, She herself,
She is awake within my heart;
Beneath Whose feet for termless times
Lies supine Eternal Time;
What measly banal Death will do
To Mother Shyama's feet this Panchanan,
He surrenders himself lowly prone,—
He dares Death, he cares a fig,
He has vanquished toils of Eternal Time.

♥ Song 257[2] ♥

Gaya, Ganga, Provas others
   Kasi, Kanchi who but yearns;

---

[1] Human beings are afraid of Death. This is a fear of the unknown. Man is ignorant of himself and death to him is darkness. This fear melts away as the being gets to 'know himself.' In the Hindu philosophy this is what is known as 'self-realization' *(atmanam biddhi)*.

The human soul is immortal. What Death destroys is merely the physical body that is built up of the coarser elements in phenomenal Nature. The sage poet has touched the feet of Goddess Mother Shyama. That is enlightenment. Mother Shyama is the annihilator of Time, which is the Domain of Death. She is both immanent and transcendent. Therefore, the sage poet who dwells on the feet of Mother Shyama has reached beyond Death's territory. He no longer fears Death.

The sage reminds Death that Lord Shiva Himself, who is Kala or Eternal Time,—He lies supine at the feet of the Mother. Mother is Supreme. She is the tormentor of Death. The poet who has taken refuge of Her cannot be touched by Death.

[2] Hindu worship and religion are full of rituals. The shastras ordain

Chanting Kali, Mother Kali
   If my life so should end;
Does he need vespers worship
   Who calls three times Kali's name;
Vespers run in search of him
   Alas, futile, he's beyond its ken;
Giving alms, *yajna*, offerings
   They all fall away behind;
Madan's worship, *yajna puja*
   They are all at Kali's crimson feet;
The puissance, power of Kali's name
   Who would ever know it, ken;
Lord Shiva, Primal God of deities all
   Whose name, in His five-some faces chant!

❦ Song 258[1] ❦

I cling on to thy feet, Mother, even then
You never care to cast a glance;
In thine own sports you are drunk and lost
Overwhelmed, oh Maiden, by thine own thoughts;

pilgrimage, sacrifice, *yajnas*, penance and many other religious practices. The poet questions all these mandates of the shastras.

   The poet has surrendered himself to the sublime feet of Goddess Mother Kali. And those feet are the final refuge, the ultimate of bliss and liberation. For the sage poet no rituals, no vespers, no holy worshipful acts,—are necessary. All such pious works, *pujas* and pilgrimages to holy places like Gaya, Kasi or Provas or bathing in the holy Ganges river,—they all seek and dissolve in the sublime feet of Mother Kali.

   Even the supreme God Lord Shiva, He has held on to the twin vermilion feet of the Great Mother. The very name of Mother Kali is the ultimate of worship. When Madan (the Hindu god of Love) was burnt to ashes by the fiery rage of Lord Shiva, he worshipped Mother and through her grace was restored to life.

   The poet thus abjures all his desires and cravings for holy pilgrimage. His only longing is,—as his mortal life ends in this world, his tongue should chant ceaselessly the name of Mother Kali.

   [2]The poet is the beloved child of the Mother Goddess Shyama. In this world of pain and chagrin he is worn, weary, lost,—weeping all the time for the sublime feet of the Mother. Yet, the mother seems careless and absent, busy all the time with her sports and playfulness in this chameleon world of illusions. Mother is the saviour, the ocean of love and compassion; and again She is the dread dour annihilator with open scimitar in hand. She is as loving as she is wild in her loud lurid laughter in her warring stance.

What is this thy game round and round
Across heaven, earth and the netherworld?
For fear the worlds their eyes they furl,
They hold thy feet—'Mother, oh Mother' call;
The final doom in your hands a toy
At your feet Lord Baba supine and coy;
On your face rolls wild laughter loud
Down your limbs cascading blood;
Tara, benign, oh Mother of weal
Sviour Mother, my fears do heal;
Do take me, Mother Shyama, in your arms,
In your arms do take me on;
Do come thou, Mother now
    In thy Tara-countenance,
In thy gracious smiling stance
    In robes pure snow-white,—
As dawn descends down on earth
    Through deep dense darkness of the night
Till now, oh Mother, I've worshipped thy image
As Kali, fearsome, dread dour visage,
Now all my worships done and over,
I pray, Mother, sheath thy open scimitar!

❦ Song 259[1] ❦

Oh thou, 'fish of life,' thy life is done,
Oh as time's opportune, the 'fisherman' Death has come;
In the pool of world's desiring 'field'
He pulls the 'line' of works and deeds,

    The poet prays as the timid weeping child that Mother, in her gracious form lift him up into her lap! Let her appear in her sublime grace as Dawn descends in the early morn swaying out in her charm from the deep awesome darkness of night. Let her resume her mellow smiling all-forgiving mother—Tara's countenance to her beloved weeping child!

    [1]The imagery is of a treacherous pool of waters where fishes dwell. This world of desires and craving for earthly possessions is the pool and the fishes are the human beings. But then there is the fisherman waiting with his fishing-net watching out for an opportune time. Death is that fisherman. He has taken lease of this pool of mortal world. He will choose his proper time and cast his net, sure and wide. The fishes (the beings) of this world have no escape. They will sure fall into the toils writhing to death.

He'll set the fishing net across the aisles;
Why did'st thou, alas, repair and dwell
In this world's miry slimy pool
Where Eternal all-devouring Death
Has right of casting his fishing net,
Do shun this sinning pool, resign,
Let's go into the waters, deep down
Where there's Mother Kali's feet sublime!

ꕤ Song 260[1] ꕤ

I have come to know, Shyama Mother's Court,
Oh, it is so loud in rack and ruins;
There's constant clamour of complainants
And those who are there in their defense;
There's no fair decrees, indeed there's little chance
There in the court of One with the serpent crown;
Alas, oh Mother, the treasurer, when
He Himself is insolvent,
What reliance's there on the verdict then!
I have briefed lawyers full one lakh,
What more, oh Mother, could I act?
I invoke thee loud, thy 'Tara' name,
Has Mother lost her hearing then?
Let me shout, call names aloud,
Is it thou hast done down thy hearing ears
To earn thine own, Kali's name!
Ramprasad laments,—his marrow, bones
Bruised, alas, she has roasted brown!

> The poet blames the foolish human being for casting anchor in this sinning pool of the world. Let him sink deeper (in meditation) where the fisherman cannot reach Death's 'net.' It is there that dwell the sublime feet of Mother Kali. There alone is the safe haven of the human being.
>
> [1]The song proceeds on the symbol of a Court of Justice. Mother Shyama has opened her court. There are countless complainants accusing others of injustice. The defendants are no less vocal. They stoutly argue their case. The whole court-scene is clamorous and distasteful.
>
> The poet is disheartened. He knows he can hardly hope for justice from such a court. The Mother, the supreme judge of the court, she too is so dishevelled and insensitive. The court's chief officer of revenues (Lord Shiva), he himself is bankrupt. He has surrendered to Mother Shyama lying prone beneath her feet.

☙ Song 261[1] ☙

Mother thou, deign the blooming lotus of thy feet
To one, who, prone, lies beseeching thy refuge;
Saviour thou, of thine eyes by a gracious glance,
Deliverer of fears all, of the offspring of the sun.
Thou the image of the primal sound
Mother Tara, queen of the Lord supreme
Thou the safe sailing craft across the ocean of the world!
Thou art the sensuous Nature's worlds revealed
Thou art aloof beyond the Nature's veil,
Thou art primal causeless subtle profound!
Thou art lotus blooming pure
   In the puissant seat of Muladhar,
Thou art unborn beyond all Ends,
Thou art the seed, thou the womb
Of all the vast universal realms
Thou art the Being Supreme
Again thou art His consort Queen!
   In the creature world in all and one;
Origin, annihilation and sustenance
   Thou art the divine Queen of all three stance;
Durga Name, it's the elixir
   The realm alone of light and bliss,—
The 'vital soul' overwhelmed in ignorance,—
He ever adores the trinal pain
   In the well of poison, squirming, vain!

The poet pleads that he has set up a lakh of lawyers on his behalf. He can do no more. These lawyers are his endless devotion and ardent chanting of mother's name. Is it that Mother has lost her sense of hearing? Ramprasad is angry and impatient. He calls her (mother Shyama) names and charges her with unjustly putting him to endless pains and miseries.

[1] The song is a massive concatenation of the endless appellations of Mother Kali. She is the queen of the eternal Cosmic Nature. She is both immanent and transcendent. She is everywhere in every creature. And again she is the Absolute, dwelling in the human body as part of the primal supreme energy of the Absolute Brahman. She is the primal cause of Creation, Sustenance and Annihilation of the Universe. She is sans beginning, sans end, beyond all knowledge. Nothing happens without her, no leaves fall nor flowers bloom without her nod; and yet she is in nothing, she is unknown and unknowable. She is the final liberation of the soul of man from out the endless cycles of births and deaths.

Ramprasad avers, so well he knows,
That's all, alas, futile and sham!

❦ Song 262[1] ❦

Jaya, oh, do not, I pray, so beseech,
    Wake up Lord Hara's queen from her sleep,
Gouri, She was awake all night
    Weeping that she has to leave;
Weary of her sleepless night
    Uma, daughter, she's now asleep;
Alas, the face as the lambent moon
    Is dark and pale in melancholy!
When she is awake from her slumbering sleep
    Plunging the Himalayas in darkness deep,
My Uma as the gracious moon
    Will depart for the Kailasa realm;
Lord Hara, he is here to take her home
    That's why I pray, do linger on,—
Let her sleep on as long as she will
    So, at her face as the moon I may look on!

❦ Song 263[2] ❦

I have come to know, I ken so well
You are the queen of sorcerer's veil;

---

[1] Gauri (Uma or Goddess Durga) is the daughter of queen Menaka and the Lord Himalayas. Gauri is also queen consort of Lord Hara (Lord Shiva), who dwells in Kailasa, a remote realm of the interior Himalayas. Gauri comes to her mother's place once every year (the four days when the annual Durgapuja is celebrated in every Hindu home) from her husband's home in Kailasa.

Gauri now sleeps at her mother's palace although it is late morning. She has to leave for her husband's place, the same day and Lord Hara has come to take her back. Gauri is sad and weeping as she has to leave her mother so soon. That is why she had wept throughout the last night and had no sleep.

Menaka pleads with Jaya, Gauri's boon companion, that she should not wake her up, although the morning is late. She is so tired and woebegone. Let her sleep as long as she would. And mother Menaka would fain behold the sweet sleeping face of daughter in the meanwhile.

[2] This song is unique in the way it demonstrates the catholicity and

Whoever which way seeks you, call
You assent, his seeking you fulfil
Foratara, thee the predators name,
God, they call you, Mother, all Christian souls.
Khoda, is thy name by which they call
The Muslim priests, Pathans, Mughals;
The 'Shaktas' fathom thee as Supreme Energy
Those who worship Lord Shiva, Mother,
They divine you Shiva,—deigner of weal,
Gouri, She,—Surya christens you
The hermit hails you Sree Radhika.
'Ganapatyas' as Ganesh chant,
Ganesha's Mother Yaksha counts;
The artist calls you Vishwakarma,
To the sailor, Badar is your name
Shri Ramdulal avers,—it's no marvel charm,
One should know the Truth, the Reality,—
My mind has erred dazed bemused
Divining dual Form of One Divinity!

❦ Song 264[1] ❦

Should I breathe my last chanting 'Jai Kali,'
   Glory be to Mother thee,—
I'd sure attain Lord Shiva's realm,
   What use to me, oh, Varanasi!

universality of the Hindu religion. Sages like Ramprasad (Sen) and, later, Sri Ramakrishna,—were worshippers of Goddess Mother Kali or Shyama. Yet it is most wonderful and revealing how they perceived the Divinity of their idol of worship.

   The poet tells Mother, she is a sorcerer and is mistress of legerdemain. In any form that anyone worships her, she is there to fulfil one's cherished dream. The Mugs (a Myanmariot) calls their god, Faratara, the Christians call him God; the Mughals declare, it is Khuda; the Pathans name him Syaid Kaji. She is called Shakti by the Shaktas, Shiva by the Shaivaites. The Sun-worshippers call her 'Sun,' the mendicant minstrel sect name her Sri Radhika. Then too she is variously called as Ganesha and Vishwakarma. And the 'sailors' clan call her by the name 'Badar.'

   But then Ramprasad says it is not sorcery. She indeed is the Absolute Brahman who assumes and appears in varied images by which she is invoked and worshipped by different sects of people.

[1] Poet sage Ramprasad was a natural composer of his devotional songs.

Kali the Image of Eternity,
Who but fathoms Kali's bourne!
A little of her marvels Lord Shiva kenned
That's why at her twin crimson feet
He has made his dwelling lying supine!

Song 265[1]

Wake up thou, arise, oh mind
From marvel's veil of slumberous sleep
How longer must thou slumber on
Unconscious in ignorance!
This sham and empty world goes on
In gustful joy and dalliance;
In flaming passion and fond desires
Thou art immersed in chameleon dream;
Should'st thou must slumber, sleep
Then in *yoga* trance you better drown
Thou would'st attain mother Kali's feet
The Treasure rare, most sublime!
In *yoga*'s radiant lambent light,—
Counsel love faith devout—

Many of his songs were composed impromptu while he sang them in his high melodious voice.

The *Srimadbhagavad Geeta* quotes Lord Krishna to say, "Ceaseless thought and chanting of my name is the most sublime way of worship." It is enough for the liberation of the bonded human being. Ramprasad was a householder. he had not formally renunciated his family life (*grihadharma*). But then he would sing and chant mother Kali's name all hours of his daily life.

This bit of a song is expression of his devout faith in the name of Goddess Mother Kali as the seed energy of liberation from the human bondage. If he should die while chanting Mother's name, he would most certainly dissolve in the Absolute All Soul, the supreme Divinity. Then there is no need of pilgrimage to holy places. Even Lord Shiva, conscious of the glory and marvel of Goddess Kali, has taken his place beneath the vermilion feet of the Great Goddess. The poet knows of the supreme Divinity of his beloved Goddess Mother Kali in her Image of Infinity.

[1]This is a pleading of the poet with his own mind. The 'soul' of the 'being' is free and unattached with the 'works' and 'illusions' of Nature's legerdemain. But the 'mind' and 'ego-self,'—they play the tricks. They are under the constant influence of the three *gunas* (or qualities, as Rishi Sri Aurobindo puts it) of Nature,—*sattva*, *rajas* and *tamas*.

Awake the indwelling conscious realm
Awake thou, oh mind, in meditation, chant
Look, the creature world's awake around!

ꕤ Song 266[1] ꕤ

The fishing net cast well spread out
There watchful sits the fisherman,
Mother Tara, alas, to me
What'll befall at the end!
In the remote unfathomed water, deep,
There abides the fishes' house,
The net is vast sweeping all three worlds.
When the fish bethinks, he will escape
Then he is caught by the hair of his nape;
For escaping there is ne'er none no chance,
Where would he flee,—into the net he returns;
Ram counsels,—do thou, call Mother, Her,—
As She'll come, dour Death away she'll scare.

Swayed by the ever-present turmoil of desires and passions of the world, the human mind and the ego-self join hands with the Nature's *gunas* and put the human soul into perpetual bondage. This indeed is '*maya*' the veil that puts the shroud on the being that builds the eternal chain of *karma* (works) and the endless cycle of births and deaths.

The enlightened Sage Ramprasad knows the Truth. He is conscious of the slumber of ignorance in which the mind is perpetually trapped. He calls upon his 'mind' to wake up in the light of consciousness. But then he gives his 'mind' another better choice; if it is so fond of sleep and slumber, then let it dissolve into *yoga*, meditation and union with the Absolute,—the infinite bliss that lies in the feet of Mother Goddess Kali. There it is all light and liberation of the human soul.

[1] The image of the world as the troubled sea is common in Hindu philosophy and literature.

In sage poet Ramprasad's songs humdrum rustic scenes and events of common knowledge are often used with great precision and lucidity for his devotional imageries. Thus, village fairs, kite-flying, court-scenes, the home-coming of the young married daughter to her parents' home,— these and many other scenes of Bengal's rural life are used with new allegorical symbolic meanings and nuance. The mystic veil of ordinary experiences is woven with a rare appeal to the intelligence of the common man. This trait in the devotional literature of India, indeed of the whole world, is rare.

In the present song the human being is the fish. He dwells in a pool of waters which is this world seething with risks and hazards. Death is

Song 267[1]

Into the Yamuna water I'll throw myself
Chanting Kali, Kali's name all the while;
I'm thy, Mother, innocent infant child,
I don't e'en know by what name to call;
I play thy sports as best I can
The way that Thou dost put me on;
Thou Brahmamoyee, that's how people call;
It's no cake, Mother, in the hands of a child
That Thou'dst snatch with thy charm and wiles,
How gracious kind thou art, Mother,
I've witnessed in the field of war!

Song 268[2]

Who is that your company, oh mind!
For whom, oh mind, you, anxious, bide your time?

the fisherman waiting round the corner. He holds in his hands his vast all encompassing fishing net. he strikes at the right moment. He casts his net wide and sure. No fish can escape. No mortal being is free from the clutches of Death.

But the poet knows there is a way out. Chanting mother Kali's name and taking refuge at her feet will save the human being from the toils of Death.

[1]The poet in this song is in a threatening mood. He is the devoted child of Mother Kali, and yet, Mother does not take care of him. The poet has earned his right to Mother's grace. In Hindu philosophy Mother Goddess, the supreme Divinity, is beholden to Her/His devotee.

The poet claims his rights of Mother's grace. He is suffering pain and misery in this world. The Mother is careless. She defaults in her duty to Her beloved child. But the poet is not an idiot. The Mother cannot play with him and deny him his rights to Mother's divine grace.

The poet threatens the Mother, if she does not relent and persists in Her careless unconcern for Her son, then he would drown himself in the River Yamuna. That is the way the poet would take revenge on the Mother.

[2]The song is a warning of the human soul to the errant mind.

It is the 'mind' of the human being that plays a dual role. When the mind is clean and pure stalled in the *sattva guna* (quality) of Nature it acts as an ally of the human soul in its transcendence to the Absolute Infinity. But most often the 'mind' is errant, wayward, wicked. It then keeps company of the meaner *gunas (rajas* and *tamas)* of Nature and subserves the six-some foes that dwell within the human being. The six foes are

Your frail carnal craft, oh, lies careened
In the miry shoal of the mortal world;
Pray, proceed, oh sailing fast and hale
In the halcyon breeze of guru's name upon the sail.
Prasad counsels,—with six-some foes along march forward
Wary, oh, straight fearless unperturbed!
Or else, the tainted seed of the dark recess
Will cloud bedim the glow of Yoga stance!

❦ Song 269[1] ❦

Get thee gone, oh Death,—what wouldst thou dare?
I have put, oh, Shyama Mother close behind the bars,
I have put her feet in shackles
   With the toils of my mind,
I've installed Her in the Prison
   Of the lotus heart of mine
I've set aglow my lotus heart
   The mind settled in 'Sahasrar'
I've resigned my soul to Kulakundalini

the products of *rajas* and *tamas gunas* of Nature which constantly battle for ascendance and hegemony over the human soul (*jivatma*); it is then the foremost enemy of the soul. It takes the divinity within man to the path of degradation,—sin and eternal damnation.

   The poet (here in this song) warns the mind that this mortal life is like the vessel stranded on the shoals of the turbulent ocean of this world. For whom is it that the mind tarries in the midst of this peril? Let it chant the *seed mantra* given by the spiritual guru—and then this craft of the mortal carnal body would sail smooth and pure across the earth's turbulent sea. The mind should beware, for there are the six-some foes as its constant companion. It should steer clear of them, or else the dark inconscience waiting within himself will spoil all his efforts at union with the All-Soul!

   The song embodies the eternal hazards of the spiritual pilgrim.

[1] The poet is happy and assured in his safety. He has put shackles round the feet of the supreme Goddess Mother Shyama. He has imprisoned her in the lotus seat within his heart. Devotion is the bond which Divinity cannot overthrow. The sage poet has tied the mother's feet with devotion's chain. and he is ever watchful. Mother as the supreme enlightened energy assumes her seat in the blooming lotus installed on the crown of the sage. And there itself the poet has set his mind constantly keeping up the vigil. And he has taken all precautions against perils and pestilence. He has taken the potion of the *seed mantra* of guru which is a panacea against all evils.

    The coiled Energy's door supreme
And then I've set up a strategy
    There's no gain should she truant flee
The devotion bailiff, he e'er patrols
    My twin eyes sleepless they are sentinels
I knew the mortal ill would chance
    That's why I did up in advance
I drank deep off the guru's lore,—
    Panacea of all miseries;
Sri Ramprasad says,—"I've shattered thine
    Firman writ so well proclaimed.
Chanting Kali, Kali, oh Kali
    Having taken leave, I now mark time."

♥ Song 270[1] ♥

As the blooming lotus blue azure
    In the frosty lake snow-white pure
My Shyama, Mother, she's installed
In Lord Hara's snowy heart;

Armed as he is with his preparations to hold Mother prisoner and to secure himself against assaults from outside he confidently dares Death to do his worst!

[1] Sage poet Ramprasad is known for his devotional songs. Most of his songs and lyrics are inspired by his spiritual union with his beloved Goddess Mother Kali or Shyama. He is a master of metaphors hand imageries taken mostly from common rustic experiences. There is an awful blend of his realization of the Infinite Energy—the supreme Infinity within his own Being. The Hindu Tantrashastra is the acme of science with meticulous anatomical analysis of the human body, the vital life-force and their intimate communion with the Universal Energy of which the divine image is Mother Kali. In this he is uniquely alone. There are other great devotional poets and composers in Hindu love, devotion and spiritual literature. Vidyapati, Chandidas, Shekhar, Gobindadas, and Jaidev in Vaishnava literature; Tulsidas, Kabir, Nanak. Chaitanya, and Shankar,—all great sages and composers chanting their songs and hymns to their beloved Divine Lord or Queen Goddess Mother.

Yet Ramprasad is alone in his strange rhythm and rhyme scheme very often choosing the words of his songs from the daily commonplace life of the rustic folk. But Ramprasad was a scholar and a masterly poet whenever he so chose to be. In the present song, for example, he is almost Keatsian in the sensuous quality of his imageries and symbols. Mother Shyama's complexion is as the dark blue cumulus clouds. Her

The countenance,—it is dark rolling cumulus
And yet this louring darkness illumines
The trinal worlds passing lightning flash.
I so yearn ever ceaseless in my mind—
How the toils torn of this mortal fair,
Those twin feet I would install sublime
In my heart with anxious care!

Song 271[1]

Tara, pray now take me across the stream
I'm caught in wheeling turbulence.
Yet, I do not know how to swim
The body, for one, is an ailing craft
And, then it's burdened with vice and sin
Where's the mooring, what, oh do I do
The world's ocean, it's shoreless main!

Song 272[2]

Save thy son oh Saviour,—
In three-some pain, oh Mother Tara

flowing swarthy hairs are like the agile movement of the storm cloud. She stands on the snowy chest of Lord Hara (Shiva). Yet, the luminous halo of her dark complexion illumines the trinal worlds. The glow of her divine splendour surpasses the lightning flash.

The song, a hymn to Goddess Shyama is highest poetry in its own right.

[1] The song is a portrait of the perilous worldly life that the sage poet perceives.

The poet is a spiritual seeker. It is as if a journey across a stubborn tumultuous ocean. The perils are legion. What is the craft on which he must ford these troubled waters? It is the mortal worldly life, the frail body in which the human soul is housed. The body is fragile and dilapidated. It is ageing, hardly able to carry the hardship of austere penance. And then it is heavily loaded with sins with which this mundane world is beset.

He finds himself, lost rudderless, without mooring, in the middle of the ocean. The poet decided to renounce the world and spend his days in worship and pilgrimage at holy Kasi (the holy city of Varanasi). But then he was caught again in the turmoil of the world.

The poet now takes refuge of Mother Tara. It is Mother's grace that alone can take him to safety and bliss across the perilous ocean of the world.

[2] This song is the wailing cry of the human soul in its spiritual journey. This world is *maya*,—shrouded in the veil of illusion. This world is full of

Day and night I'm so singed
Do not put me to agony, tears
For nought, endless, unremiss
Embalm the pain of thy wretched son
Oh Mother, slayer of all miseries;
I won't be amiss again, oh Mother,
With the cherry fruit of the world mundane;
I have tasted enough of that fruit
There's no savour or no good,
It's soaked in poison, as one partakes
Of it, it yields pain and injuries;
As the fruit I swallow I lose the light
I remain forgetful of thy sight,—
Being Mother, thou,—pray, do not, Mother,
Give thy son the poisoned fruit!
'This is mine,' oh 'this is my own'
Like this I'm drunk, sans surcease
My senses all, my wife and sons,
I divine they are all my own,
But then I fail to know and ken
Where is this 'I' as I bethink;
Tell me, oh Mother, which is the way
That, Mother, I should find that 'I!'
No longer, Mother I beseech,
This wretched Rama beguile confound!

⚘ Song 273[1] ⚘

Can I blame thee, Mother, oh?

desires. The human being is perpetually caught in its web. From desire come worries and then despair. We seek possessions,—of fortunes and then of wives and sons and kith and kin. But there is no peace, only ceaseless pursuit of the elusive chimera.

One constantly thinks of 'me' and 'I' and 'mine.' But as the sage bethinks, he is lost. He wonders, who is this 'I'? Whence they come and where they go—vanish, leaving the being all alone.

The real 'I' the human soul is aloof and alone,—part of the Absolute Divinity. Sorrows come from attachments and these attachments are the veil of the Mahamaya,—the Queen of this transitory world of illusions.

The poet begs of the Mother to tell him who is this real 'I' so he realizes himself.

[1]The sage poet knows he is an idiot in his ways in this world. The

It's my own fault that I suffer so;
Leaving its 'master' as roams the dog
Greedy around the sweetmeat shop,
So chasing pleasures I roam the world
Unconcerned of thee in oblivion!
Thou dost pull me on into thy presence divine,
How does he, Mother human turn?
To Prasanna so gracious thou,
I move in the human world,—that's why,—
Prasanna is thy silly child
In words so fond, in work so vile
Do take him to task, punish oh Mother,
    Pulling him hard by the hair
Smite him (on the neck) with shoes
Hit him twice hard and square.

Song 274[1]

To dwell in a place of pilgrimage, it's futile
It's futile in a holy pilgrims' place to dwell;
Where is that holy place, which one
Beyond Shyama Mother's feet, oh mind?
I've heard it, people say,—to Ayodhya shrine
To that distant city as one proceeds,—
And then should he witness there Rama's sports,—

Mother's grace is all there—but he turns his eyes away, wallowing in animal pleasures of this world. He is like the silly goat that is tied hard to his tether. In his eagerness to graze in this world's senseless pastures he pulls hard at the peg, and as he does so he tightens his own stranglehold,—bleats in his self-inflicted pain and agony.

Mother calls him, open-arm, all the time in her divine grace; yet, the beast persists in its beastly life chasing the chameleon of animal pleasure. The poet pleads with the Mother that She pull him up, punish him hard and square. Then only he would know the truth. The poet is in agony! But he knows, all that is his own fault, of his own making. He roams the world like the miserable greedy dog searching for futile pleasures that lure him in this world. He forgets his real home and Master. The Mother is not to blame. The human being has only to turn to the gracious divine Mother,—and peace, joy and bliss are all his for the asking.

[1]This song is something of a veiled pride of the poet of the supremacy of his own beloved Goddess Mother Kali over the other great gods of the Hindu pantheon. The great trinity of the other three gods of the Hindu religion are Lord Rama, Lord Krishna and Lord Shiva.

Then all his sins are past and gone!
But then the Vedas,—they oft announce
The same Rama when he was trounced,
With crimson hibiscus at Kali's feet
He worshipped for Ravana's defeat and death;
In—Dwaraka, royal Mathura realm
Sri Vrindavana, and all else then
Where Lord Krishna, playful, had his sports,—
When that same Krishna as he was born
And King Kansa would kill him there and then,-
Krishna's life in maya's marvel shroud
It was She who then did save and shield!
Lord Siva's own domain, the Kasi realm
Of all the shrines, most holy and supreme
Whoever has been ever there,
His emancipation has attained
That same Lord Sambhu who enshrines
Everlasting that Kasi realm
Himself repaired to the crematorium
Holding to His heart those feet sublime!

    Rama is the royal king of Ayodhya. Ayodhya is thus a place of holy pilgrimage. But that great Rama was powerless when the mighty demon Ravana had to be slain. He had to worship goddess Durga (another image of mother Kali) with scarlet hibiscus flower to give him the puissance of the Mother when alone he could destroy Ravana.
    Dwaraka is the place of Lord Krishna and is a place of pilgrimage. But then when the life of the child Krishna was in peril at the hands of the murderous King Kansha, it was mother Kali who had cast the veil of illusion under which Krishna was taken out of the prison by his father Vasudeva.
    Even the great Shiva who dwells in the holy city of Kasi (Banares) had courted Mother's twin feet. For Lord Shiva (in Hndu mythology) lies supine with Mother Kali standing on his chest.
    The poet concludes, one who has installed steadfast his soul at the Mother's feet has no need for pilgrimage even to the most sublime of holy shrines.
    Outwardly, the sage might sound a little parochial, claiming a more elevated place of his own Divinity over the other great gods of Hindu pantheon. But the poet knows they are all one and the same. It is the Absolute Brahman that assumes images of multiple divinity. Goddess Mother Kali is the Form of this same supreme Absolute.

☙ Song 275[1] ☙

How will it profit thee my errant mind,
From pilgrimage,—whence this illusion thine?
The fruits of thy worship in billion holy shrines,—
They are all there in Shyama Mother's feet sublime.
In enlightenment's holy Ganges
    Do thy hallowed bath
In the holy Kasi of the body
Take to meditation's path
Contemplate within thy mind
    The image of the 'Self,'
Of the sole saviour supreme
Of all the existential worlds.
On the sixteen-petalled blooming lotus,
    There dwells the Lord supreme
From Muladhar in the spinal wheel
At Sahasrara behold the Queen!

☙ Song 276[2] ☙

When will it be that time will come, when

[1] The song enshrines the cream of the revelations of the spiritual progress of the Tantra *sadhaka.*
Goddess Shyama is the supreme Godhead, the Absolute Infinite Energy. She resides within the human body in her eight successive seats along the spinal cord. Lowest at the bottom of the spine is the Muladhar seat. Here coiled (like the serpent) Energy lies sleeping and dormant and so long as it is not awakened, man is weak and ignorant. As the *yogin* progresses in his *sadhana* (spiritual path), this energy is unleashed and human being receives a kind of new joy, new light, peace and vision. The *yogin* goes on ascending along the seats of the Primal Energy till it melts and unites with the All-Soul, the Brahman that dwells on the sixteen-petalled lotus on the top of the brow, called Sahasrara. Then it is that the human body itself will become like the holy shrine of Kasi and enlightenment will flow inside like the sacred current of the holy river Ganges. Conscious of this Absolute Truth the poet is no longer interested in visiting holy places of pilgrimage.

[2] The song is a symbolic craving of the soul of the poet for absolute dissolution with the Infinite Being in the image of Mother Tara. By the constant repetition of the word 'Tara'—as the name of the Goddess Mother Kali and also the Bengali word for the pupil of the eye,—the poet creates the chanting rhythm of the whole being with his beloved Goddess Mother.

My last breath will leave with Tara, Tara, Tara's name,—
From then on when I will learn to ken,
I'll, aching ask how, Tara, Tara, Tara I'll gain;
When Tara, Tara as I'll chant and call
Will stand staid and still my twin eye-balls.
Then it is, oh Tara, in worship Thine
My eye-balls will dissolve in thy name.

❦ Song 277[1] ❦

Tara, Thou art Supreme Mother divine!
Oft thou art the Male Supreme,
Thou art then, the maiden of sixteen;
Thou art Enlightenment in dark ignorance.
Deigner thou of devotion, deliverance;
Across this tormenting world's ocean, Mother
Thy feet the sailing craft, sole assurance;
Thou art the Image of all three worlds,
Thou art the cause of all three worlds,—
Tara, Mother,—thou the slayer of all three agonies;
Glory be to thee,—of the worlds thou royal Queen!
Do vouchsafe this wretched poor

The sagely soul of the poet will dissolve in the Infinite Absolute freed from the bondage of the mortal world and liberated from the chain of endless births and deaths into this world of pain and sorrow. In Hindu philosophy the ultimate aim and craving of the spiritual seeker is liberation from the chain of works and its fruits—that is the primal cause of bondage, and that is what keeps apart the human soul from the Absolute Brahman.

[1]The song is a poetic hymn of the great Goddess Mother's varied charm and grace. The Mother is the image of the supreme Divinity. She often assumes the Male form (as in Lord Krishna) and then sometimes she appears in the image of a young maiden of sixteen. One would observe in this song a unique perception of Hindu metaphysics. Mother is the image of the Supreme Energy—who sometimes stays still, inert, immobile, transcendent as the Supreme still Brahman; and then often this same supreme Energy appears as the immanent dynamic Mother Nature,—the primal cause, existence and sustenance and then of annihilation of the whole phenomenal Nature and the existential system. The form and shape that is assumed by this Infinite Energy (mahashakti) is thus a matter of indifference.

This mother Nature, the supreme goddess Mother Kali,—she is everything and she is everywhere. Nothing is except Her; nothing happens without Her. She is the ordainer of deliverance; She alone is the refuge of the human soul. It is Her grace that is the last resort of the human being.

at thy feet a place,
Repository of grace, oh Mother,—
By thine own mercy, grace,
If thou wouldn't deign forgiveness mercy
Oh Shankari who would but then forbear?

❦ Song 278[1] ❦

Mother, you cast me, sure, out of mind
(Yet) I am so troubled with Him insane
He laughs and weeps ever absent lost,
Save me He knows none, is unconcerned;
Fond of hemp, Mother, He's ever so drunk,
That's why I'm ceaseless so concerned;
I must lift it, mother, to His mouth
Or else, He'll forget His food and drink;
As I bethink of Him insane
Sure, I'm lost, I'm out of mind;

The sage poet turns to the Mother in utter devotion for his escape from this world of bondage pain and miseries.

[1] This is one of the rare songs of sage poet Ramprasad.
Goddess Durga (Her maiden name is Uma or Parbati) is the daughter of the royal King, the Himalayas. Uma's mother is Menaka, the queen of the Himalayas. There are quite a few songs on Menaka's grief and lament over Uma's absence or short sojourn at her mother's place. Menaka cannot bear to live without her charming little daughter who must now live most of the time at her husband, Lord Shiva's abode at Kailasa. And then Menaka is unhappy with the nature and way of life of Lord Shiva or Lord Hara. Shiva (Menaka's son-in-law) is half-insane, absent, living on alms, roaming half-naked in leopard-skin.

In this rare song it is Uma who talks to her mother Menaka. She tells her mother, as if, of her woes and troubles at her husband's place and in dwelling with her half-wild Lord. Yet, the song embodies the unique divine love of Uma for her husband. She pleads with her mother her trials and problems in coming to her mother's place, leaving her helpless, absent husband behind alone. He is careless, half-insane, roaming round, unable to look after himself. He does not remember to take his food unless she takes care of it. He does not know anyone else but her. He is like a child not knowing what he does. Uma is so afraid lest he should go somewhere, deserting his home, in her absence.

The loving wife's devotion and love for her Lord, with a rare blend of openness and modesty, have seldom been enshrined better or more eloquently in the compass of a short lyric anywhere else in literature of love,—mundane or divine.

As I cajoled Him when I left (Oh Mother),
He all but swam in streaming tears
I fear lest he should quit alone,—
So absent careless lost where else is one!

⚜ Song 279[1] ⚜

Tell me Tara, then, what use reposing trust in thee,—
If the fruits of all my works are destined to me?
Along the path that you steer and lead
That is the way I proceed
How is it then that you make me share
The fruits of pleasures and agony?
Kamalakanta has this prayer
(Brahmamoyee, Mother, thou)
Were it, oh, the human being,
Of dreaded Death he had no awe!

⚜ Song 280[2] ⚜

Shiva's queen you mountain-maid
With heart of stone for termless times,—

---

[1] Hindu philosophy ordains that every bit of thought and action is followed by its fruits, and the fruits carry their own seeds of further thoughts and action. The chain of works and the fruits of works thus build up a closed wheel that spins for eternity. This is the essence of the philosophy of birth, death and rebirth of the human being moving as an eternal chain in this mundane world. This cause-and-effect cycle is inviolable working as Newton's Third Law of Motion or as the Psychic Law of Compensation of Ralph Waldow Emerson.

The poet questions this fateful law and challenges Goddess Mother, why that should be so. The Mother is the ordainer of every single movement in this phenomenal world. Not a single dew drop nor there is the 'batting of an eye' without the Mother's consent or desire. If that is so, why is it that the sage poet should be made responsible for his actions. For is it not that what he does or how he behaves, is all as the Mother has willed?

The poet prays to the Goddess Mother Tara that she consider his appeal and set him free from the fruits of his work and from the fear of Death.

[1] The song is a marvel of blend of occult mystery and poetic charm. The Hindu legend and image of Goddess Mother Kali is that of a dark awesome maiden, unrobed and with flowing locks, standing like a be-

Amused at your sporting stance
At your feet supine Eternal Time:
You are crazy Mother, in battlefield
You roam round where dead bodies burn
With sprites of weird all spirit worlds;
You have bemused all creature realms
By casting toils of your marvel veil;
Who knows, (oh mother), Shiva's queen
What is your 'Self' and occult ends,—
You charm creatures with marvels sham,—
Do be kind oh Shiva's queen
Wipe out of this your lowly page
Chain of all his works and sins.

༤ Song 281[1] ༤

Who is that One who dwells upstairs,
Tie up, worshipful, oh, that One, sure,

witching colossus across the snow-white chest of her Lord Shiva who lies supine at her feet. The poet talks to her as the closest of kins,—his dear mother. The language of the song brooks no distance or conventional homage. He takes all the time complete liberties in talking in his various moods,—a kind of intimacy to which love alone is privy!

Lord Shiva is the supreme Absolute Divinity. He is amused at the Mother's (his own queen) wild warring stance. That is why, as if, he lies quiet still at her feet in fun and wonderment. And how wayward are the ways of Mother. The *burning ghats* and crematoriums are her favourite wonted haunts. And then who are her vassals and companions? It is the ghoulish denizens of the spirit world with dark powers and lurid horrors. And the Mother herself is the supreme sorcerer. She has cast her veil of strange marvel across all three worlds. No creature is ever free from the bewitching toils of the Queen of Illusion *(Mahamaya)* which eternally keep the creature-world bemused and ignorant of the Supreme Reality. But the poet knows the Truth. His prayer to the Mother is that she lift her veil and set him free from the *chain of works* and the termless cycles of incarnation in this sham world of desires and illusions.

[1]Spiritual seekers and Hindu sages proceed along different paths of progress. Some do worships and *yajnas* and propitiate the gods of their devotion, some renounce the world and take to *sannyasa* and hermitage. Still other, follow the Bhakti cult, singing and chanting the name of the Divine Image of the Absolute. The path of spiritual seeking is rugged and steep strewn with vicissitudes and hazards. The spiritual guru is a great help in all these pilgrimages to the Divine.

And take Her in into the hall of grace,
Of enlightenment and lore abstruse,—
Gurus you possess,—but whose, of what are they?
Some deign learning, lore some initiate
They are mere steering wheels they only show the way!
But the guru that is the real one
That is ordainer of all weal
That one dwells within the temple
   of your own heart concealed
In arrays of lotus blooms
   petals spread in legion domes,
Swarms of blossoms
   in her twin shining flames
As upon the slender nape
   of the tender lily bloom.

⚘ Song 282[1] ⚘

Take back your sack and gypsy gown
No more, pray, oh, mother Kali,
   benight and do me down;

    Sage poet Ramprasad is a *bhakta* (devotee) of Mother Kali. His relations with the Mother Goddess is close and intimate. He is the Mother's own child. And by virtue of his great love and devotion to the Mother, he often weeps, then often he prays to her for liberation and again he takes her to task for all his pains and agony in this miry world of desires and miseries. He is *sadhaka* in the Path of Tantra Philosophy. He has realized, witnessed Mother Goddess within himself. He does not need any other guru to tell him the way to liberation. The fulgent glow of enlightenment and the supreme bliss of the human soul dwell on the lotus seats within his own body itself.

    [1]This song has a rare diction and way with words. The poet knows, this world is a chimera. Sorrows and laughter, pain and pleasures, joy and despair—all come and go as shadows in a pantomime. Nothing is real. Nothing ever lasts. As the other poet had said, "It (this life) is a tale told by an idiot full of sound and fury signifying nothing."

    Truth is elsewhere, in the sublime bliss that is the feet of the supreme Goddess Mother, Kali. But then She is also the queen of sorcery. For, all these ephemeral world of phenomena is the sports and playground of Mother Shyama. All is her tricks and legerdemain. And her marvels and sports are infinite. The soul of the sage poet knows it all, and yet he is caught again and then again in the varied endless *maya* (illusions) of the sorceress Mother.

You sent me down to the world alone
    to play tricks and legerdemain,
Oh, tell me, Mother, Shiva's queen,
What was it, you did bethink,
You sent her down with endless tricks
    Her the queen of sorcery;
Bewitched and lost in marvels sham
Donning gypsy robes and form
However so I play on tricks
    again and then again,—
Mother, thou, thy sack unending,
The toys and tricks of trade go on,—
The sack is ne'er empty, ever, ever done!
I often bethink, I'll now refrain,
I'll call it a day and end the game,
I would tell the sorcerer queen
To take her leave and quit the scene;
But then, oh mother, alas, again,—
How strange is the charmer's chameleon chain,—
I fall victim to her legerdemain!
The fatal all-consuming charm,—
Oh, thou the royal sorcerer queen,
Whence but did'st thou all this glean?
Oh Shyama, mother, I'm so tired, spent
I no longer can tell thee, oh then,
The voice of the weary soul within,—
I so love, worship thee, oh Mother,
Is't that's how, thy son, thou dids't adorn,
Him in the robes of the gypsy clown!
Oh, thou mother, *gracious queen*,—
The name, 'Gracious Mother,' that very same
Oh Mother, Kali, you blasphemed!

❦ Song 283[1] ❦

Do tell me, what kind is this stance,—
The eyes,—they are moist filled with brine

    The poet is so tired and miserable. He prays to the goddess,—let her quit her tricks and marvels. She should have mercy and shower her grace to her devout child Ramprasad. Let her not play with him any more. Let her not blaspheme her own name as the 'gracious mother!'
    [1]The sage poet experiences marvels in his body and limbs. As the

The tongue,—it rings on Kali's name,—
You are a most learned wise far-seeing soul
Tell me, without a doubt, the final call!
Let me say what I so wish and yearn,—
This body true it is wet-wood in water sunk
Yet, that dull, rolling water burns in flame
In the fire in the tongue of Kali's name,
Furling eyes I dream of *Eternal Time,*
Lest slumber sneaking should invade betimes,—
Lord Shiva,—Ganga flows upon his crown,
The stream of water, mingling pure and clean,
Guru, he has sure avowed
The final shrine is the brow, sans doubt,
Of Ganga, Yamuna,—the sacred two-some streams,
The culmination and the end sublime
Prasad says,—my friend, oh mind
I beg of you, the last and only alms
Have me a place near you at the confluence.

❦ Song 284[1] ❦

Lift thy head, thou Lord supreme,
    thou Madan's foe, tormentor doom,
I must leave for father's home,

spiritual seeker proceeds advancing on the spiritual path strange powers, light and vision visit him. There is a shiver in the limbs. The eyes fill with tears with some kind of unknown emotions. The body is dull and earthy; but suddenly it is set aflame with the chanting of the name of Kali by the tongue.

The poet himself does not know the meaning of all this,—why these strange things happen to him. He asks the wiser souls to explain and tell him why. The Immanent Energy of Divinity is suddenly awakened within the body. And then all barriers are broken, all limits are washed away like bars of sand in the rushing waves of the sea. The poet now is face to face with the Supreme Lord Shiva as the symbol of Brahman on his brow. The two rivers the Ganges and the Yamuna,—they are images of the flow of infinite power which merge on the brow as the seat of supreme bliss and enlightenment.

This, the sage poet has learned from guru,—and there is no doubt about it. If the mind cooperates, in absolute meditation and ceaseless contemplation,—then the place of the human being at the seat of this confluence of bliss and light is assured indeed!

[1]This little lyric is one of the sweetest songs of the sage poet Ramprasad.

The prince of mountain, he is here
   to take me to his place along,
Vouchsafe thy consent, oh thou Lord,
   prince of *yogins* all supreme,
My father's here, he is immobile
   he tells me to speed up hasten along
The twin eyes, they are so tearful,
What, oh Lord Pashupati,
   is thy pleasure and thy will?
As days go on and on and on,
Mother, how she weeps along,—
I'll soon return my lord, sure I won't be long!

♀ Song 285[1] ♀

I'll let you know what's Mother's pain
By keeping your Ganesh here interned;
How it hurts the Mother's heart
You'll suffer yourself and know it then,

The pain and melancholy of parting of the daughter from her mother as she leaves for her husband's place is the theme of quite some songs of the peot Uma (the maiden name of Goddess Durga) is so beloved of mother Menaka. She is unreconciled! Her grief at the parting of the daughter for Her husband's place echoes the universal mother's grief when the young daughter is given away in marriage, and when, after short visits to Her mother's home She has to return to Her husband's home.

   This song embodies the pang of the husband (Lord Shiva) when his consort Uma, leaves him for Her mother's place. Lord Shiva's image in Hindu philosophy is that of the supreme Divinity, the symbol of all-eroding Eternal Time *(mahakala)*. He is the dread dour God of annihilation wild in dance,—just as he is the absent forgetful mendicant, half clad, most ascetic, the prince of *yogins*—and so easily propitiated with a *bael* fruit and some leaves of the *bael* (wood-apple) tree.

   In this song that same Lord Shiva is the loving husband, pining and so reluctant to let His consort (queen,—Goddess Durga) leave for Her mother's place. Uma consoles Her husband.

   His eyes are full of tears. Uma assures him that She won't be long away. Her Father, the Great Himalayas is waiting so anxiously. But without His (Lord Pashupati's) permission the wife cannot depart.

   The song is a unique human perception of the sweet love of the supreme Twin Divinities of Hindu philosophy.

   [1]Mother Menaka cannot bear to live without her daughter Uma or Gauri (the maiden name of Goddess Durga). But Uma is married to Lord

Who's there save you that is my own,—
The Mountain home was dark inane,
I'll not send you back again,
From Kailasa when He comes to take you home;
The son-in-law, He's very own son, as well
What harm if here He should come and dwell
Let him frolic round and err in joy and sports,
The King will proceed himself and Him escort;
He's so used to erring wandering here and there
Whoever calls Him beckons, to Him He repairs,
The royal King's-in-law son, He will here abide
I'd rejoice as I watch the two-some side by side.

♀ Song 286[1] ♀

By your ways and stance I now know for sure
You are most stingy, miserly demure,—
'You are bounteous to your devotee,' that 'say'
Of the sacred Vedas, it is mere hearsay;
In all the creature worlds that you revealed
To whom have you deigned vouchsafed,—oh tell me weal?
All you have given is thy marvel's veil,

Shiva who lives in his abode at Kailasa far into the recesses of the snowy mountains.

Menaka will take revenge on her daughter Uma for Her heartlessness in deserting Her Mother and going away to Her husband. Uma does not seem to know the pangs of the mother in parting from her child. Uma is now mother herself. Young Lord Ganesh is Her son. Menaka will take Ganesh away from Uma. Then will Uma herself know the agony of separation from her child.

Menaka has another idea. Shiva, her son-in-law,—He is very like her own son. Why can't He come over with Uma and children and live with Menaka in her vast palace of the Himalayan kingdom! Lord Shiva will be so welcome. Uma's father, the royal king of the Himalayas, he will go himself to warmly receive the son-in-law in their palace. Then Menaka would be so happy to have her beloved daughter with her. She would rejoice watching the two—Shiva and Uma together. Lord Shiva, He is by nature a wanderer,—roaming round the three worlds. He too, therefore would have no qualms abiding away from His own home.

The song is the simple tale of the mother's sorrows and desires round her little daughter who grows up and then goes away to her husband's place.

[1]This song is altogether in a different mood of the poet.

You have tied them all in pain, travail.
I hear, thy name renowned as 'Bounteous Queen'
(Yet) Shulapani, He begs for alms;
Sorely starved galling poison He consumed,
Unrobed you are bare with nothing on;
Kuvera's queen mother, thee they call
(Then) why thy nape adorns necklace of skulls,—
Deadly hooded snakes thy ornaments,
I now know (Oh mother), thy laurels, stunts

☙ Song 287[1] ☙

The gnawing endless pain and tears
Mother Tara, that you ceaseless shower,
I've learnt they are tokens all of your grace,
Oh thou, of grief and sorrows deliverer!
The Mother scolds the child
    for the sake of His boon and weal
That's how careless I carry so

    Mother Goddess Kali or Durga,—She is known everywhere as the gracious Mother, the queen of bounty. But the poet is disillusioned. He questions the Mother, where is Her grace and bounty. She is the mother of the worlds. Yet what has she done to its creatures? What weal and grace has She showered on them? She has merely eluded them all with Her charm, sinking them into grief and miseries of the world!
    Then, Her own husband, Lord Shiva, (Shulapani—lance in hand) He is a half-clad beggar ill-fed who consumed the poison that came out of the churning of the ocean in search of nectar, the poet claims that He did take poison from the agony of starvation. And then Mother herself,—She is bare, naked with ornaments of snakes round Her and necklace of human skulls round Her neck.
    How can Mother, whose ways and appearance are so uncouth and beggarly ever be called gracious and bounteous?
    [1]The song is a total submission of the poet to the gracious Mother.
    The poet suffers pain and miseries in this world. But then, he knows that all the grief and sorrow that he suffers is Mother's grace. The worldly man who is full of joy, immersed in pleasures he is apt to forget the Divine Goddess. Pain is a reminder that the world is no refuge of the human soul. The Goddess Mother, She alone is the house of bliss.
    The poet reminds himself that the Mother scolds and punishes the child for his good. The poet knows that his pains in the world are Mother's blessings. He carries them with joy and gratitude. The poet has his rare treasure, that is the name of the divine Goddess Mother. When he chants the name 'Tara' (Mother Goddess Kali) he is lost and overwhelmed within

the can of miseries and ill;
As I possess the treasure, one, supreme
The gem of Brahmamoyee's name,—
As I call you loud by Tara name
I lose myself in oblivion;
You are, oh, saviour of the lowly poor,
Of those who seek refuge the sustainer,—
I'm most depraved, I've sorely sinned,
That's why from you I'm lost and torn;
I'm your caged bird, your parrot pet
Whatever you teach I learn by rote,
Ram you have taught the 'Tara' name
That is why I 'Tara,' 'Tara' chant.

✽ Song 288[1] ✽

Howsoever I teach you, mind, alas, you ne'er learn,
You do not contemplate your most cherished end;
At the end of the day e'en in error, chance
Kali's name you forget to utter or to chant;
You had been a yogin when you were in the womb,
You had passion for pleasures the moment you were born,—
You were a soul of attachment shorn,
Steeped in elixir of Shyama's name,

himself. The poet knows that he has sinned, departed from his spiritual path; that is why he has not attained the sublime feet of the Supreme Goddess. In a spiritual seeker, this awareness and ceaseless agony for the Mother is worship indeed.

The poet knows and tells Mother that he is like the caged bird under Mother's complete command. Whatever he says, does and thinks,—that is ordained by her.

The mood of the poet is utter devotion and submission to the Mother. He gladly bears all the pains of this world, happy in his total bliss in which he is immersed as he chants the name of the Mother.

[1] The poet often talks to his errant mind. It is the mind that takes the human soul astray. The mind plays with the *gunas* of Nature and embroils the 'vital-soul' *(jivatma)* in the desires and cravings of this world.

The poet is most unhappy with the mind. Sunk in worldly pursuits, he (the mind) forgets to chant the name of Mother Kali. When the soul was unborn in the Mother's womb, it was a *yogin*, untrammelled by the toils of the world. As soon as he was born he became involved in the pursuit of worldly works, giving up the ambrosia of the Great Mother's name.

(But) you turned a seeker of fortunes, gain
This poor soul, he, most fervent pleads
Forswear you fancy with passion, greed;
Those six, they have their six-some ways
(Now) they hold you firm bewitched.
By the might of the senses
   as Lord of heavens
Now you are swollen vain
   with pride and fortunes,—
(But then), the crown and kingdom
   will lie low in dust
When all the ten senses
   lie supine inert!

⁕ Song 289[1] ⁕

Do burn the passions
   you will get perfect cleansing ash,—
You wash the mind
   (then) all shoals and sands,
   of the mind all stains

   The poet, humble as he is, pleads with the mind that he forswear all desires and cravings of the world. Unhappily, the mind has been plagued by the company of the six-some evil companions. These are the enemies of the human nature and dwell within the body. These are *kama* (desire); *krodha* (rage and anger); *lobha* (greed and avarice); *moha* (confusion and ignorance); *mada* (vanity and ego); *matsaryya* (hate and jealousy). These negative forces within man are Nature's creation. They ceaselessly play with the mind swaying him from the path of bliss and light. The poet warns the mind that he thinks he has achieved supreme powers with the help of the sensuous organs but these will perish with the death of the mortal body.
   This song carries the message of the cream of penance and spiritual purification.
   The poet tells himself (his own mind), let the desires be set on fire. As desires and cravings are burned they will leave ashes. And this ash will be a good detergent, a cleansing material for purifying the mind. And when the mind is so washed clean, all perils and hazards will vanish. Then the cleansing water must be soft and clear. Such water is there in the Kali-pool *(Kalidaha)*. The reference is to the name of Mother Goddess Kali, in which all stains and slime will dissolve. Then the cleansing mixture must be boiled in the way of the washerman. The fuel wood should be the sins and vices. The vat and the vessel in which the boiling will be done is man's own consciousness.

They'll all vanish, melt awashed as trash.
Let's go, repair to the Kali-pool
The water there will clean, wash well
(Then) light the fire with the woods of sins,
In the vat of consciousness boil in kilns;
Neelambara—he is tired worn
It is nigh futile to tell the mind
Is there a foe beyond the fold of mind
He is either gold or useless trash.

♀ Song 290[1] ♀

What fears oh mind, so why bemoan
Durga, Durga,—chant the 'name'
She is saviour Queen of immortal gods
Extirpator of the demon hordes;
Of Death, his dread puissance She usurps,
Of the weak, infirm, She is support;
The name so balmy blissful cool
Turns death so gracious, cause of weal;
Prasad is sad so melancholy
Oh mind, thou truant ceaselessly,—
The forest-fire, it's ne'er tranquil still

However the poet is sad. He has been telling his mind all these means and methods of self-purification. But then, the mind doesn't seem to obey. The mind, alas, may be the worst of enemies, just as he can be the best of friends of the human being.

Poet habitually takes scenes say, the village fair or kite-flying and events (e.g., a man who is just dead) and common trades of the artisan (e.g., the trade of the fisherman, the potter, the washerman and so on) and turn them into symbolic process of spiritual pursuits. Just as Lord Sri Ramakrishna (about a century later) was the spiritual teacher of the common man, Ramprasad was bard and singer of rustic songs that had taken ascetic search for spiritual emancipation to the homes and hearths of the common villagers and ordinary householders of the world.

[1] The poet assures his own mind. The mind is ever errant and worried. The poet tells the mind to forsake his fear. He should chant the name of Goddess Durga. The sublime Goddess is the saviour of the gods and the slayer of the demons. She is the subduer of death. She is also the might and safety of the weak. As one chants the name of Mother there is no fear of death. Death itself is then a bliss. But then Prasad is sad because his mind is so fickle and unstable. It is like the wild flames which consume the whole forest.

It razes verdant woods, burns sylvan vales.

❦ Song 291[1] ❦

Thou hast me bewitched becharmed,
Of all three worlds thou enchanting Queen;
On the Lotus sublime in Muladhar
Thou art resonant in the tune of lyre,
Thou dost orchestrate the body's tune
In sushumna and other instruments
In the varied *gunas* of Tantra profound
Thou dost roam in *all three sounds;*
The image of Bhairava in the inner realm
On the lotus of *sixteen leaves,* the gracious Queen;
In Manipura, thou art the sound of heaven,
In the spring of seasons, the fulgent radiance;

Unceasing desires and passions set the mind in constant turmoil. Such passions and craze are like the wild conflagration of the forest fire. It consumes peace and weal of the human being.

[1]The song is an esoteric description of the various stages of spiritual progress of the sage on the path of Tantra philosophy.

The Tantrashastra is most scientific which works on the vital energy enshrined but dormant within the human body. The coiled seat of energy (Kulakundalini) is located at the bottom of the spinal cord just above the anus. As the sage practises penance, *asanas* this dormant energy is opened up. The human being has strange perceptions,—occult tunes and light—as the energy goes on upward toward the crown of the spine.

There are six seats of the vital energy along the spinal cord. The Tantrashastra is a system of penance for rousing this infinite energy that dwells within the human body. Within the spinal cord there are three arteries—Ida, Pingala and Sushumna. Ida runs along the left side of the spine, Pingala along the right and in-between dwells *Sushumna.* These three arteries together consititute the core of the arterial system of a human body. Within the arterial channel there are six wheels. *Sushumna* begins at the bottom of the spine just above the anus and proceeds upward to the crown of the head. Here it dwells coiled up like the coiled serpent in the wheel which is called Muladhar. By the practice of *Pranayam,* the penance and cultivation of the vital winds, the profound energy of Kulakundalini, (the serpent energy) is roused. Then it rises up along the spine and as it happens, the sage progressively experiences strange powers and bliss. When this *coiled energy,* in its upward journey, reaches the crown of the head the sage attains eternal bliss and liberation. The Yogin through penance and practice of the vital winds (*Pranayam*) rouses this dormant energy. The sages along the Tantrashastra have special Tantric *asanas* and practices to reach the same enlightened status.

In the occult chamber of the soul
The lilt of purest music rolls
In pitch and tune and pause and tone
Piercing trinal seven realms of sound.
In thy numbing toils thou sorcerer Queen
You hold fast embroiled in no time;
As truth in the world of thoughts you shine
Frozen, still, the lightning stands.
Sri Ramprasad says,
   The truth, it's ne'er steadfast
The veil of the Reality
   To that I'm tied true and fast.

The six wheels within the arteries in the spine are:

1. *Muladhar:* It is located at the spinal root just above the anus. Its form is a four-petalled lotus. It is the dwelling house of Lord Shiva. The eternal energy is coiled up with its mouth on the source of elixir from the organ of Shiva. The energy lies dormant or sleeping at this stage.
2. *Swadhishthana:* This wheel is located above Muladhar, at the bottom of Lord Shiva's genetic organ. This is a white lotus with six petals. It is the seat of Lord Varuna and the wild energy of the vast moving waters.
3. *Manipur:* This wheel is located at the bottom of the navel. It is a scarlet lotus with ten petals. Here dwells the power of the God of Fire.
4. *Anahata:* This seat is within the heart. This is the lotus wheel of sombre, grey with twelve petals. This is the seat of power of the winds.
5. *Bishuddha:* This is the lotus wheel in the region of the throat. This is a blue lotus with sixteen petals. It is the dwelling house of Lord Shiva and the power of the God of Fire.
6. *Ajnachakra:* This wheel is located between the two eyebrows on the forehead. This is the lotus seat yellow and with two petals where dwells Lord Shiva in the form of his genital organ as the seed of creation.

   A little above this lotus seat dwells the blooming lotus of thousand petals, which is the seat of the Supreme Brahman. This is the Sahasrara lotus.

   Thus the Sahasrara, thousand-petalled lotus is separate and dwells above the six wheels within the spinal cord.

   Sushumna is the primal channel which carries the infinite energy of Brahman. Ida and Pingala are born of the human system and they sheath and uphold the supreme energy from its origin at Muladhar upward till it reaches the seat of Brahman. According to Tantra Shastra these upward moving stages of the spiritual seeker is known as the piercing of the six-some wheels till the sage reaches final bliss and

♀ Song 292[1] ♀

In the world's realm of thoughts
   Thou art the royal Queen
As if in the white frosty lake
   The blue azure lotus bloom
The twin blessed feet, they shine
   Surpassing the nascent purple sun,
The array of nails as crescent moons
   Cloakless naked maiden form;
Thighs as buxom banana plant,
   Navel deep as lake profound,
Legion demon-hinds adorn
   Round the waist as ornament;
What bowl of nectar grace benign
   The twin bosoms full and round,
Which, e'er savouring, gods and men,
They relish bliss and joy sublime.
In the four hands beam and shine

    liberation. Ramprasad had reached this final stage of fulfilment and sublime divine bliss.
   [1] The song is an example of the highest mystic poetry in devotional literature.
    The Hindu image of Goddess Mother Kali is that of a buxom maid with an enigmatic facial expression. The stance of the Goddess is of a warrior woman. Mother Kali is symbol of supreme Power and Energy. She is Chandi (the Dread Power *mahashakti*) who is the slayer of the demonic forces of evil. She is the extirpator of all that is dark and demoniac. But then She is also the Mother of all phenomenal worlds. She is full of grace. She has four hands which carry the open scimitar, the weapon of war and destruction; She is also the epitome of grace with Her hand upturned in blessings and bounty. She wears a wreath of severed human skulls, symbolizing the mortal forces of the transient world. She wears venomous snakes as ornaments. Then Her mount is Mahakala (Lord Shiva) who lies supine beneath her mobile twin feet; the symbol is the dual play of creation and annihilation that goes on eternally across Termless Infinite Time.
    To the casual eye of the thoughtless ignorant observer, the image might strike as one of a lurid Primitive Goddess that strikes awe and terror to the human world. But the sage poet Ramprasad knows. The song is a rich poetic critique of the apparent enigma of the Mother's image.
    Mother Kali is the Queen of thoughts. She is the spring and fountain of all desires and wishes that flow ceaselessly within the human being. Her twin feet are aglow as the fulgent sun. Her buxom bosom is the bowl

The scimitar skulls and precious boons,—
Thee, tormentor, dread, of evil foes
    E'er saviour of the devoted one;
Shyama, She, face awesome dread
    Fanning fearsome tongue in deep scarlet,
Teeth, they shine as pilgrim shrines
    In loud lilt of laugh sublime!
The Sun, the Moon, the flaming Fire,
    They beam aglow in the trinal eyes
Vermilion charming on the brow
    Echoing the lambent half-moon glow.
From off the twin pendant aural lobes
    Two nascent corpses dance and swing
The heavenly flash e'er plays around
    Across the e'er smiling lips;
The tresses flow in cascading rolls
    They kiss the feet low down below
As if the drunken bumble bees
    Surround the fragrant lotus bloom,
Complexion dark as young rain clouds
    Fountain of rare unequalled charm
The treasure supreme of sages all
    Of Yogindra, of his bosom's gem.
Thou Mother Kali, dread of Death
    Panacea of trinal pains
Thou, oh, Prasad's deliverer queen
    Thou the Image of Brahman Absolute!

Song 293[1]

At long last now I have thought it right
My own salvation I'll find it out;

of nectar that is the ultimate home and refuge of gods and men. She is at once the refuge and solace of all who surrender to Her grace and the dread tormentor of the wicked and the evil.

And then the poet perceives the overwhelming splendour of the Mother's Image. Her hairs are like cascading darkness; Her eyes are blazing like the Sun and Lambent as the Moon. The long dark hairs kiss the purple feet as the swarthy bumble bee kisses the blooming flowers for honey and elixir.

[1] The poet is aggrieved at his own Mother Goddess Kali. He has worshipped, adored and loved Her all his life with single-minded devotion.

I won't, no longer call you 'Mother,'—
Step-mother, to her, I'll now repair,
By whose sight and holy touch I'll attain,
My desire seeking cherished end;
Being as I am, thine very own son
Should I take refuge of step-mother mine,
It's your shame disgrace you'll then discern
And pull me on to thee only then alone.

❦ Song 294[1] ❦

What fears have I, oh Death, of thee,—
Within whose heart dwelleth She,
Of swaying stresses, abode in the *burning ghat*?
I'll ever chant and sing 'Kali,' 'Kali's' name
Thou'rt powerless to thwart, contend the same,—
In Kali's name I'll sound the trumpet,
Fear of Death I'll waive and spurn disdain.
When from Death the call should come
I will show the letter then, by Kali signed,
The letter's content as 'he' will ken,
He will cower and slowly then return;
The son of Kali,—twice born, callow young,
Being mother, oh Mother, thou

Yet, for this supreme love and loyalty to the Mother, he has been deprived of Her love and grace.

The poet is now an angry child. He warns the Mother, if She should neglect Her child as this, he would shift his loyalty to the step-mother, the holy river Ganges. Mother Ganges is known in Hindu mythology as the consort of Lord Shiva. She dwells on the plaited hairs on the crown of the great sage, Lord Shiva, who is also the Lord consort of Mother Goddess Kali. That is how the Goddess Mother Ganges is the step-mother of the sage poet Ramprasad.

But then the poet's quarrel with his own mother, Goddess Kali is only a sham show of anger. He knows, as he should shift his love and loyalty to the step-mother, his own mother Kali would become jealous. It would be such a shame for the Mother that Her own son (the sage poet) should desert her. It is then that She would relent, and turn Her grace to the aggrieved son and lift him on to Her lap. And that indeed is the real craving of the poet. His threatened turning to the step-mother is only a ploy to draw the attention of his own mother whose love and grace is the final aim of the sage poet.

[1]It was Francis Bacon who said, "Man fears Death as children fear

Forswear thy such hostile stance;
I'll repose, safe, on the mother's lap
Who's there who would tear away me thence?

ꕥ Song 295[1] ꕥ

On the earth the joyous blissful soul is one
    Who knows the queen of bliss supreme,
That one, he never proceeds
    To pilgrimage or holy shrines,
Save his ears embalmed by hymns
    And chants of Kali's name
For worships vespers he has little charm
    (Let) what Kali does, be done, he deems.
The one who has done Kali's feet
    The sole and lone essence,
Who is oft amiss forgetful absent
    Of caring worldly things
He will reach the shores of the ocean world,—
How but he would lose his roots, can you divine?
To such one as this, Ramkrishna says,—
'Why heed others' abuse, be ashamed

darkness." Death is the fear of the unknown which is the product of ignorance.

Hindu philosophy does not suffer such ignorance. The Vedantas and the Upanishads have declared that the soul of man has no death. What dies is the coarser physical body of the human being. The human soul is a parcel of the Absolute who is infinite.

Mother Kali is the image of the Infinite Being. The supreme Being is still, inert, transcendent. Nature is the mobile Infinity, revealed everywhere, pervading and immanent in the phenomenal worlds. This Nature, this infinite supreme Energy is Goddess Mother Kali. She is the sole refuge of the human soul. She is the supreme Divinity that dwells as the 'soul' in every creature. And She is revealed and attained through devotion, love, and contemplation.

The sage poet has installed Mother Goddess Kali within himself; He has touched the pool of eternal bliss. Therefore, the poet is beyond the reach of Death whose domain is the mortal mutating phenomenal world. He can claim the physical body of man but the poet is safe in the lap of his Infinite Mother.

[1] The Hindu shastras—the Vedas and Brahmanas, mandate various methods and rituals of worship. There is *yajna*, giving of alms, pilgrimages, penance and austerity and so on.

The eyes half-closed, lost slumberous
Drunk with the elixir of Kali's name!

☙ Song 296[1] ☙

Listen, oh my mind,—
Confecting sweet delicacies should you divine,—
Then, oh, Kasi's sugar,—most sweet is Kali's name
In the vat of your open mouth,—pour it on
Then counting letters of the alphabet
Array them all in the ordered set;
Then renouncing sloth, languor idleness
Move your tongue fast ceaseless in harness,—
In the bi-petalled wheel between the brows
Hold the primal seeds of elixir,—
Then drink off it, so be immortal, then
Set up abode in the deathless blissful realm!

The sage poet knows better. The ultimate bliss is the Mother Goddess Kali, who is the Queen of supreme bliss and joy. The sage and the seeker who knows this and chants Kali's name and ceaselessly thinks of her, he enjoys bliss and salvation. Such a person does not go for pilgrimage. He does not do any kinds of rituals, vespers or morning *puja* but spends all his time in thought of Goddess Kali and singing Her name. He has set his home on the feet of Kali; he forgets his daily chores and is absent in worldly affairs. Such a person has his mooring firmly set and he will cross the world's ocean, safe and secure.

Such a person need not worry or care about what others say of him. He is lost in his own thoughts and meditations with his eyes half-closed and careless unconcern for all things of the world.

[2]The poet here weaves his spiritual counsel to his mind round the symbols of the confectioner's process of making sweets.

The confectioner has a vat in which the syrup is boiled and thickened. The confectioner's vat is the hollow of his mouth. Sugar is to be put into the vat. Mother Kali's name is sweet and mellow and it is the sugar. Plenty of that sugar must be put into the mouth. Then the sugar in the vat must be constantly moved and churned with the ladle. The tongue is the churning ladle. And then Kali's name will be constantly rotated and turned by the tongue. The poet will chant and sing the Mother Goddess' name. And from out this constant churning in the confectioner's vat will come out the cream and nectar which will accumulate in the bi-petalled lotus wheel located between the two eye-brows on the forehead. This lotus wheel is the seat of Mother Goddess as the image of the Absolute Brahman. The human soul as it dwells on this seat of Brahman dissolves into Him as part of the Absolute Infinity.

Song 297[1]

Ignorant my absent mind, that's why
It would Mother's image build with clay;
Mother maiden, is She an earthen girl!
How futile, with clay and clods I ever toil;
Scimitar in hand and wreath of skulls
That Mother,—is She e'er an earthly girl,—
Mere earthen clay,—could it soothe and balm
The mind's pain and the singeing flame?
Mother's complexion's dark, I'm told
That darkness yet illumines the world;
Is it that, that dark Mother's sombre hue
Can e'er be etched on the earthen clay?
Mother's eyes,—they are three-some fare
The Sun, the Moon, the flaming Fire
Is there any one such artisan
Who would sculpt such another one?
Kali, extirpator of evils, sins
Is She mud and clay and straw and hemp?
She will dissolve erase mind's taints and slime
To Prasad revealing her Kali's form.

[1]They say, Hindus are idol worshippers. In the Chicago Parliament of Religions in 1893, Swami Vivekananda had done some profound explaining of the meaning and symbolism of the Hindu idols of gods and goddesses. A dark speck on the Western sky in the month of Baisakha presages a thunder storm. The distant inaudible faintest simmer and rumbling forewarns the devastating earthquake. That is the nature of Energy in its concentrated essence.

Long before Swamiji or Sri Ramakrishna, in fact from the hoary ages of Hindu religious philosophy this *consciousness* pervades all imageries, images and idolatry of the Hindu gods and goddesses. That is how the Vedic religion and the Hindu pantheon of gods and goddesses are so different from the Greek and Roman deities. The Vedanta concept of Brahman, the supreme Absolute, Purushottama or the Supreme Being of the Geeta,—it is not the same as pantheism as understood by the Western metaphysics. Then it is not the same as monotheism, or henotheism or any other 'theistic' pattern conceived in the religious discussions in the world body of religions. The duality of the Absolute in His simultaneous transcendence and immanence in this phenomenal worlds is peculiar to Hindu thoughts. Savants,—in the East and the West,—have read in Hinduism the 'Mother-Seed of Religions and Religious Thoughts' of the world.

Song 298[1]

On mind, why but all these worries thine
Call 'Kali' once and then sit down in trance,
Should'st thou worship with pomp and loud fanfare,
Pride, vain glory clouds the mind's subconscious sphere,
Do thou worship, lonely behind the veil,
No one else will know for sure in the world,
Bronze or Stone or idol of earthen cast
What need hast thou for such relief and bust—
Make Her in thy bosom's lotus throne;
Sun-dried rice and offering banana ripe,
What use all thy trappings, array of things?
You offer, feed Her, devotion's elixir,
Propitiate, please Her within thy mind alone!
What use chandeliers, loud luminous lamps
What would you do with such show and brilliance,—
Why not set alight, the jewel candle of they mind,
Let it burn then shine lambent day and night;
Sheep, goat, buffalo and such others all
Why must thou sacrifice them at all;
Rather sacrifice the sinful six-some foes,
Hail 'Kali,' 'Kali' as you cry, extol;
Prasad says,—Oh trumpets, drums

Sage poet knows, the idol of the Mother Goddess is not of mud and straw and bamboo sticks (the basic materials of the frame of the idol). The Mother is not Mrinmoyee—an image built of mud and clay. Her idol is merely a symbol. The essence of the image is the supreme enlightenment and consciousness that permeates the created worlds.

The song enshrines the cream of Hindu metaphysics.

[1]This song is an eloquent message of Hindu worship and spiritualism. Like other religions, Hinduism too has many rituals and customs and ways of worship enshrined in the *Yajurveda* and other scriptures. *Yajnas* and penance were quite popular in religious ceremonies.

However, for the devotee and the spiritual seeker no elaborate preparations, illumination and music is necessary. Only devotion and meditation of the divinity is enough. The poet tells his mind, it has no need for fanfare or decoration of the image of the Goddess Kali as it worships Her. The mother's image in the mind is enough. She should be installed on the lotus seat within the heart and given offering of the elixir of devotion. Ceremonial sacrifice of animals should be shunned; instead the six-some foes (*kama, krodha, lobha, moha, mada,* and *matsaryya*) within man should be sacrificed at the altar of the mother Goddess.

What profit thine such loud alarm?
Call 'jai Kali,' loud as you clap your hands
On her twin gracious feet instal your mind.

☙ Song 299[1] ☙

This time, Kali, I'll thee devour
(Oh, I'll devour thee, I'll eat you up
    Oh, gracious queen of the wretched poor);
Tara, oh, I was born in the wicked fatal star
Who in that dark astral conjunction's born
    He turns devourer of his mother own,—
This time either you eat me up
    Or, Mother, else I devour thee
One of two, sure, I will accomplish;
I'll gorge the mincemeat of the curry
    Of the apparitions and evil sprites,
I'll snatch from thee thy wreath of skulls
For savour as salt and pickles spice,

Then, the lamp of the mind should be lit with the light of consciousness; luminous lamps and chandeliers are useless.

Prasad assures his mind that no pomp, show or fanfare,—no illumination or beat of drums are required. Only sing and chant the name of Mother and clap your hands in tune with it. That indeed is the most sublime worship.

[1] The poet here is an altogether different mood. It is one rare element in the various songs of Ramprasad that he shifts relations with his Goddess Mother Kali. He is sometimes angry with the Mother, often weeps as the whining child. He takes the combatant's stance and fights his battle out with Mother. He is often overwhelmed by Her charm and grace. And then he uses language and allegories from commonplace life. It is sometimes the Court of Law, or the scene and metaphor of kite-flying. He takes the symbol of the merry-go-round or the potter's wheel. He devotes a song to the image of the fisherman casting his net wide in the pool of the world. Yet everywhere the words and the metaphors are charged with the inner spiritual symbolism. The poet was a scholar well-versed in Bengali, Sanskrit and Persian. He was a liberated soul and reached the end of Tantra *sadhana*. When he chooses he uses a diction which is highly resonant and Sanskritized. But mostly, the words, rhythm and diction echo the rustic dialect of the people. Many of his words are used in 'pun,' carrying double or multiple sense.

In this song the poet warns the mother that he would swallow Her up. He would join a battle with the Mother when it would end with either one gorging up the other. But then, he would not allow mother to sink

I'll paint my hands and face, all limbs
With deep and dark and swarthy hue,
When Death will come and tie me tight
I'll dye his face with that inky hue.
I say, mother, I'll eat you up, devour and swallow,
Yet I won't put you deep inside my belly,
Here in my lotus heart Thee I'll install
And worship you in my mind's inner hall
If it's so, should I swallow ink, then,
I might get stuck in Death's domain,
What fears have I in that—for then
I would call, 'Kali,'—and Death defy.
Ramprasad,—he is Kali's son
I would tell him that true and well,—
I will either win or lay down my life,
Sure, I'll let it happen what it will!

☙ Song 300[1] ☙

Oh mind, why not have a game of dice?
You cast the dice so quick, oh mind
That all desires melt away;
You set up the board in Durga's name
In the chequered homes arrange the pawns,
At seventeen, eighteen throw the dice

down to his stomach. He would hold Her within his heart and install Her on the lotus seat in his bosom. And he would prepare various dishes and cuisines with the mother's companions of the spirit world. He would also use the human heads (image of mother Kali is adorned with a necklace of bleeding severed human heads) in his cooking as spices and satellite dishes.

And he would dare Death (Kala) with the name and trappings of Mother Kali.

The poet here asks the mother to the final battle of life. Victory or defeat,—either way the poet wins.

'The song is a fancy of the poet in which (as often) he talks to his own mind. The symbol is of a 'game of dice' which is a favourite foil of the poet's portrait of his devotional desires.

The stake in the 'game' that he suggests to his mind is wiping out the last trace of desires. The dice-board should be set up and fenced with the name of Durga. Then the dice must be cast with a high stake. Three dies together are cast. Each one has the highest value of six. Thus the highest possible stake in one throw of dice is 3 x 6 = 18.

Shatter, break Death's vested house.
Should you six-and-twenty throw the dice
The game will be lost in erring device;
At home the six-some foes are there,
They will ridicule and laugh and jeer;
The day's lost if the die is not cast,
(And) if you play, you err, a cruel lot;
Oh cast the die in Tara's name
Build your castle in the dice game.

❦ Song 301[1] ❦

Oh mind, get wont to the saviour's feet
If thou should'st sail safe across
The fearsome sea of dread, torment,—
Those feet, they are vanquisher of Death,—
Those contemplate, oh mind, in safe retreat;
The treasure of which feet is treat
Of the Trident Lord supreme, as if,
Beyond, alas, of temporal reach;
Chant shrill and loud, chant, oh tongue,

But if the die is cast wrong and the right face does not turn up then the foes within the human being, they would exult and take the upper hand. Sage poet Prasad warns his Mind to play well and safe. The name of Durga and casting the dice with the name of Tara is most essential in winning the stake of life. Then alone the human being can destroy the *niche* of Death and escape his overwhelming clutches.

[1]This song is a lyric of devotion of the poet to his Mother Goddess Shyama.

Mother's feet are the saviour, the safe sailing craft across this world's ocean of peril. One who dwells on the Mother's feet he escapes death— for Mother herself is the Supreme Queen whom Death serves as slave and servant. The human mind is ever beset with worries and agony. Man is ever afraid of death, who is lurking close to him. But one who installs his whole thoughts on the twin feet of the Great Goddess is freed from fears and dangers.

Mother's feet is the treasure-house. One who attains those feet is freed from the 'sense of seeking.' He then has no desires, no craving, no charm for worldly possessions, joys and sorrows.

The poet enjoins on his tongue that it should constantly chant and sing the name of Mother Kali. Prasad is eager to drink deep off the elixir of Mother's name. That way he has no doubt that he will gain all his desires and fulfilment.

Shyama on Her seat of corpse, Lord Shiva's Queen,
Thee I worship, adore and chant
To Prasad, deign thy boon, oh, gracious Queen!

⚘ Song 302[1] ⚘

Mother, art thou everywhere!
Thou dwell'st vast in cosmic form
In the atoms thou, in the tiny acorn;
Whichever way, when I roam around
Whenever, where I look and ken
I behold discern and find you there
Mother's there, thou, oh, everywhere.
Be it the vastest universe there
Or water, earth, the winds and fire
Mother, they are all image of thine,—
The limitless worlds all universe,
Be it the mountains, creatures marine.
The winged birds, the earthly beings
Prasad kens thee in all creature worlds
Mobile, inert still in the charming vales.

[1]The song embodies the highest Hindu metaphysics enshrined in the Vedantas and the *Srimadbhagavad Geeta.*

The perception of the Brahman, the Supreme Absolute Divinity in Hindu philosophy, is a strange dual image. The Supreme is transcendent. The Absolute Brahman is still, quiet, immobile, silent, sans beginning and termless, indestructible, immutable and changeless—the Akshara Brahman. This is the undimmed, undying, still Energy that is the seed and origin of all manifest universes.

The other image of the Brahman is the dual kinetic form of this Supreme Energy—the *Mahashakti.* This Energy is the Immanence of the mobile Energy of the Brahman. She is Mahakali, the Great Goddess Durga or Kali. This Energy is ever mobile, ever-mutating, pervading every movement, every single creature of the universe,—animate or inanimate, mobile or inert, big or small—from the vastest to the tiniest manifestation of the revealed worlds.

The poet discerns this Absolute truth. He finds her, the supreme immanent Goddess, everywhere—in hills and dales, on land and waters, in every creature in every form of revelation in all three worlds.

And it is this perception where there is increasing harmony between the findings of modern science—the Quantum Mechanics and Particle Physics on the one hand and the Hindu metaphysical literature on the other.

❦ Song 303[1] ❦

Oh mind, even in error, absent mind
Can't you see your errant way?
Lest you should lose sight of your roots,—and then
Do go about in search of it;
Brothers, friends, wife and sons
All your other kinsmen then,—
The same you contemplate as Mother's form!
The tiniest atom, the termless seed,
On which all forms are built, revealed,—
They all unite and must then decay
Bethink, who is one's own and who away;
Sri Ramprasad,—he does proclaim
In dales and banks you roam around
Brahmamoyee—She is there in every form
She's the seed essence, you do divine

❦ Song 304[2] ❦

Oh my mind, must you take some potion, then,
There's Srinath Datta,—He's *Patal Sattva,*—

[1]The poet here, as it is often his wont, remonstrates with his mind. The human mind is notoriously fickle. It is restless and error-prone constantly playing with the three *gunas* (qualities) of Nature's illusions—*sattva, rajas,* and *tamas.*

The mind misleads the 'being' *(jivatma)* enshrined in the human body, the soul; this soul is the seed and origin which is parcel of the Absolute Divinity. The poet pleads with his mind that is must not forget its origin. The mind is the source of desires and attachments in this world. The love and affection of man for wife and children, for friends and kith and kin—it is the property of this mind who suffers illusions and is caught in the Nature's toils of such bonds and attachments.

But the poet has a solution. Mother Goddess,—she is immanent, She is everywhere, in every creature. Let the mind behold Her in whomsoever it loves most. Let it not forget, that She (the Goddess Mother) is the seed and origin of all. She is the element from out of which comes all shapes and forms and thoughts and emotions. These forms and passions all arise out of the elements and then, soon, melt and dissolve into the original Infinite.

Let the mind go about everywhere but let it remember and perceive the Goddess Mother in everything that it beholds.

[2]This world is a place of perils and pestilence. Desires and temptations,

That recipe you seek from time to time,
All good fortunes,—them you banish send away
Adore, worship Lord Mrityunjaya,—
It is then alone, Ramprasad says,
You will be cured of the world—disease.

♀ Song 305[1] ♀

My mind oh, it so yearns to go, resort
To the garden of joy and bliss;
Thou art, Mother, Queen of thoughts,
Why not to this mind, thou deign'st solace?
Varanasi, by Shiva installed
That Shiva, on thy feet he dwells
Yet, for Kasi the mind so yearns
How is it I stay behind?
Thou the image of bounty Queen
Five *crosas* beneath thy feet supine
With Ganga, Manika, thy nails, they shine
On thy twin feet the purple glow
Of Varuna, Asi, casts halo

worries and attachment,—ceaseless longings for worldly gains,—and then hate, jealousy, despair and chagrin,—all beset the mind and destroy peace and tranquillity of the human being.

The poet finds this worldly existence as disease and dangers. Therefore, antidotes must be found for immunity and cure from infection and ailment. The poet suggests to his mind the kind of potion that it must use. There is a great panacea—a herbal kind of medicine *(patal sattva)* by Doctor Srinath Datta. The name of the Doctor is a play on words. Srinath is the name of the Divinity. The mind should take doses of the name of the Great God, that should save him from infection and cure him of all disease.

And then a patient should practise austerity in food and habits. He must avoid pleasures and all excesses. He must practise penance and abstinence. He must abjure craze for fortunes and a loud life. Lord God Shiva, and Goddess Mother Kali,—they are the refuge from Death. Let the mind pay heed to worship and meditation of supreme Divinity.

[1] Sage poet Ramprasad is a devotee of Mother Goddess Kali. His relation with the Goddess is that of the child with the mother. But then, the poet is not an orthodox or parochial worshipper of a personal god or goddess. He is a philosopher with full consciousness of the immanence and transcendence of the Absolute Godhead. Mother Goddess appears

Let thee grant, I behold and ken
Thy lotus feet with eyes mine own.
Prasad bides with grief beset
Soothing him is becoming, meet,—
What profit repairing to holy Puri town!
Do vouchsafe, thou, Mother sublime
   At the time when this life doth end
The vital wind, let it quit in fine
     Cracking through the roof of the helm of crown.

❦ Song 306[1] ❦

I die of the load of thankless work in thrall,
In my purse I have no means none, no wherewithals;
Myself, I am the common porter
   I work for others, vain futile
I work each day on daily wages,
     The five elements,—they ursurp it all;
The five elements, the six-some foes
     The senses-ten,—they are all arrant rogues;

in an image of Kali or Shyama but She is the symbol of Divinity,—who is one and the same as the Absolute Brahman.

   The poet is in search of bliss and emancipation. In the Hindu religion, the spiritual seeker proceeds on pilgrimage and Varanasi is one such foremost shrine. Varanasi (Banares), is the dwelling and abode of Lord Shiva. There also abides Goddess Kali, in the image of Annapurna, the Supreme bounteous Goddess Queen. The rivers Asi and Varuna bathe the two banks of the place, as if washing the vermilion feet of Mother goddess Annapurna. The poet often pines for that holy place which appears in his spiritual vision as the ultimate of emancipation. But then as he reflects, Lord Shiva himself lies supine holding on to the feet of the goddess mother and Prasad is her child. Why is it then that he should move about to Kashi or Puri (another holy shrine) when the two sublime feet of the mother are in his possession.

[1]The song is the poet's introspection of the futility of the works, worries and anxiety of this worldly life.
   This body and the physical world is composed of the five coarser elements,—earth, water, fire, the wind, and space. And then within the human body, commanding the errant mind, are the six-some foes,— *kama* (desire and lust), *krodha* (anger and rage), *lobha* (greed and avarice), *moha* (error and confusion), *mada* (ego and pride), and *matsaryya* (hate and jealousy). These are the driving forces that move and control the thoughts, desires and actions of the human being. The 'self,' as such, the soul of the being is thus tormented biding its time in utter slavery of

They, none, no one, heed none of them,
My days, alas, oh, lost and waste,
As the one who is sightless blind,
   As he his steering staff regains
He holds on to it fast secure,—
That's how, likewise, I'd hold fast, Mother,
(Yet) oh, it slips, escapes the clutch,
   It's my fault, sinner for sure I am such;
Prasad pleads, oh Brahmamoyee,—why not—
   Oh the bond of works, pray, cut the knot
Do vouchsafe, thou, Mother sublime
   At the time when this life doth end
The vital wind, let it quit in fine
   Cracking through the roof of the helm of crown.

⚘ Song 307[1] ⚘

The elephant queen wild in must
Dancing naked roars rushing past;
The dense dark heaps of tresses entwine
Caressing the twin speeding feet along;
The nascent morning rays shoot off the array of nails,
Behind the dancing feet
   Lotus blossoms off the trail,

the five elements and the six-some foes within the human body. The poet is conscious of the error and the futility of his worldly works and pursuits. That is why often he seeks to free himself from these turmoils and hold on to the feet of the Goddess Mother. But then he is ever frustrated and carried away by the turbulence.

The poet's prayer to his Mother Goddess, as the image of the Absolute, is that She vouchsafe and free him from this eternal bondage of works. She should grant that as he quits this life, the Vital 'self in him should melt and dissolve in the Infinite Divinity.

[1] The song is a portrait of Goddess Kali wild in her warring stance as She roams round the worlds, annihilating the demonic spirit of evil. The image of Goddess Kali in Hindu mythology is of a graceful swarthy buxom woman, all naked with loose long flowing tresses overwhelming her limbs to down below Her waist and entrapping the thighs.

Her movement and gait is like that of a wild queen elephant in must. Barebodied as the dark rain-clouds She stalks as a towering column swaying in war-dance. The loose locks play around Her thighs and legs; the nails of the toes are dazzling scarlet showering as if rays of the

The limbs bathed in floral nectar
   The bumble-bees hum on their way;
Laughter lilting dazzles all the time
   As lightning flashes, legion off and on,
Setting the dark looming clouds aflame!

❦ Song 308[1] ❦

Oh mind, do tell me, by what pain travail
You got this strange dark swarthy girl?
Looking at the glowing darkness' grace
They were lost benumbed—the mind and the eyes;
At whose place abode this charming lass
You lured, brought here, by what device?
As the morning sun at the break of dawn
So, glow the Mother's feet sublime.
Sambhuchandra, twice-born, he proclaims,
The hibiscus flowers upon those feet,—
It were so becoming, gracious meet.

❦ Song 309[2] ❦

Do not call out, seek, 'Mother' any more, oh mind,

morning sun. Lotus blooms on the spot where tread Her gracious feet. Her limbs spread aroma all around inviting swarms of bumble-bees with the fragrance. Loud laughter flashes as lightning from Her open mouth overwhelming all worlds with blinding light.

The portrait of the Mother is an amazing blend of grace and horror. The image of Kali in Hindu metaphor and mythology is a rare union of grace and benevolence with the supreme puissance that enshrines the infinite mobile energy of the Absolute Godhead. Mother Kali is the embodiment of the ever-mobile mutating Nature—revealed and rotating through the vast phenomenal worlds.

[1]This song is the poet's enchantment with the grace and beauty of Goddess Mother Kali's image.

The poet asks the mind how it came by such a bewitching dark maiden form. What was the penance and worship that the mind had done? The poet wonders where, whose home this gracious maiden had adorned. Just as the morning sun sets the dawn aglow, like that there is radiance around the twin feet of Mother.

The poet bethinks within himself, how the scarlet hibiscus flower would perfectly match the Mother's twin radiant feet.

[2]This song is the poet's resentment against his own Mother Goddess

Where is it you'll find her, oh, my friend;
Had she been there she'd have come in sight,
The 'queen of ruins' she is not alive.
In *burning places*, in spirits' haunts
In all the shrines and holy lands
In search of her I'm worn, woebegone;
Why then, alas any more this torment!
To *step-mother's banks* I'd now repair
I'd cremate her *kusha image* in fire
Then at the end of the days of penance,
Offering food to the departed soul
I'd proceed to the distant Kasi realm?
Dwija Narachandra,—he, sure, divines
Oh mind, of mother why're you so concerned,
Mother's gone,—(yet) there's the Name Brahman
There's sure, no fears of deliverance!

☙ Song 310[1] ☙

Listen, Mother Shyama, my yearnings hopes
I'd tell, Mother, thee seated on the corpse,—
My tongue as I die, let it, deign, oh, chant
Mother Kali, Kali's honey name again;

Kali. The poet tells his mind no longer to search for Mother. She has deserted Her own child, put him to miseries and gone away. She must be dead. The poet has searched for Her everywhere possible,—in the *burning ghat* (a customary haunt of Goddess Kali), shrines and pilgrimages,—but to no purpose.

Now the poet will do the duty of the son. The dead body of Mother must be burned by the River Ganges. But Mother's body cannot be found. Therefore, the poet will build an image (idol) of Mother with grass and twigs, and burn it by the Ganges. Mother Ganges is the poet's step-mother as both Goddess Kali and Mother Ganges are wives of Lord Shiva.

Then the poet, after his period of austerity, usual after death of parent, will go to holy Kasi. But then the poet is not worried. Mother is not there but Her name itself is the Supreme Brahman the refuge and saviour of all.

[1]The song is a simple prayer of the poet to his Mother Goddess Shyama. The poet has forsaken all worldly desires. His only craving is that when this mortal life ends, his tongue should remember to chant and utter the name of Kali. When the dying body of the poet will be taken to the bank of the Ganges (as is the Hindu custom), let Mother appear in the poet's mind and reveal Herself. The poet would worship with hibiscus flower

You gave me the gall of world's fortunes,
You usurped my all, left me in ruins;
When they would bid me adieu at last,
Do Mother, thou appear within my heart;
It's then that in my mind I'd glean
Hibiscus flowers in sylvan dens;
Mingling devotion's sandalpaste
I'd give flower—offerings at your feet;
Half-immersed in the holy Ganges
On the bank with half my limbs,
Someone will etch upon my brow,
Array of Kali, Kali's name;
Someone else in my ears will pour,
Loud, cascading Kali's name,
Still some others,—Hari, Hari will chant
As they clap their hands in echoing stance.

☙ Song 311[1] ☙

Oh mind, let me but ask you this,
Who's that, of whom you write income debts?
You never tallied, oh your own account,
Debts, overdrafts, deficits, gains;
As days go by, expenses mount
The earnings wane, deposits dim;
There's no longer time, oh, settle accounts
The day of reckoning will come so soon;
Be steadfast, oh mind, so Kumar says,

that he would glean with his thoughts. He would mingle it with devotion's sandalpaste and offer it to the Mother's feet. Some would write the name of Kali all over his brow; other's will call out loudly the name of Kali into his ears. And still others would clap their hands as they chant the name of Lord Hari.

The song is token of the overwhelming love and devotion of the poet and his absolute renouncement of worldly interests and possessions.

[1] The human being works all the time for pleasures, gain and prosperity. And in the process he constantly calculates the pros and cons, the gains and losses of all his moves and actions. Thus life's accounting—keeping records and books of accounting—absorb all his thoughts, time and energy. Such pursuits possess him all his life as a passion and obsession. The poet asks his mind a most fundamental question. The books of

Or else, you'll sink in dark disgrace;
Beware, lest you lose your own and gains
Stand condemned before eternal Time.

❦ Song 312[1] ❦

Oh mind, hush, just keep quiet and calm,
The Tara-bird, I'll trap it for you in charm;
On the fourteen-petalled lotus,—oh mind,
Set up your trap and sit veiled behind,—
But then have a watchful eye askance,
The moment she comes, pull it fast at once;
Holding her in, in your bosom's cage,
Call out,—'Kali, save the page;'
All kinds of speech she fathoms, knows,
Like the winds of hope she ceaseless blows;—
With devotion's cord with anxious care
All doors closed you watch your snare
For, oh, at the same place she never lies
On waters, earth she roams with equal grace.

accounts that occupy the mind and keep him so busy and worried without rest and respite,—whom do they concern? The wealth that he chases and the gains and losses that he calculates, are they not all sham and futile?

The real aim and wealth of the human being is his spiritual emancipation. His only pursuit is contemplation of Mother Goddess Kali and ceaseless devotion and chanting Her name! The poet reminds his mind that time is fast wearing out, life soon comes to an end. His real income, the deposits in his life's balance-sheet are thinning out. The way the mind works, erring into the path of pursuit of worldly gains will soon leave him bankrupt and the day of reckoning—the time that life's balance sheet must be closed,—is drawing all too near.

Poet Ramprasad had worked for some time as an accounts clerk in a zamindar's office. The metaphor and symbolism of the books of accounts,—the accounts of income and expenses, and the balance-sheet of life,—appears in his songs every now and then.

[1] The song is a gem of poetic imagery in which the sage poet weaves his spiritual experience as a *sadhaka*—the spiritual seeker with the symbol of trapping a wayward wily bird, ever fickle, wary in her stance. The mind of the poet is the hunter. The cage is the bosom of the poet where the trap is set. The soul and the vital energy of the human being must be awakened through deep and patient contemplation. The lotus seat within the human heart must be kept ready where to install this supreme 'bird' of Mother Goddess Kali. But the bird is ever mobile,

♀ Song 313[1] ♀

My Mother She is so concerned
Save Her devotee She knows no one;
Open thy heart and call Mother, loud
All your cherished dreams,—
   They'll be fulfilled;
As you call mother by 'Mother' name
The parched soul is cooled in balmy rain
She is gracious loving queen benign
In Her whelming love She calls all men,
Oh listen, hark, my brothers, ears intent.

♀ Song 314[2] ♀

My mind, is it, you have gone insane?
Or else, how is it you avow,—my Mother,
She stands on the chest of Her consort King;
That chaste Mother, is it meet, in accord
   That She should tread upon Her Lord,

evanescent, most difficult to spot and then to hold on to it. The mind must be wary and watchful too.

The trap must be set well and firm. The strings of the trap well-tuned with which the 'mother-bird' must be tied and imprisoned in the unalloyed devotion of the being. Devotion alone and nothing else will tempt the bird near the cage. Like the skilled hunter the mind should pull the string as soon as the bird is near. And the 'bird' must be trapped within the cage by uttering loud the name of the goddess Kali. Her feet should be tied then most tenderly and with utter care with the string of devotion.

[1] The song is an overwhelming hymn of the poet to his beloved Mother. The poet tells himself and all his other fellow devotees to chant Mother's name. The very name, Mother is so sweet and balmy. As one calls Mother in deep devotion, all one's worries disappear. One's whole being is filled with joy and peace. All that one cherishes, all one's dreams and seeking are fulfilled.

And then, Mother is fond, so concerned of the weal of Her devotees. She is the saviour and refuge of all who seek Her with devotion and submission. She is waiting open-arm to receive in love and affection everyone that bethinks of Her, chants and contemplates Her in love and devotion.

[2] This song is a soliloquy of the poet in which he puzzles out a paradox of the image and stance of Mother Kali as She is portrayed in Hindu mythology. But then, he uses his own mind as the foil in debating the

The same queen that quit her life
  As She heard Her Lord's name blasphemed?
Mother, who has done Her five-some penance,
  Accomplished Her consummation,
By installing whom Supreme
  In Her thousand-petalled lotus seat,—
Oh, how did you dare e'er suggest
  That same She, She stands on Her husband's chest?
Do not blame, oh, my Mother,
  Blame it on beneath Her feet,—
By Mother's touch that corpse, it Shiva turned
  And caused Mother shame default;

question and presents his solution to the riddle in the form of catechism. Goddess Kali is portrayed as standing unrobed with flowing enveloping tresses on the bare chest of Lord Shiva. Lord Shiva is Mother Kali's husband lord. The husband of a Hindu woman is most revered and is worshipped! That is why the poet is puzzled and unreconciled. He asks his mind if it has lost its sense, has gone mad to bethink that Goddess Mother Kali,—she treads on the chest of her Lord spouse Shiva ? Does the mind not recall that it was the same Mother, Sati (Goddess Durga) who was so seized of grief and remorse at some wicked word spoken of Her Lord Shiva, that She chose to die and quit her earthly life?

The reference here is to the well-known annals of Hindu mythology. Sati or Durga, the same as mother Kali was married to Lord Shiva. Sati's father was Daksha, the royal king of the mountains (the Himalayas). King Daksha had celebrated a great yajna, Daksha (as well as his queen Menaka, Sati's mother) was never happy with Shiva as his son-in-law. The ways of Lord Shiva are most unorthodox by royal standard. He is half-clad and roams round as a mendicant. He wears a loin cloth of tiger-skin, smears ashes on his body, has plaited unkempt long hairs and wears a serpent round his neck. Daksha made some scoffing remarks on Lord Shiva. Sati, the loyal and devoted wife of Lord Shiva was incensed at this and ended her own life. Upon this Lord Shiva was roused to violent rage and with the dead body of Sati on his shoulders danced round the worlds in violent thunderous roll. All creations were on the verge of annihilation, when at the request of the gods in heaven, Lord Vishnu cut the body of Sati into 52 pieces with his famed Sudarshan Wheel. The 52 pieces of limbs of Sati's body fell scattered round the land,—and each such place where the torn pieces had fallen is a renowned shrine and holy pilgrimage of the Hindus.

The poet here refers to this Hindu annals as proof of the adoration and love of the Mother for Her husband Lord Shiva. And so it is most absurd that that same mother should stand with Her feet on the chest of her beloved lord. In fact, the poet avers, the truth is elsewhere. It is not the fault of the Mother but of Her feet. Her feet are so sublime that as

The wise soul says, it is no fault,—
   It's pure serene those twin feet,
Or else why, Lord Shiva, Father
He should hold it, ceaseless, on his lotus heart!
Charan proclaims,—it's not quite that
What they say, it is not right,—
Mother's fate,—it's all but sealed
   She is past beyond reach of all qualities
For why else, tell me, should on his brow She dwell?

☙ Song 315[1] ☙

Oh mind, why, tell me, to Kasi would you roam?
Listen, oh mind, you'll get all you want
   As you sit quiet at your home;
Why not you close your eyes and look within,
Varanasi there lies at Shyama's feet supine;—
There flows all the three-some wealth of streams
Jahnavi, Varuna, Asi,—there they gleam;
How then you are so crazy, insane,
Your cherished fruits you seek by devious means?
Oh, the fruits of emancipation,
They grow ceaseless at those feet sublime.
In righteous ways as life should end
You will win Her grace then alone;
To dwell in Kasi, that's not the end;
There are barbs and faults, unseemly mines.
Look, upon the chest of your Kasi's king
She stands,—with rolling tresses,—oh She my Queen!

they touched a corpse, that dead corpse became the Supreme Lord Shiva himself! And then, the poet argues, had the mother's feet not been so gracious and sublime, were it that Lord Shiva himself would hold them on so close to His chest?

Yet, the poet has a final deviant thought. It is the lot of the Mother that She is beyond all *gunas* (qualities) of Nature *(Trigunatita)* or else, why should she dwell on the brow of the great Lord Shiva? In the brow is the lotus seat of the Supreme Brahman of which Mother Kali's is the image.

[1] The spiritual seeker believes in pilgrimage and worship at holy shrines. But then, sage poet Ramprasad knows better. Mother Goddess Shyama (Kali) dwells within the human body. She is the ultimate of worship. One who knows this and contemplates Her ceaselessly, has no need to go on pilgrimage or visit holy shrines.

❦ Song 316[1] ❦

As a porter I have spent all my days—oh Kali
(Oh Mother) you wear me down with burden (Mother)
The more it is as I lose my strength.
You are daughter, oh, of mountain stone (Tara Mother)
You never cast, oh, once a look,—
Oh mother, no more I can bear the strain;
My span of life I lose unceasingly,—
Should I go on in peril and pain
Then how do I at those feet dissolve and end!

Varanasi (Benares) is the holiest shrine in Hindu philosophy. The sacred river Ganges, the pure waters of rivers Varuna and Asi,—they bathe the land of Varanasi. But Kasi or Varanasi, that itself dwells at the feet of Mother Goddess Shyama. Worship at the shrines or pilgrimage may bring fulfilment, joy and pleasures to the human being. But then the final fruit of emancipation comes only from total devotion to the Mother Goddess.

Even when one repairs to Kasi one is not freed from desires and the foes like *kama, krodha, lobha, moha, mada,* and *matsaryya*—who dwell within the human body, linger on with stubborn roots.

Sage poet Ramprasad is amused at the folly and ignorance of the mind. The Great Goddess Kali with flowing tresses,—She Herself stands on the chest of the Supreme God Shiva. And that queen of Goddess Mother Kali dwells within the devout heart. One who is conscious of this is the real liberated soul.

[1] As he does it often, the poet here mourns the arid futility of his worldly pursuits. The poet Ramprasad was born in a commonplace householder's family and himself was married early in life. His father died early and the worries and anxieties of a family man beset him most of his life. His passionate love and devotion of Goddess Mother Kali drew him inexorably to the path of spiritual penance (*sadhana*) but he suffered constantly a twang of pain and remorse for the hardship, often penury, of his wife and mother. The burden of the family and the pangs and worries that went with it, seldom deserted him.

Yet, the sage poet was a conscious enlightened soul. All the work in this world as a householder was but the burden that a porter carried on his shoulders. All worldly works are useless but that it merely earns a few coins for livelihood. The real work of the human being is along the path of his spiritual journey for the ultimate emancipation of the soul. But, alas, the poet knows, Mother's will prevails and man is destined to obey Her ways.

The poet pleads with the Mother that She deign Her gracious look at him. She herself is daughter of the mountain King (the Himalayas) and has a heart of stone. Let Her take a kindly stance and relieve the poet of

❦ Song 317[1] ❦

Is it there still left aught of misery—
Why not draw the balance and pay the debts
And reckon what is left of it!
I worry ever of food and fares
I die of fever of anxious cares
I'm left no urge to behold thy face.
That's why thee, at Kali Temple
By thy Tara name I call,
Food and clothing, I am left without,
Cheerless, Tara, is my gloomy world,—
You ne'er cast, oh, Tara, a kindly eye,
Should you so bestow such pain and misery?

❦ Song 318[2] ❦

You will no longer be born again
You won't be born in the mother's womb,—
Should you call chant Her, 'Uma,' Ishana's Queen
Shyama, Baba's spouse, of penance supreme,
Beyond the Vedas, sans limits, bourne.

his arid burdensome worldly chores.

[1] Sage poet Ramprasad is often sad and full of remorse. He is a great devotee of Goddess Mother Kali. His whole being pines for attainment of the Mother's feet. He is tired of his worldly pursuits. But, alas, he is tied to his earthly chores. He possesses a family,—wife and mother. He is beset by poverty; the family is poor, the poet must make a living,—must take care of the need for food and clothing for himself and his wife.

The poet constantly suffers the agony of conflict. His thoughts and passionate devotion are with the Supreme Goddess, Mother, yet he is torn and harassed by worldly worries of the poor householder. In many of his songs this pang and remorse of the sage poet finds expression as his sorrowful pleading to the Mother to stop this perpetual grief and harassment. The poet wonders if there is an end to his miseries. The poet laments, he is so toiled up with worries and useless works in this world that he has little time to turn to the Mother and seek her gracious appearance. He is ever cheerless and melancholy. Let Mother deliver him from this perpetual agony.

[2] This song is a hymn to the Goddess Mother Kali.

According to Hindu metaphysical perception of the 'self' of the human being, (as enshrined in the Upanishads and the *Srimadbhagavad Geeta*) the human soul is immortal, alone and aloof and parcel of the infinite immortal Absolute Divinity. But the 'vital self' *(jivatma)* of the 'being' is

Her marvels splendours,—he alone,—
Lord Shiva, Shankara, he has known;
By chanting, oh, my Mother's name
Legion sinners gained deliverance,—
Oh Mother, the Kailasa mount that realm divine,—
That, pray, reveal to me, oh Mother, this time!

❦ Song 319[1] ❦

(Mother) pray, as life ends I do attain those feet;
Wert thou stingy, Shiva'll bear witness to it;
If Shiva, Lord, he is sworn to Truth
Were it then thee that I so entreat?
They say, thou art daughter of rocks and stone
That is how (Mother) I'm so fearful worn.

toiled up with the *gunas* (qualities) of Nature *(sattva, rajas,* and *tamas)* and is chained eternally by the bondage of works. This causes the endless chain of rebirths of the soul assuming physical bodies in this mundane mutating world.

The ultimate spiritual aim of the human being is emancipation of the soul from all attachments which is caused by the chain of works with desires and expectations for fruits of works. But one who takes Mother Shyama's name with single-minded devotion is freed from the bondage of works and chain of the cycles of births and deaths. For, Mother Shyama is the image of the Supreme Divinity whom the holy scriptures, the Vedas, the Shastras cannot fathom. She is the final ordainer and arbiter of everything that happens, every movement in the phenomenal Nature and it is Her grace alone that can emancipate the human being from the chain of desires and repeated births in the mother's womb. Only Lord Shiva, the supreme Male, the Lord consort of the Queen Mother Shyama,—he knows the essence and Truth of the Mother.

The poet prays to the Mother Goddess to vouchsafe Her grace and reveal to him, the heavenly Kailasa, the supreme abode of bliss and emancipation

[1]This short scrap of a song is both a sweet hymn to the Goddess Mother Kali and a lambent lyric with rich poetic cadence.

Among many sages in India, who sang and wrote and chanted of Divinity such as Kabir, Tulsidas, Nanak, Sri Chaitanya,—Ramprasad is unique in his singular personal relation with the Mother Goddess Kali. There is no liberty with the Supreme Divine Mother that he does not take. He is his Mother's own son. He demands of the Goddess the same love and caress that the young child claims from its mother. Goddess Mother must take him on to Her lap. The poet is often angry with the Mother and calls Her names. He threatens Her that he will report to Lord Father Shiva against Her misdemeanour. He sometimes plays on

Song 320[1]

Have thy pleasure, oh Mother, I know thy way,—
One who propitiates pleases thee
   Him thou punish'st, Mother, twice bitterly,—
The one who, prayerful deep devout
Crying 'Mother, Mother,'—follows thee,
You torment him singe with pain and misery,
Then throw him into the lair of louring Death.
Who is e'er attained with ease, facile,
The current's fast through narrow aisle,—
The one who, Mother, is ever stubborn,
By might and force he is free all trinal time;
Unless one should put one's finger in thine eyes,
Is it thou would'st not judge the right from wrong?
Hara's craze, thy twin feet,—for fear
You surrendered them to the demon's care;

Her jealousy as if the great Goddess Mother were human. He warns Her that if She does not remove his sorrows and miseries, bestow Her grace on him, then he would turn to Her co-wife, the other wife of Her Lord Shiva, the holy Ganges. Then the poet shows his consciousness again and again that Mother Shyama (Kali) is not merely an image and idol built of clay and grass; She is the Absolute Supreme Brahman—immanent and transcendent. The combination of this human love and demands on the Mother as the human child and the highest enlightenment of the absolute divinity in Mother Goddess Kali is unparalleled in Hindu devotional songs and poetry.

In this song the poet prays humbly to the Mother that She should deign Her sublime feet as the last refuge at the time when the poet quits this world. But then the Mother is stone-hearted because She is the daughter of the Mountain King, the rocky Himalayas. The poet pleads in the name of Her Lord consort Shiva that if She should be miserly and not grant him his prayer, it would be so cruel of Her. The Upanishads and the Vedas are the sacred words of Lord Shiva. If those words were true, and Mother Goddess is all gracious as ordained in the shastras, then there was no need for the poet to submit his prayers to the Mother. But then the poet is afraid because the Mother is born of Mountain Lord, the Himalayas.

[1]The poet is in a complaining mood. The Great Goddess, Mother, She is not fair. Sage Ramprasad is her child. He is utterly devoted to Her. He chants Her name in sleep and waking day and night ceaselessly. He worships Her in every form, follows Her devotedly like the child craving for her mother. Yet, the mother is careless, unconcerned. She puts the poet in utter grief and misery. She has no love, no compassion for Her grieving devotee.

Whoever, dour, dares talk back to thee,
Whoever dread fearsome weapons wield,
You forever in his thrall abide,
As captive ward for fear of life;
Ramprasad, he will be blessed pleased
By the might of a tiny bit of grace,
Oh, do worship Mother Shyama's feet sublime
Within this house of windows nine.

☙ Song 321[1] ☙

What good turn you have done, oh Kali,
I have need no more of your helping hand;
Bid adieu, Mother, pray graciously,
Let me leave, oh, ere the sun has waned;
How warm fervent, Mother, is your grace,
I have fathomed, kenned, oh, sans surcease;
I have so learnt it legion times
There's no way but the one destined;
You have borne me, oh, in your womb,

But then She is soft and merciful to those others who are stubborn and hostile. The demon Mahisasura, is such a dour hostile enemy. But she has given him Her sublime feet even while she slays him. The symbol is the image of Goddess Durga, who in Her puissant stance puts the warring demon king Mahisasura beneath her feet in mortal war. The poet charges the mother with iniquitous unfairness. She is perhaps afraid and seeks to pacify those with Her gracious attention who are stubborn and who contend with Her.

Ramprasad, the obedient child prays for Her mercy and grace and craves the sublime feet of the Mother to hold them fast within the bosom of this house (body) which has nine adits—the two eyes, the two ears, the two nostrils, the mouth, the genital organ and the anus.

[1] This is a song of the poet's despair. The poet is the beloved child of the Goddess Mother. All his devotion is bestowed on the feet of the sublime Mother. Yet nothing good has happened to the poet. He goes on suffering pain and agony of this world.

The poet has now lost faith in the Mother's grace. He now wants to take his leave of the mother. Now he knows, what is destined will happen. But then the poet appeals to the Mother. He is the Mother's own child who is born into this Nature's world which is the vast womb of the eternal Mother. It thus does not behove Her to spurn and neglect Her own child. The poet yearns to know from the Mother, the way he may attain liberation from the bonds of this mundane world of grief and sorrows.

Pray, oh, Mother, do not so spurn;
Narachandra,—he so bethinks,
What is the way of deliverance!

☙ Song 322[1] ☙

The one who is daughter of mountain stone
Is it in Her heart She has compassion!
Were it She wasn't so cruel heartless,
Could She have kicked at Her Lord's bosom!
Thou art world-renowned as the Queen of grace
In thee, of compassion there's none no trace;
With wreath of human skulls your neck you'dorn
By shearing off heads of others' sons
'Mother,' 'Mother,'—howsoever I call
You listen, yet, ne'er care or heed at all;
Nara,—to stunning kicks he is immune
He ... calls thee, yet, by 'Durga' name!

☙ Song 323[2] ☙

The one who Tara's feet bethinks
Is it he e'er caught in grief, chagrin!
Those feet are Brahman's feet tranquil,

---

[1] The poet charges his beloved Mother Goddess Kali. Mother Kali or Durga, She is the daughter of the mountain lord, the Himalayas. She is thus the daughter of stone. No wonder then that She herself is stonehearted, without mercy or compassion. Were it no so, would She have stood with Her feet on the chest of Her beloved Lord, Shiva. The allusion is to the Hindu image of Goddess Kali, where She stands naked, in Her dread louring visage on the chest of Lord Shiva who lies at Her feet supine, as a human corpse.

The poet has no doubt that the mother is cruel and heartless. For, she wears a necklace of human skulls. Those wretched human beings whose necks are severed must be sons of other people,—for whom the Mother has no compassion.

The poet chants the Mother's name ceaselessly. But She is unconcerned. Even then the poet is not dissuaded. He has become immune to Mother's cruelty. His devotion to the Mother is undiminished.

[2] The song is the sage poet's hymn to Mother Goddess Kali. As is usual with the poet, he plays on words and on sounds with dual meanings, in his worshipful homage to the Mother. Mother's feet (*pada*) are the saviour.

The deigner of emancipation, weal;
What can he do,—All-eroding Time
When Eternal Time's at Her feet supine?
As you call, 'glory to Kali,'—loud
Death,—at once he flees in awe and dread;
Mother's marvel, it's vast sans bourne,
The termless, e'en He, knows no bounds
The Kali 'mantra'
   It's death to all-devouring Time,
She is saviour,—
   She, the 'trinal' qualities, the womb;
My Mother She's bounteous gracious Queen
But oft She's dour dread, the Image of Ruin
And then sometimes She's Lord Banamali
Or again, She's Radha, the balmy stream.

❦ Song 324[1] ❦

You didn't care, oh mind, to obey my will;
Pure lotus-honey you abjured
To get drunk with fortune's poisoned pill;
The coiled supreme serpent power
E'en waking it, oh mind, you did not care;
As you met a treacle-pitcher
   You fell into indolence, sloth,
Oh, how is it alas you became so loath!

   One who contemplates those feet is delivered from all danger. Mother's feet are the sole refuge and the Brahman itself. Worship of those feet vouchsafes liberation to the human soul.
   Death (Kala) cannot torment such a devout soul because Mahakala (Lord Shiva), He himself lies supine under Mother's feet. Mother's marvels are endless, Even the Infinite Absolute (Lord Shiva) is ignorant of Her charms. Mother is the repository of Nature's three *gunas* (*sattva, rajas,* and *tamas*). Often She assumes Her fearful form, and then again Her mellow countenance. She then takes the form as Krishna or his beloved Radha.
   Reference is to the annals that to protect her from the rage of her husband (Iyan Ghosh) Sri Radha asked Lord Krishna to take the form of Kali and Mother appeared in Her divine form. Ramprasad knows that Divinity is one although he appears in different forms and shapes according to the devotion of the devotee.
   [1]Sage poet Ramprasad is a conscious enlightened soul. He knows that his real self,—the soul of the human being is immortal, as parcel of

This body, a vase of sundry flowers,—
You failed, let slip the harvest hour,—
Prasad says—forsaking treasure
Your fault you wander here and there!

☙ Song 325[1] ☙

Crimson lotus in scarlet hands
On scarlet feet the lotus red;
On coral lips the flaming smile,
Ruddy wreath on cherry feet;
Trappings scarlet, crimson clothes,
Mother's rosy trinal eyes;
Legion flaming suns and moons
Lie supine, oh, on coral nails;

the Supreme Infinity. But then the vital soul *(jivatma)* is perpetually veiled and clouded by the mobile turbulent forces *(gunas* or qualities) of Nature. These Nature's *gunas* are three: *sattva, rajas* and *tamas.* Each one has its own property,—*sattva* for calm, quiet harmony and wisdom; *rajas* for violent passion, greed, perpetual combating energy; and *tamas* for sloth, languor, indolence and dark ignorance. The 'mind' of the human being is that which plays sports with these Nature's *gunas,*—swaying, mutating and quivering all the time with desires, passions and worries born of Nature's marvels and sham illusions of love and hate, sorrows and exultations.

This fickle wavering 'mind' is the perpetual enemy of the human soul which constantly careens and swerves from peace and tranquil meditation of the Supreme Divinity by the influence of the mind.

In this song here, the poet remonstrates with his mind. He admonishes it, that it has played truant and has not obeyed the wise mandate of the soul and real self of the being. The worship,—chanting and meditation,—of the Goddess Mother is the pure honey—the nectar and elixir of the human soul. The errant mind has forsaken it. Like the suicidal fly it settles on the slimy treacle of worldly desires and passion for wealth and fortunes. It has infinite energy of the Infinite within his own body, lying dormant and slumbering. It has not bothered to take pains and wake it up to realize the Supreme Godhead within. But then, enamoured of the world's treacherous lures, it has been forgetful and indolent—so losing the treasures which he has inherited.

[1]This song is a lyrical hymn in which the sage poet portrays the charm and grace of Goddess Mother Kali.

It is often that the poet is overwhelmed by the radiant beauty of the Mother's person as a young bewitching woman. In such portrayals, the poet and the philosopher in the sagely Ramprasad merge and mingle and the outcome is an awful lyric. It is as if the romanticism of John Keats and the poetic spiritual vision of Sri Aurobindo—unite and melt all in one image and symbol of the Supreme Mother.

Blundering with the feet as lotus pink
Rush bumble-bees in endless swarms;
Who's that charming maid of cirrus tresses
As one calls Her, cool the soul's embalmed.

❦ Song 326[1] ❦

Oh thou Death,—look, here I fearless stand
Secure by the charmed fence of Kali's name;
Kali's twin feet, they rest on Eternal Time,—
Those fearless feet who holds in his heart and divine;
One, who, bethinks Mother's saviour feet—
How it ails him, oh, the fear of Death?

❦ Song 327[2] ❦

I shudder, my little mother, as I bethink,

The Mother's hands and feet,—they are like the crimson lotus. the Mother's image is in Her warring gait. She is out destroying demons and all evils of the phenomenal world. Scarlet blood envelops Her limbs. Her mouth and lips are red like cherry, Her smile is radiant like the vermilion morning sun. Her trinal eyes are ruby red, Her lobes are florid, Her nails are shining coral,—as if legion suns and moons, they nestle nudging at Her feet. The bumble-bees roving around for lotus honey descend on Her feet mistaking them for crimson lotus flowers in full bloom.

As the poet broods and meditates that enchanting woman he is filled and whelmed with a strange joy and bliss.

[1]This scrap of a song is the expression of courage and daring of the poet before the all-consuming God of Death. He confronts Death himself and tells him on his face that he (the poet) is not afraid of Him.

What is the poet's strength? How does he hold the mighty all-eroding Death in utter contempt? The Poet is a conscious enlightened soul. He knows that the human soul is immortal, a spark of the supreme Brahman who is sans beginning, sans end and immutable. The 'soul' is beyond the reach of Death whose domain is the mortal human body and the mutating phenomenal world. The poet has touched the 'seed' and the source,— that is eternal. He now dwells at the feet of the supreme Infinite Divinity, the goddess Mother Kali. The name of the Mother is the 'fencing' within which there is the domain of eternal bliss. The poet has set up his abode in this safe territory, out of bounds of the mortal touch of Death. Mother's feet is the refuge of the human soul. The 'being' who has reached this haven is freed from the fear of Death.

That is how the sage poet Ramprasad stands intrepid and fearless before Death outside his reach and compass.

[2]Unlike other devotional poets and composers of the land, Sage poet

He'll take you away tomorrow morn,
I die of fear how, there in Kailasa realm
Her days, oh mother, She will bide and spend.
The sun and moon,—they are concealed,
Dense coils of clouds,—they cast a veil;
Demons, sprites—they ceaseless swarm
Who is there who will Her attend?
As he returns with his bowl of alms,
On the fire they'll put the cooking urn;
How do I, oh, reconcile,
I'm fated doomed, who'll beguile?
In his whims he dwells that crazy one
How do I argue, he is hardly human!
How can he attend, he'll need your care
He'll swallow drugs, not á day he'll spare!

Ramprasad is equally facile on profound philosophical themes and most mundane and commonplace human touches. Mother Goddess Kali is the poet's image of Supreme Divinity. The poet is a realized Kali-*sadhaka* (an emancipated sage along the spiritual path of Tantrashastra). Mother Goddess Kali is his image and symbol of worship and devotion. Yet he knows the Reality and the sublime unity of the Supreme Divinity, the One and the Same, appearing in his varied images in Male or Female symbols according to the creed and inclination of the spiritual seeker. That is how, Goddess Kali or Shyama or Shiva or Krishna—they appear off and on, in his songs as the varied revelation of the same One Supreme Godhead.

Uma or Pravati is the maiden name of Goddess Durga,—who is none else than another image of Mahashakti,—the Goddess Mother Kali. Mother Menaka is the mother of Uma,—whose father is the Lord of the Himalayas. Uma is married to Lord Shiva. In the Hindu mythology, Lord Shiva is half-clad in tiger skin. He lives on alms, indulges in wild dances and is half mad. He is an addict of marijuna. As the 'prince of yogins' *(Yogishwara)*, his way of life is far removed from the royal ambience in mother Menaka's place of the Himalayan kingdom. Understandably Menaka is unhappy with her wayward mendicant son-in-law. She is ever worried of her daughter Uma at Her husband's place. The abode of Lord Shiva is the playground of denizens of the spirit world. It is dark and dim beyond access of the sun and the moon. Shiva, He himself is half-mad, ever drowsy with drugs and narcotics. He is not fit to take care of Uma. Indeed, it is on Her to take care of the absent, careless husband. Menaka is thus sad and anxious all the time for Her little child Uma who must dwell in Her husband's place.

❦ Song 328[1] ❦

Pray, hearken thou, oh sombre Night
To thee I pray in my plight,
Withhold thy motion for just today
To this inert soul have mercy, pray!
This thy page importunes is't for naught,—?
Ah alas, oh Night as thou art left,—
My Uma, balmy Moon, She'll depart,
Darkening deep the Himalayas;
What do I tell thee, oh, Night divine
Thou knowest all in the other's mind,
The pain and grief within my soul,
In thine own mind thou knowest all!

❦ Song 329[2] ❦

The withered Tree—it does not sprout,

[1]Mother Menaka pleads with the dark night to stay still, tarry and stop its movement toward the break of dawn. The sorrowing mother's heart is unreconciled. Her little daughter Uma is set to depart from Mother's home and proceed to Her husband, Lord Shiva's place as the night is past and the morning breaks. Thus, the only way to prevent Uma leaving Her mother's place is for the night to never end.

It does not occur to the grieving heart of the mother that what she asks of the Night is unnatural, beyond the bourne and compass of the cosmic laws. But the unreasoning love and pain of one so overwhelmed with grief knows no reason. And mother Nature in the poet's heart is no alien. She is but the image of the all-loving Mother Goddess Kali or Durga.

That is why the Night is part of the immanent Divine Goddess and She knows all. She knows that Uma, the beloved daughter of mother Menaka, She must desert the Himalayan kingdom and leave Her mother's home to join Her husband Lord Shiva in his abode in Kailasa.

Sage poet Ramprasad is a natural poet. In this small lyrical piece he powerfully portrays the mother's love and sorrow as her young married daughter who has come to her mother's place for a little sojourn leaves for her other home, that is her husband's place. The night is personified and is invoked to relieve the mother's agony. In poet Kalidasa's *Meghadutam*, the *yaksha* youth had pleaded in the same way with the cloud to do him a favour by carrying his message to his distant sorrowing beloved woman.

[2]The song is a beautiful lyric that blends poetic imagery with metaphysical symbolism.

I'm frightened, mother, lest it should snap,—
The Tree,—it e'er wavers in the mighty winds
I shiver, mother, so, as I bide in it.
I had hopes so fond in my mind
From this Tree, mother, fruits I'd glean,
The Tree doesn't sprout, the branches wither
The six-some flames redoubled singe.
Kamalakanta,—he has but one way out,—
From birth, withering age and death
Saviour Tara's name,—Her name for safety shout!

❦ Song 330[1] ❦

My heart, I've turned it desert—waste,
For, thou art fond of the 'burning ghat'
That, Shyama, dweller in the land of waste
Should dance sans surcease, surfeit,
I've no yearnings of the mind,
In the mind the singeing pyre,—it burns

The phenomenal world of creatures is likened to a giant tree that rests upturned with its roots pointing to the heavens and its branches, twigs and foliage spreading dense wide and sprawling downward. Two birds—twins and of the same tribe—sit on the bough, one careless with its face upturned heavenward and the other bemused looking down and away into the widening foliage. The first bird is the immortal human soul parcel of the immutable Absolute Brahman, alone and aloof,—*(Paramatma)* and the other involved and attached to the Nature's world *(jivatma)*.

This human life is the symbol of the tree. The leaves fall and the twigs break; the tree is mortal. It tends to spread its foliage downward and away from its roots which is its source and origin, the eternal absolute Brahman.

And yet the human life, a precious perch on the phenomenal tree has its great promise. The flowers may bloom and the Divine grace may drop like elixir on the human soul in its abode in the bosom of the tree. But, alas, it is not happening with the poet. The twigs and the lean boughs are all drying up. They can snap and break any moment, sending the poet down to his fall. There are six-enemies *(ripus)* —desire, rage, greed, confusion, pride and ego, and hate and jealousy,—which are constantly wearing down the poet's refuge. But the poet knows, he has one salvation,—that is the name of the Mother Goddess Tara,—which is the saviour from all perils and the last refuge of bliss and emancipation.

[1] In Hindu religious practice the dead bodies of people are cremated; they are not buried or interned. The place where such ceremonial burning takes place is the crematorium, also called the 'burning ghat.' The *ghat*

Oh Mother, pyre-ashes in all corners four
I've spread, so thou should'st come perchance;
Lord Mrityunjaya, the Eternal Time,
Keeping Him, Mother beneath thy feet, supine
So come, Mother, in rolling rhythm dance,
So, I should shut my eyes and behold thy stance.

☙ Song 331[1] ☙

Thou art, oh Mother so fond of desolate waste!
Then why is it you left me so and went away?
Where else in the whole expansive world
Did you get such vast waste awesome dale?
Just come behold what all has happened here
Thirty crore corpses sprawling everywhere;
Legion gnomes and spirits they dance,
They play and sport in bizarre stance
Phantoms, sprites, spectres, ghouls
They dance trumpeting cheek by jowl,
And along with them the jackal hordes,
As you catch one you let others go;

is a place usually on the bank of a river earmarked for bathing or the landing place for the ferry across the river.

The *shmashana* or the 'burning ghat' is usually a desolate lonely place somewhat away from the village or habitation, visited by jackals and vultures and haunted by sprites and denizens of the spirit world. In Hindu annals and mythology, Kali or Shyama is fond of dwelling in such deserted, grey and lonely burning-ghats. The companions of Goddess Mother Kali are gnomes and spirits of various order. They have all frightening looks and take to dances and merry-making in the desolate burning ghat where the human being leaves his worldly body and joins his companions in the spirit world.

Poet Ramprasad knows the Mother's ways and favourite haunts. That is why he has made his own heart arid and desolate, as proper ambience for Mother's playground. He has renounced all rosy desires and charms of the world. Lonely and desolate, pining for the Mother, the poet implores the mother to come and dwell and dance within his heart. She will find her coveted playground there—pale, arid and ashen, smeared with the ashes of the burnt bodies on the pyres. Let Her come with Lord Shiva beneath her sublime feet as is Her wonted stance. The poet will keep time with the rhythm of the Mother's dance and he is well prepared with his eyes closed in contemplation.

[1]This singular song is poet Ramprasad's vision of this waste and

Pray, Mother Shyama, you come here and dance,
Shiva at your feet, will don corpse's stance;
All realms will fill with rolls of kettle-drum
Will behold the whole world with eyes upturned.

♥ Song 332[1] ♥

Shyama Mother, some device she has set up
Mother Kali, She's coined a 'trap;'
In this trap of five feet and half or so
What varied funs She's kept on show;
Dwelling within the device herself,
She turns the springs for legion fun;
The 'trap' divines it turns itself,
It does not know the wheel who turns;
The 'trap' which that 'one' has known
Will no longer need be 'trapped' again;
Then there are 'traps' by whose devotion's strap,
Herself Shyama, She is entrapped;

desolate world. Legion people here roam this land like gnomes, spirits and phantoms doing their lurid sports and playing pranks in loud lilts of laughter. The poet finds the world cheerless and gloomy. There is peace of death, no joy and sublime bliss. It is a vast arid lonesome desert echoing the dismal grey ambience of the crematorium where dead bodies are burnt and the denizens of the spirit world have their playground.

The world is a picture of the arid ashen desolation of the poet's own heart. He is miserable amid the filth and squalor of the world. People here chase their passions and desires in unseemly rush and pursue their wicked ends. Indeed, they are all dead men without the lambence of their soul.

The poet knows Mother Goddess Kali loves such desolation and grey waste as Her favourite haunt. That is how the 'burning ghat' *(shmashana)* with a look of grey desolation is the usual abode and field of sports of Mother Shyama and her companions of the spirit world. The poet pleads that the Mother with consort Shiva, who lies supine beneath her feet as a dead corpse—should come and dance in Her wild tumultuous stance as on the date of annihilation.

[1]This song is a typical example of the singular powers of the sage poet Ramprasad of evoking the highest metaphysical lore within the compass of a commonplace symbol.

In this song he likens this human body to a strange device. There is a body—rather weak and small—of flesh and blood. And the body and the limbs are ceaselessly at work. But then, within the body there is something which we call the mind, and which we cannot see hear or perceive. But all the time we are conscious of it; we refer to it and talk

For so long, in the 'trap' as Kali dwells,
The trap's devices, they run so well;
Kamal says, when Kali quits,
The 'trap's' alone, none comes near it.

♀ Song 333[1] ♀

If Shiva, Mother, is thy husband, Lord,
At thy feet why is it He does roll?

about it and say that we think so, we know this and that or that we feel so happy or so sad.

But then who is this One (the so-called mind) who thinks or feels or knows? As one reflects one becomes aware that one can do what one thinks or wills but one cannot decide or will what one thinks. The poet knows that herein lies the eternal illusion and riddle of the human body. Mother Goddess Kali has the appellation of *Ichhamoyee* (the Queen of Thoughts and Desires). The ceaseless thoughts that arise in the mind of man are indeed the thoughts and wishes of the Supreme Mother, and the human mind merely mirrors them, just as a dumb doll that is set adance by the invisible hand of the Master.

The error and illusion of the human being stems from his 'ego': This 'ego-self' intervenes between the Supreme Divinity, the mother Goddess Kali and the mind of the human being. This 'ego' gives the illusion to the human being that he is the 'do-er;' that it is he that 'wills; or thinks or does.' The conscious enlightened person knows that he and his body is the mere 'Instrument,'—a mere 'device'—by which the Supreme is working out His will and purpose. Once this consciousness dawns on the human being and takes firm roots, the person reaches enlightenment and emancipation. Godhead is revealed to him. Sage poet Ramprasad is one such sagely enlightened soul.

A disciple once asked Sri Ramakrishna Paramahansa,—"Sir, can you see God?" The answer came ready from the great sage,—"Yes, why not?"

Surprised, the disciple persisted,—"But how?"

The sage asked the disciple,—"Can you see me?"

"Yes, of course."

Then Sri Ramakrishna took out his large napkin *(gamchha)* and spread it close against the eye of the disciple and asked,—"Can you see me now?"

"No, Sir, but you have shut my eyes."

The guru said, "Yes, just so your 'ego-self' is shutting your inner eye. The moment this 'ego-self' takes leave, you will see God!"

Ramprasad knows it all. He also knows that, so long as Mother dwells within this 'device' (the body), the body is divine, the temple of spiritual emancipation. But as Mother leaves the body it is dead and deserted and no one cares to touch it or go near it.

[1] In the Hindu religious thought and social system the husband of a

He opens up His chest in fear,
On thy face, Mother, His eyes ne'er dwell;
Thy twin feet, they bewitch and charm,
Is't why, Shyama, to His bosom He holds them on?
How but, oh Mother, you've husband, thine,
Thou, Mother, 'Mother' thou that's they all divine;
The rolling earth rocks beneath thy feet,
Does it not hurt him with thee upon the chest?
Or else tell me, Lord Shiva, how,
He holds thee on His lotus heart?

❦ Song 334[1] ❦

Is it, my Shyama Mother,
    She is swarthy dark?
They say, Kali, she is sable black
But then, oh, my mind disowns

woman is her foremost object of reverence,—even of worship. The husband is known as the 'god of the wife'—*(pati-devata)*. Also, in Hindu mythology and religious image, Mother Goddess Kali is the spouse of Lord Shiva. She is the consort of Her Male Divinity, Lord Shiva, to whom she is eternally united as the female partner.

And then again Goddess Kali or Shyama is portrayed and imaged as standing with Her two feet apart, somewhat like an advancing colossus,—on the bare chest of Her Lord consort,—the Divine Shiva, who lies supine under Her feet.

The poet is puzzled. If Lord Shiva is Her esteemed Lord husband,—adored of the wife, then how is it that She stands on him, supine beneath Her feet! The poet wonders,—is it that Her twin feet are so charming and blessed, that the Lord Shiva holds on to them close on his chest ? Is He awed by Her countenance that He lies supine, eyes half-closed, like one dead, without even looking at Her face? And then the poet is confused. Mother Kali is the divine Mother of the Universe,—known to the creature world as the Supreme Mother. How does it behove that even She should have a Lord husband?

Beneath Her feet the whole world trembles in awe and fear. Is it not that Lord Shiva finds Her awesome weight aching and tormenting? Perhaps not; or how else He should take Her colossal presence upon his lotus heart!

[1]The song is a piece of supreme abstract poetry. Mother Goddess Shyama (Goddess Kali),—She is imaged in her dark sombre complexion. But then the poet wonders,—his thoughts tell him otherwise. The poet has installed Her within his lotus heart. And as he has done so, he finds that his whole being is lighted up in a heavenly glow.

It swears She isn't dark.
In her swarthy charm, She's robed in space
My lotus heart, oh, She illumes,—
Oh, is it that my Mother Shyama—,
She wears a veil that leaves no trace;
Shyama, She is often snowwhite
    Often yellow pale
But then sometimes She's blue azure
    Again, oh, She's aglow,—
What indeed is Mother's stance
I cannot fathom, never know,—
As I bethink endless on and on
    My life is close upon its end;
My Shyama, Mother, is it then—
Shyama, She is oft the Supreme Male,
She is then sometimes, the cosmic Queen,—
And then again, she's the vast inane;
As He Divines Mother's varied charms,
Kamalakanta,—He has turned insane,—
Is it that my Shyama Mother, then.

    Mother is immanent and ubiquitous. She is undefined,—She is manifest in every form and hue. She is ever mutating mobile—in Her shifting chameleon colours. She is sometimes pure white, often yellow, scarlet red or blue azure. The poet has spent his lifetime in Her contemplation. Even then he does not know. The Divinity in its absolute form is unknown and unknowable.
    And then the Great Mother is coequal of the Supreme Absolute Brahman. And then She is the Supreme Male *(Purusha)*, one with the Primal seed of all creations. And again She is profound, abstract,—abstruse and unrevealed, veiled in the void inane. The more the poet bethinks Her and contemplates, the more is he lost, confused—out of his wit's end.